William Burgh

A Scriptural confutation of the arguments of the one Godhead of the Father, Son and Holy Ghost

William Burgh

A Scriptural confutation of the arguments of the one Godhead of the Father, Son and Holy Ghost

ISBN/EAN: 9783337284220

Printed in Europe, USA, Canada, Australia, Japan

Cover: Foto ©Lupo / pixelio.de

More available books at **www.hansebooks.com**

A SCRIPTURAL CONFUTATION

OF THE

ARGUMENTS

AGAINST THE

ONE GODHEAD

OF THE

FATHER, SON, and HOLY GHOST,

PRODUCED BY

The Reverend Mr. LINDSEY

In his late APOLOGY.

By WILLIAM BURGH, Esq.

THE SECOND EDITION.

OMNES AD SACRAS LITERAS SUNT DUCENDI, UT INDE TALIA HAURIANT, QUÆ, NISI DEO SEMET PATEFACIENTE, COGNOSCI NEQUEUNT.
GROTIUS.

YORK:
Printed by A. WARD, for the AUTHOR, and sold by W. NICOLL, in St. Paul's Church-Yard, London; and by all Booksellers in Town and Country.
MDCCLXXV.
[PRICE THREE SHILLINGS.]

DEDICATION.

TO

EDMUND BURKE, Esq;

SIR,

WHEN I first committed the volume, with which I now present you, to the public, I was actuated purely by a desire to stop the progress of errour, which I feared, from the sacrifice that had been made to her, would be mistaken for truth; and as such embraced by many unsuspecting, and many indolent persons. A train of thinking, upon one side of the question, had been prescribed to them, and the conclusions, set up for their assent, abetted by proofs of sincerity, which I apprehended such men would consider as the criterion of truth. For their benefit I ventured to interpose, and, to the best of my power, have pointed out the only premises from which any conclusions in religious enquiry can result; and from which they may proceed

intention, and thrown a weight into the opposite scale, sufficient to preponderate against his huge mass of human authority. I have the honour to be,

Sir,

With the greatest respect and esteem,

Your much obliged,

And most obedient, humble servant,

WILLIAM BURGH.

Advertisement.

IN the following sheets, which I am desirous of rendering universally useful, I have taken care to write the third and fourth chapters in such a manner, as that they may be read separately by persons to whom the preceding part of the work might be difficult or unnecessary.—The plan I have pursued throughout is as follows.——Having, as I think, set aside Mr. Lindsey's foundation of argument in the introduction, and shewed the fallacy or inconclusiveness of what he builds most upon, I have in my first chapter stated the proper premises upon which our reason is at liberty to act with respect to scripture truths. In my second, I have endeavoured to shew the nature of the evidence which is borne to that great scripture truth to which our faith is required. And in the subsequent parts of the work have shewed what the evidence itself is.— I have but one request to make of my reader, which is, that he will do by me as I did by Mr. Lindsey; and when he is reading my book, that he will place the

Bible beside him; for, by my agreement, with that only do I desire to stand; nay, if I shall be found to disagree, I wish to fall. In some few instances, for the sake of continuing a sentence, I have changed the person used in a scripture precept, and, instead of absolutely adhering to such words as *do ye*, have sometimes said *we are desired to do*, &c. and in a few instances have omitted a multitude of nominatives, where one answered the purpose full as well, as in Rev. vi. 15, 16, where it is said that *the kings of the earth, and the great men, and the rich men, and the chief captains, and the mighty men, and every bond man, and every free man hid themselves in the dens, and in the rocks of the mountains*; in such cases I have used only the first. Of this I think it necessary to apprize my reader, lest he should charge me with inaccuracy in my quotations; whereas I will promise him that, throughout the whole work, he will not find the smallest alteration made in the sense. The passages with which I have taken this liberty are but very few also; but let him lay the Bible before him, and there is no great danger of his being misled.——Sometimes instead of quoting I have paraphrased;

phrafed; but that will always appear in the inftance. — In the 66th page I have made a comment upon John viii. 58, and confuted an objection brought againft it by an author who ftyles himfelf "a Lover of the Gofpel." The paffage which I have treated of was pointed out to me; it remained on my mind, and by miftake I have afcribed it to Mr. Lindfey. This is but of fmall importance. I mention it only that I may apologize to him for it.

A

SCRIPTURAL CONFUTATION, &c.

INTRODUCTION.

THE conduct of Mr. Lindfey, in refigning the vicarage of Catterick on certain fcruples, excited my curiofity to know what his particular objections to the fubfcription of the articles of the church of England were. His refignation was foon followed by a book under the captivating title of " The Apology of Theophilus Lindfey, A. M. on refigning the vicarage of Catterick, Yorkfhire." With this book, which was greedily bought up, I alfo furnifhed myfelf. What I expected to have found in it, is of no confequence to the public; but I did indeed find a much " larger circuit taken" than the title promifed, and that " the defign was not barely to offer a vindication of the motives and conduct of a private perfon," but to affail every fundamental doctrine of the church, from the miniftry of which he had retired; to degrade the God of our falvation; to fnatch from us the object of our religion; and to evince, that Jefus Chrift is not one, with the Father and the Holy Ghoft, God. Upon what foundation he has raifed the flimfy fuperftructure of his own doctrine, or rather with what engines he has endeavoured to fubvert the fixed fabrick of our religion, and force it from the bafis of revelation, I fhall proceed to fhew; and without infinuating

nuating pretenſions to divine aſſiſtance, from the grant of which it might be inferred, that my cauſe had the particular favour of heaven, I hope to evince the divinity of our bleſſed Lord and Saviour Jeſus Chriſt, and, in oppoſition to all the human authority convened by Mr. Lindſey, to ſhew that God himſelf has borne teſtimony to it; and if, from his revelation, it be clearly ſet forth that Jeſus Chriſt is both God and man, I hope and believe the poſition will be acceded to, however unable reaſon may be to comprehend it, or how numerous ſoever the voices may be which have lifted themſelves up againſt it.

Before I enter upon the ſubject propoſed, I think it neceſſary to remove ſome prejudices which favour Mr. Lindſey's cauſe, prejudices ſo natural to the mind of man, that he has been aware of their uſe, and, with ſuperfluous diligence, beſtowed near half his book to inſtill them. The influence of theſe upon my readers I muſt, however, try to avert before I can hope for an impartial hearing; for I have reſigned no vicarage; I have puſhed from me no worldly advantages; I have given no proofs that a little, with a ſettled conſcience, is preferable, in my eyes, to great riches retained by acquieſcence in that which I do not believe; all of which he has done, and for which let me freely pay him the tribute of my praiſe; let me declare that I honour the ſincerity which ſuch a conduct demoſtrates; but let me never ſay that, from the rectitude of his heart, I can deduce the rectitude of his opinions. Such proofs of my ſincerity, it is true, I have it not in my power to produce; but even Mr. Lindſey has borne ſuch teſtimony to the troubles of an unquiet ſpirit, that no man will conceive that I ſhould ſeek to incur them by a voluntary engagement in the cauſe of falſehood, or look upon the ſalvation of my immortal ſoul as a matter of

ſo

so little importance to me, that I should maintain a doctrine, connected as this is with the felicity of a future state, if I were not clearly convinced of its truth.

Unless then I am to consider it written with a view to prejudice the Reader, the aim of the long chapter of sufferers for the maintenance of Mr. Lindsey's doctrine is altogether inexplicable to me, because I am unable to deduce the truth of a system from any other source than that of reason or fair argument. Submission to misery, in preference to the concession of an opinion, does indeed prove the sincerity of the sufferer, but by no means the opinion for which he has suffered; it may prove the weakness of his understanding, but by no means the strength of his cause. In India the distortions of the Bramin are the testimony of the divinity of his Ixora; in the holy office, the submission of the Jew to the extremest tortures, is the testimony that our Saviour had not even divine assistance; and now in England we find a number of unhappy wretches suffering under equally unjust and cruel inflictions, to prove a negation of our Saviour's divinity; and this list of miserable creatures is held out to the public by a gentleman who has voluntarily added himself to the number. I have already said that I considered such a conduct as a proof of sincerity, but I cannot submit to allow it the name of martyrdom, or in the least degree a proof of the justice or truth of the opinion for the maintenance of which it is sustained; doctrines the most contradictory would else be true. Papal supremacy and regal supremacy have almost mingled their blazing testimonies, and were they both truly to be maintained? What horrible proofs have been given to the world that flour and water are flesh and blood; and will any man declare that the contrary doctrine has derived validity from equal, nay greater, streams of blood

poured

poured out to testify that they were flour and water still? No man, surely; because this is a position, the proofs of which are submitted to all men, and a stronger degree of testimony, than my stedfastness, may be and is borne to it by the senses of all mankind. Both sides of this question have had their bleeding advocates, and are they therefore both true? I will go yet farther and say, that were I to undergo the sharpest afflictions for entertaining the opposite doctrine to that of Mr. Lindsey, (and I would undergo them rather than depart from the belief for which I think I have so sufficient grounds) yet I should not conceive that I had added even the slightest proof of the truth of it. My sincerity the world would, I believe, allow, but what could my sincerity evince? I suffer for a position, and because I have believed it upon arguments seeming sufficient to me; if they be in fact sufficient, I have done well to adhere to them, and they were as valid before my suffering as afterwards; and if they are defective, my miseries cannot alter the conclusions following from them. Their truth or falsehood, the justice or injustice of the inference are pre-existent to my testimony, and so absolutely independent of my belief, or any proofs that I may give of the sincerity of my belief, and are so far from deriving strength from my suffering in behalf of them, that they would have been precisely the same though I had never been born, as if I had made my exit at a stake. I am anxious to establish this point, and therefore dwell upon it, for I fear that too easy credit may be yielded to a doctrine held forth by a claimant to martyrdom; the seal of blood has given a seeming validity to many a position, from which the assertors had before derived no glory; the stake, where it has been the only argument, has sometimes been considered as a very convincing one; and a departure in flames has been thought to have revealed

vealed the angel, where the precepts for which they are sustained had perhaps only shewed forth the contemptible man: But martyrdom is not now to be deduced from sincerity, which is all that can be concluded from strenuous suffering. The apostles indeed were martyrs, they bore testimony to facts submitted to their senses, and had even a sensible perception of divine assistance, of which also they gave proofs to the world: They bore testimony, and they would not recede from it; what they testified they knew, and promulgated by extraordinary aid, of which they were eminently conscious; what they knew, not what opinions they formed without divine assistance, was their doctrine; and from the testimony of what they knew they would not be deterred; they suffered, and their constancy was a proof of their sincerity: But they were sincere, not in the maintenance of dubious controvertible doctrines, but in having testified, that what they had preached they had known. As then they were sincere, and had proved themselves so, we must conclude that they did know what they had preached, and consider their stedfast adherence to what they had set out with as an exceedingly strong testimony borne to the truth of it; and such a testimony as this is what is properly called martyrdom. I hope that this may be sufficient to warn my readers from looking upon sincerity as a proof of the opinion sincerely believed; let it recommend the heart, but by no means the head, the errors of which may be as sincerely believed as the best established maxims.

The prodigious number of names, only pretending to human authority, which are produced by Mr. Lindsey to support his doctrines, might perhaps be well opposed by citing as great a multitude of eminent men, who have agreed with the church of England, and ascribed divinity to our blessed Saviour. Were it only to
satisfy

satisfy him, with whom, I fear, the authority of the scriptures will signify but little, I would purſue this courſe of argument (if argument it may be called); but I ſcorn any other foundation than that of God himſelf, whoſe written word, not ſeen through the medium of a comment, is alone evidence to me; let it not therefore be inferred, that I am unable to meet him upon his own ground, becauſe I chooſe that which is better; for I could, to him, oppoſe as good human authority to maintain my belief as any ten Dutch women in Europe, however ſtrenuouſly they might have ſuſtained and ſuffered for the doctrines of Anabaptiſm.

The diſpoſitions of mankind lean toward thoſe who flatter their reaſon, and endeavour to reduce all things to her comprehenſion, or to thoſe who abet that pride with which ſhe is deſirous of rejecting whatſoever ſhe cannot comprehend; from this principle it is that they who familiarly illuſtrate the moſt unfamiliar difficulties, or flatly deny the exiſtence of that which tranſcends the faculties of man, are heard with partial ears. Againſt this prejudice alſo, in favour of Mr. Lindſey, I am obliged to guard; for he has declared, that " our Saviour Chriſt teacheth no myſterious doctrines". As I have already ſaid, that the ſcriptures ſhall be my only appeal; to this denial of a myſtery, nay to that ridicule with which the word *Myſtery* is treated throughout Mr. Lindſey's book, I ſhall oppoſe the ſerious declaration of St. Paul, who, ſpeaking of the goſpel of Jeſus Chriſt and him crucified, and that not with enticing words of Man's wiſdom, but in demonſtration of the Spirit, that our faith might ſtand not in the wiſdom of man, but the power of God, declares, " we ſpeak the wiſdom of God in a myſtery"; and this he ſays he does " by the Spirit of God, by which alone the deep things of God are ſearched"; and he farther declares,
that

that "the spirit compares spiritual things with spiritual; but that these things are foolishness to the natural man who receiveth not the things of the Spirit of God." See 1 Cor. ii.

Will Mr. Lindsey now persevere to say, that the doctrine of Christ is not mysterious? The moral doctrines delivered by himself I grant, indeed, are not so; but on the contrary most perspicuously clear; but a manifestation of him who delivered those doctrines, and a revelation testifying of him, and setting forth who he was, and is, and shall eternally be, and that "in him dwelleth all the fulness of the Godhead bodily," Coloss. ii. 9. Is not this a mystery? "Now, without controversy, great is the mystery of godliness; God was made manifest in the flesh, justified in the Spirit, seen of angels, preached unto the Gentiles, believed on in the world, received up into glory," 1 Tim. iii. 16. Let us then beware of the philosophy of the natural man, of the enticing words of man's wisdom, which St. Paul has warned us against, because he well foresaw that it would stand in the way and preclude "the acknowledgment of the mystery of God, and of the Father, and of Christ," Coloss. ii. 2. This warning to beware of the deceits of philosophy is given at such a time, and in context with such a doctrine, as makes it utterly astonishing to me how any man in his senses should attempt to warp it to the purposes of overturning our Saviour's divinity: We are desired to beware of it, because it might be opposite to the declaration which immediately follows, that "in Christ dwelleth all the fulness of the Godhead bodily;" that "Christ is all in all;" that "Christ forgave us all;" that "of the Lord we shall receive the reward of the inheritance, for we serve the Lord Christ;" that "whatsoever we do, we should do it heartily, as to the Lord, and not unto man."

man." In short, St. Paul has given us this warning in the midst of his epistle to the Colossians, to which I refer as a most explicit declaration of our Saviour's divinity throughout. Let us just consider now, whether this warning can have any other object in view. Mr. Lindsey's principal objection to the Godhead of Christ, is, that it is not reconcilable to reason; St. Paul says, that the Greek requires wisdom. Mr. Lindsey says, that it is a doctrine fraught not only with impiety but absurdity; St. Paul says, that it is to the Greek foolishness. Of what doctrines, of what philosophy now was St. Paul afraid? Will Mr. Lindsey say, that he feared that the Greeks would, from their demand for a reasonable doctrine, adopt a doctrine contrary to what he thinks reasonable himself? Or will he say that the apostle apprehended, from their aversion to that which was foolish, their adoption of a doctrine which he himself declares to be foolish? If this be his mode of reasoning, it is so self-subverted that it requires only to be read for its own confutation. His assertion, that the Trinity is an idea adopted from Plato, is full of impiety, and so extreamly weak, that I am sorry to see any man capable of promulgating it; and, were I not assured of this gentleman's sincerity, from the proof which he has given to the world, that upon the whole he disbelieves our Saviour's divinity, I should incline to conceive that he meant to impose this on mankind upon the faith of a martyr. I will now advance one of the like nature, and assure Mr. Lindsey that the idea of the Unity of God is derived from the philosophy of Socrates, who, notwithstanding his having been educated in a country where such a doctrine was esteemed impious, yet dared to preach this imagination of his own brain. How does this sound? Just as well as the other, and is advanced with fully equal truth. For my own part, I must now declare to this gentleman, that (so far from

having

having drawn my faith in the Trinity from Plato, the only book I have ever read on the subject, (except his own, which I was led to look into by my curiosity to see the motives of his uncommonly conscientious conduct) is the Bible. That I have thence deduced the doctrine of the Trinity; that both the Old and the New Testaments evince it; the Old by typical and verbal prophecies; and the New, by the events which justify the prophecies; that our Saviour's life and lessons teach it; and that the more explicit testimony of the Holy Ghost declare and enforce it; that, in the epistles of St. Paul, evaded or trifled with, it is delivered in nearly so many words. But I must farther declare, that though it be not precisely so denominated there, or in any part of the scriptures, I cannot form an idea why I am not at liberty to give a name to that, which another shall so describe as to put it into my power to give it a name for the benefit of communication. The Godhead of the Father, and of the Son, and of the Holy Ghost, is a doctrine which I deduce from the sacred writings, and to these three persons I am surely at liberty to give a name that shall at once comprehend them all, and serve the purpose of more expeditiously conveying my mind on the subject, whensoever I shall fall upon it, without levity. From the same source also I deduce the being of but one God; and as I have before given the name of Trinity to the three Persons, to this Godhead I give the name of Trinity in Unity; and what shall preclude my giving a name where the scriptures have given the substance, I own I do not see; nor can I conceive this objection to the Trinity of persons, and the Unity of the Godhead, to be a bit better grounded than that of the Quakers to the use of the word *you*, because the term is not to be found in the Bible. It is objected also to the doctrine of the Trinity, that the word was not formed till

B   late

late in the second century. As to the date of a word I cannot see it to be of any sort of consequence, if the idea to which it is annexed be but conveyed by it. If we had not been termed Christians by the people of Antioch, and that the professors of Christ's religion had, as yet, continued without a name, would posterity deny the existence of Christianity, or dispute the propriety of the term, because it was of the eighteenth century? The word *Christians* was equally applicable to us before we were called by it at Antioch, as after; and the word *Trinity* was equally applicable to the three persons of the Godhead before mankind agreed to call them by it, as after.

But if the name only were in debate, I should be but very little concerned about it, the Unity of the Godhead, and the Divinity of the three Persons being allowed, I care not by what appellation they are called: But I am sorry to see, at a time when I believe the *doctrine* is what Mr. Lindsey would confute, that he is weak enough to conceive that a disapprobation of the *name* will in the least contribute to his purpose; for either he must conceive that it does, and so trifle; or not conceiving so, acknowledge that he is talking about words only; and surely nothing can be more uncandid than such a process. He must assuredly know that his delicate conduct will procure him more readers than he could with modesty have hoped for, had his book been put forth without such a concomitant circumstance; and also that, in the multitude of his readers, understandings of every size must be numbered; and it is therefore impossible but he must have foreseen that some will be of so contracted dimensions, as to reckon the dislike of the word among the arguments against the substance named. To what purpose else than that of deception is it advanced, that to Luther " the word

Trinity

Trinity sounds oddly, and is of human invention, and that it were better to call Almighty God, God, than Trinity." And that Calvin says " I like not this prayer, O holy, blessed, and glorious Trinity, it favours of barbarism." Are Luther and Calvin among the opponents of the doctrine of the Trinity? No such thing; and Mr. Lindsey himself shall tell you that they were well known and warm contenders for what is called the doctrine of the Trinity, though they expressed such a dislike of the word itself. I cannot see his inference, unless he would insinuate that a dislike of the word, is a dislike of the doctrine, and therefore avail himself of the authority of these " virtuous holy" men: But that authority is altogether against him, as himself acknowledges; and Calvin, by a horrible instance, proved the sincerity of his belief in the Trinity, for he actually brought Servetus to the stake for opposing it.

If this delicacy of Calvin, concerning the barbarism of a term, be admitted in argument, I see no reason wherefore we should reject a classic mythology; or why, when we speak of our Saviour's incarnation, we should not use the words with which Erasmus ridiculed the fastidious wits of Leo's polished court, and say, " E cœlo descendit filius Jovis." In short, I can see no reason wherefore we should not, like Leo himself, pass judgment upon the whole of the sacred writings, declare them barbarous, and never read the Bible for fear of spoiling our taste. And with respect to what is said concerning Luther, however it may be asserted that he prefers the calling upon God, by the name of God, to the calling upon him by the name Trinity, it is deducible from this assertion, that he looked upon the two words as synonimous, and consequently that the word *Trinity*, though it might sound oddly, was expressive of the idea, which he chooses rather to express by the term God; a term perhaps more pleasing to his ear.

Thus far I have written, not with a view of derogating from the real worth of Mr. Lindsey, nor of lessening the value of such worth in the eyes of mankind; but with a purpose of preventing the merits of the honest conscientious man being carried over to his cause, and concluded to be the merits of his argument. I am myself desirous that the favour which is due to his virtue should attend his person, but not be converted into partiality for his cause. I seek not to obtain the favour of the public to myself, but their unprejudiced ear, and that men should yield their convictions to truth only, and not take prepossessions for conviction. Preliminaries being, I hope, settled, I shall now no longer withhold my reader from that line of argument, by which alone it seems to me possible to inquire into the subject before us, and by the pursuit of which, I trust, I shall be able to evince the Divinity of our Lord and Saviour Jesus Christ.

CHAP-

CHAP. I.

On the Province of Reason, with Respect to its Enquiry into Scripture Truths.

MR. Lindsey commences with an assertion, that "the unlearned reader sees at once, that the God who made him, and whom he is to adore, is one, without multiplicity or division, even as he knoweth himself to be one, being one person and not many;" and on this position he proceeds to argue. If Mr. Lindsey means by the unlearned reader, the reader of his book, who has never read the Bible, perhaps he is right; but I believe that every reader, who has read the Bible, will see the fallacy of this great foundation of all that follows in confutation of a trinity of Persons in the Godhead. On a supposition that nature has suggested, and philosophy refined upon the suggestion of a God, I do not doubt that natural religion might acquiesce in this assertion; but are we to come to the scriptures, which all men allow to be the foundation of our religion, with a religion already formed, and to judge of the revelation made by the God of truth, according to its correspondence with our previous persuasions? Are we to exalt our own reason, and say, that it is a standard whereby to measure the infinite extents of power and wisdom? or are we to set bounds to infinity, and annihilate all that stretches beyond the grasp of our limited comprehension? The short-sighted man may, with equal truth, and equal wisdom, deny the existence of all objects beyond the reach of his vision. And yet one of these consequences must be inferred from the assertion, either that our reason is infinite

nite to measure infinite wisdom; or that the wisdom of God is finite, and narrowly limited, in order to be conformable to our reason; for the faculty must be commensurate to the object, before it can take it into observation and determine upon it.

I should be sorry to have it understood, that I wish to set up one boundary which original nature has suffered reason to pass. I think, however, that, as there are boundaries already formed, beyond which she is not permitted to expatiate, it is an object of consequence to mankind to find where they are fixed; for, by an acquaintance with our limits, we shall also possess a definite idea of that which is within our comprehension; and so, instead of idly squandering our useful hours in pursuit of knowledge that is too high for us, and which, when we conceive that we have attained unto it, terminates not in conclusion, but at the very best in specious fallacy, we shall turn the force of our faculties against objects which must yield to our vigorous exertions, atchieve that which, retained, may be serviceable to ourselves, or, communicated, prove beneficial to our fellow creatures.

My purpose is only to inquire into those limits by which reason is circumscribed with regard to scripture truths, and into the proper conduct of reason within those limits.

By the word *Reason*, I mean that faculty of the mind by which it perceives the relative qualities of the objects of our perception; by which it compares the objects of our perception; and, upon comparison, sees the conclusions, of whatsoever nature they be, which result.

The

The word *Comparison* I use in an extensive sense, for every manner of laying together the relative qualities in order to infer; and I choose to say, that reason sees rather than forms the conclusions, because I suppose them to have been formed, and existing at all times, whether observed or not, and no more to be annihilated by my withdrawing my observation, than Mr. Hume is by my blowing out the candle, by the light of which I had (according to his own philosophy) seen him into existence.

That great truth of Scripture which I wish to hold forth for the assent of mankind, and which I wish also to prescribe and pursue a proper manner of inquiring into, is, that Jesus Christ is one with the Father and the Holy Ghost, God.

It has often been asserted, that reason absolutely contradicted the possibility of such a union of divine perfection and human imperfection, and thence the impossibility of such a union is inferred, and the Godhead of Jesus Christ denied upon this unweighed assertion; whereas, were it considered, that the relative qualities of God and of Man are the objects of comparison, and that the incompatibility of these two natures, upon a perception of the qualities of each, must be seen from the comparison, perhaps men who deny our Saviour's divinity would hesitate a moment before they would even pronounce that their reason had, upon natural premises, given any testimony whatsoever concerning him; for, in the process, it must be enquired into, whether the objects of the comparison be really the objects of their perception, how far even the nature of man is within their comprehension, and how far the nature of God is beyond it; and if, upon enquiry, it be found, that the relative qualities of the two natures are altogether unknown, reason must be declared incompetent competept to make a comparison, and consequently to see any conclusion whatsoever. Reason, therefore, can never have denied, that Jesus Christ is both God and Man, however ignorance and presumption may, under her respectable name.

I do not desire, on the other hand, to conclude a belief in scripture truths from the unassisted light of reason; I only desire to put that religion, which we may imagine nature has found by that light, out of the question; and then first to call for the observation of reason, when maxims, whence argument may proceed, are established; when we first find objects which we may compare, and from the comparison of which we may conclude: But till such are found, and agreed upon, we must walk upon uncertain ground; and if we should happen to come right in the end, it must be by ways of which we could not have been certain while on our progress. To fabricate maxims is not the office of reason, but to observe upon such as are ready made and submitted to her cognizance, I therefore ask no aid to my cause from any suggestions that she may be supposed to have made, nor will I allow that she can have afforded any to infidelity. I wish only to dissuade from looking upon a negative as proved, because the affirmative does not follow from premises not cognizable: From such premises we never can argue to any conclusion whatsoever; for no relation being visible, no result can issue. A declaration from natural religion that God is omnipotent and all-wise, can by no means set aside a declaration that he has done that which to us may appear weak and foolish; we must be competent to judge of infinite power and infinite wisdom before we can compare the act with the agency; and we must be very sure that the act which is inconsistent with our degree of wisdom, must be inconsistent with a greater height than our own,

before

before we can pronounce that it is impoffible for infinite wifdom to fee a reafon for fo acting. Even in the courfe of worldly tranfactions, how often has a man of fenfe accounted for imputed abfurdity of conduct, and, by fhewing us the grounds of his action, extorted our applaufe where we had before been too liberal of our cenfure? The reafons which influence man are intelligible to man, and therefore, when affigned, may indemnify his act; but the reafons of the conduct of our infinite Maker muft be incommunicable, becaufe unintelligible to our faculties, unlefs our minds were enlightened above our fphere; that is, unlefs mankind were placed higher in the chain of intellectual beings, which fomewhere requires the exiftence of fuch a creature, and fo fhould not be man. We cannot then argue, from any idea we are able to form of any attribute of God, to the action properly proceeding from it; and therefore can never deny an act, by himfelf afcribed to any of his attributes. Has infinite mercy let loofe the bloody tyrant to fcourge mankind? Or does infinite juftice choofe to afflict the meek and benevolent heart? Can the affumption of flefh, and fubjection to the infirmities of man, be imputed to the wifdom of God? Or does infinite power and glory beam from a helplefs bleeding body hanging on a crofs? And yet as reafonably may thefe two latter inftances of impotence and folly be afcribed to infinite extents of power and wifdom, as the two former, the profperity of the wicked, and the broken heart of the benevolent, to the infinite extents of mercy and juftice. If then the conduct of the affairs of this world be not reconcilable to our ideas of infinite faculties, we muft, if we interpret from the act to the agent, difprove the exiftence of thofe attributes with which we cannot reconcile fuch conduct, and confequently the exiftence of the being in which we had before conceived them inherent; fo that returning to God by the fame road by which we defcended from him,

him, we no more find him, and the infinitely great Creator of all things we then difcover to have been a meer Creature of our own imaginations.

Such is the procefs of unconducted reafon: With the fame arguments fhe conceives and annihilates her God: At every turn fhe finds and lofes him, yet ftill regrets the lofs, and though fhe cannot maintain the poffeffion, relinquifhes it with reluctance. If from our longing after immortality, our immortality is to be concluded, from our longing after an acquaintance with an intimated God, we may likewife infer the reafonablenefs of a revelation admitting us to that acquaintance, and helping us to a permanent idea, which nature was never enabled to acquire of herfelf. It feems then an act confiftent with our previous perfuafions, in which even reafon acquiefces, that a God, endowed with benignity, fhould ftretch forth his hand to mankind thus wandering in eternal intricacies, mercifully vouchfafe himfelf to become his guide, lead him to truth, and make his own way ftrait before him. This mode of argument, however, I do not infift upon, I make ufe of it rather to illuftrate than infer. I can do without any conceffions from reafon; for, at all events, I am certain, that, if fhe does not affirm, fhe cannot, upon the principles which I have already laid down, deny the confiftency of fuch an act with the agent of whom it is fuppofed; but if the ftrongeft external teftimony bear witnefs, that God has revealed himfelf, and that reafon be incapable of producing any evidence to the contrary; nay, if a revelation be what reafon might have herfelf prefcribed, and hoped as a guide to her own errors, wherefore fhould we not acquiefce in it when related, and look upon it as a fact, that God has actually revealed himfelf? The nature and validity of the teftimony, upon which the affertion is made, is extreamly well worth

enquiry,

enquiry, and certainly fhould be inveftigated by all who entertain any doubt of the fact afferted. For my own part, I am fatisfied; and Mr. Lindfey has exempted me from the neceffity of going into the enquiry here; having acknowledged that God has revealed himfelf, that the fcriptures are his revelation, that they afford " an evidence which no fair mind can refift," and that they are " the only rule of faith and confcience to Chriftian men:" In all of which I perfectly and entirely agree with him. The credibility of God, whom all allow, and who has pronounced himfelf to be the God of truth, is a ground whereon to build our faith in whatfoever he fhall relate of his own incomprehenfible majefty; and, as I have faid before, that the conduct of God can never be meafured by his attributes, fo I now fay, that there lies no appeal from his credibility, from his truth to the infcrutable nature; we muft acquiefce in that which he has faid; it muft be; it is true.

Having admitted the fcriptures to be the word of God, and that whatfoever is fet forth in them is true, we are not yet to conceive that he has fo far fubmitted himfelf to our faculties as to enable us to draw any argument from him; for we are not yet to compare his conduct, as revealed therein, with God himfelf, nor to judge of the confiftency of any act therein declared to be his, with the infinite Agent ftill left incomprehenfible; for to render him otherwife to us, the enlargement of our faculties muft attend upon a revelation of all his glory, and therefore a revelation of all his glory is not to be required. Perhaps the diftinction is not here fo clearly marked as I could defire, and that what I have laft written may feem to be only a repetition of what immediately precedes it; it is not fo; what I wifh to inculcate is briefly this, that, as in natural religion, no comparifon can be had between the attributes of God, and the moral evils of the world submitted to our observation, and yet that we do not quite consent to annihilate an original to nature, because his government seems to argue against him; so we should not, when revelation declares a course of conduct, which we cannot reconcile with the attributes ascribed to him, any more deny that course of conduct, from its irreconcileableness with God, than we should deny the existence of moral evil, because we had by nature pronounced that Original to be great, wise, and good: For if moral evil were incapable of rooting out the acknowledgment of the existence of a cause supremely good; so a conduct, not understood to be wise, should not be admitted an argument against the existence of a revealed God; but we cannot deny the existence of moral evil, and yet nature says there is a good God; wherefore then should we conceive, that an acknowledgment of a conduct confessedly not understood, and therefore not to be reprehended, can militate against the acknowledgment of the God who has revealed himself? Let us then, if we admit a good cause consistent with moral evil, not argue against the consistency of an incomprehensible God, and an unintelligible conduct: There may subsist an unseen relation in this latter case; whereas an eventual evil, resulting from a supreamly good cause, seems actually to contradict our reason. The purpose for which I have written this, is to put men upon their guard against any suggestion, that the revelation of God, made by himself, should convey an adequate idea of his great glory. That it should do so to man I have shewed to be impossible. It has indeed declared him infinite, but a declaration that God is infinite, is a declaration that he is incomprehensible: An indefinite majesty is all that can possibly be ascribed to God; and, in the conduct of incomprehensible wisdom, it is not probable that much can occur exactly conformable to our faculties. If then,

even

even a revelation be unable to make him comprehended, we are still to confider him beyond the reach of reafon; and when he relates his own actions, still conceive that the agent is not cognizable, that he should be compared with them. To make us better men upon hope grounded on his mercies, is the moft beneficial purpofe for which we can conceive it poffible for God to reveal himfelf; and to this very purpofe we find a revelation made, wherein that providence which extends to us is declared. To what end fhould God lay before our eyes the government of all that we are not concerned in? That he has created and redeemed us, is a motive to gratitude and to brotherly love; it is fufficieut to fhew in him a power to be feared for its extent, and adored for its beneficent exertion. To evince that he has promifed to every man the reward of his works, and pointed out thofe works which lead us to hope in him that is faithful, is a fully fufficient motive to faith, hope, and charity; that he bears the relative fuperiority of a creator over his creature, is a fufficient motive to us to pronounce him our God, and afcribe to him all honour and glory, without feeking for a farther revelation of the exertion of his infinite power, which we are not concerned to know. But in the government of the univerfe, it may be faid, he has felected this little orb, rolling through infinite fpace, as a fcene of a moft wonderful tranfaction in which we are certainly concerned; for it is afferted that our falvation is the confequence, and was the end propofed; and are we not yet to comprehend him? By no means; the infinite wifdom which dictated and knows wherefore fuch a tranfaction is the fitteft means of our falvation, has not yet fubmitted itfelf to our inveftigation, nor directly told us why this was the moft adequate means to fo beneficent an end; he still remains incomprehenfible, and that tranfaction by which we are become partakers of eternal life, being revealed,

amounts

amounts only to a foundation and motive for us to rely upon God, and act according to his will thereby declared to us, and not to a display of all that must necessarily exceed the limits of our perception. We are not called upon to account for his conduct; but we are required to love him, to hope and to trust in him. A declaration of his power, and the exertion of so much of it as bears relation to us, is all then that was necessary for those ends; these are best declared by a revelation of the conduct of God towards man. Such a revelation is made, and there is much in it that we cannot understand; and such must ever be the case, for in whatsoever action we look upon, proceeding from a higher intellect than our own, we shall see somewhat not intelligible till the grounds of it are communicated. In whatsoever action of God, made perceptible to us, we look upon, we shall see somewhat which must eternally continue unintelligible; for it proceeds from infinite heights of intellect, and consequently must be incommunicable.

Reason is, as it were, the eye of the mind; and as the eye is incapable of comparing invisible things, or visible with invisible, so is reason incompetent to bring together objects not perceptible, or to compare that which it can perceive with that which is beyond her perception. A view into that which is invisible, is not necessary to give existence to that which the eye has seen; neither is the comprehensibility of objects not perceptible, necessary to the existence of that which is submitted to the perception of reason.

Having, as I hope, now proved that there can subsist no visible relation between the conduct of God and the uncomprehended God of natural religion, and therefore that reason cannot deny that he has revealed himself;
and

and having farther fhewed, upon the fuppofition that he has revealed himfelf, that it was neither neceffary nor poffible for him to render himfelf comprehenfible to our faculties; and therefore that his conduct, as revealed, cannot be brought into comparifon with himfelf, that it fhould be denied of him by reafon; we muft come to this conclufion, that God is not an object of our perception, and confequently his faculties are not a ground whence argument can proceed, that which is incomprehenfible not being to be brought to the teft of reafon, nor by her made a meafure for any thing which may be afferted concerning them. About matters which we do not comprehend, it is obvious that we cannot with certainty fay any thing. The incomprehenfible attributes of God then are not fit premifes, no conclufion poffibly following, from any comparifon of them with whatfoever may be revealed to have been effected by them.

The infinite and incomprehenfible majefty of God then is an object beyond the limits of reafon; we are incapable of forming any idea of him; and confequently, from whatfoever ultimate maxims reafon may proceed with relation to fcripture truth, fhe is debarred of any appeal to God himfelf, or to any imagination fhe may conceive herfelf able to entertain of him.

But the fcriptures are admitted to be the word of God, and whatfoever is fet forth in them is admitted to be true; henceforward reafon may proceed. The fcriptures are that ultimate, that axiom, beyond which we are not to feek for the grounds of whatfoever is afferted in them; they are the word of God, and they are true. This is granted, and from this datum there lies no appeal.

Come

Come on then, for reason has now found a commencement to her work; and first she says, the scriptures, being true, contain no contradictions, the truth of contradictories being impossible: Her business then it is to reconcile what seem to be contradictions, to compare, one with another, the passages which lead to particular conclusions, and to yield her assent to that which she cannot understand, referring it only to the credibility of him who is the author of it; to acquiesce in the conduct of infinite wisdom, and not seek for principles beyond her own limits. By such a process she will never pronounce any thing to be impossible, the impossibility of which she does not see upon a comparison of perceptible qualities; but, acknowledging herself incapable of giving counsel to her Maker, believe that he has employed means for our salvation which we cannot look into; trust him with the means who has so graciously employed them for such an end; look upon the end not with vain and impious curiosity, but with unbounded gratitude; habituate our minds by such a prospect to love him, and from love and gratitude ascend to the desire to please him; seek from himself the means of pleasing him, and with renewed love and gratitude learn that to bear good will towards man, is the conduct most conformable to his will, that by which we shall best ascribe glory to God on high, and by which we shall procure to ourselves eternal happiness through Jesus Christ our Lord and Saviour. Is this a conduct beneath the dignity of reason? It is a glorious undertaking which is committed to her charge.— Let us now come more directly to the point.

If then the testimony of our Saviour be allowed, and the testimony of the Holy Ghost, to which he refers enquirers into his nature, be admitted as credible; and if by these it be declared that Jesus Christ is God from everlasting,

everlasting, I see not how a doubt is to be entertained that he is God, one with, and equal to, the Father: But if his having appeared clothed with flesh among men, as a man; if his sympathetick tears; if his apprehensive agonies and prayers to have the cup of evil put away from him; if his having fallen under the severest afflictions, and even having suffered an ignominious death, added to his own testimony and that of the Holy Ghost, be admitted as evidence that he was man, I see not how a doubt can be entertained that he was Man, inferior to God, as we are inferior to him: and if these be both admitted, it must necessarily follow, that Jesus Christ is both God and Man: But if both God and Man, I do not see the force of the objection to his Godhead, that he has acted and suffered as Man; that he refers the preservation of his human nature to the power which is alone equal to the preservation of it; that he prays as man for the world, which he sympathizes with; that he declares his human nature and the man Jesus to be a messenger to man, and acting with power derived of God. For as I believe that men, who make a difficulty of believing that any union between the two natures is possible, will hardly insist upon their own capacity to explain the manner of it, or to shew that, upon such an union, so much of the divinity is derived to the manhood of Christ, as to render it independent of God, and able to act for its own purposes, without farther application than the exertion of this derived power: so I will not admit of their explanations of our blessed Saviour's prayers, and declarations that he was sent; for these prayers were breathed by the man Jesus; and this commission to die for and to adopt a world, was given to the human nature by God, and not to the divine nature of Christ, which was itself the power, one with the Father, God Almighty, which had so sent forth this man to atone for us.

us. I am far from saying that I am myself able to explain this union, God forbid; but that I am not able to explore the ways of an Almighty God, whose little creature I am, is not a reason why I should doubt his word, when he is pleased to reveal any part of them to me. We are told, that the ways of God are not as our ways, nor his thoughts as our thoughts: And shall we attempt to contradict the declarations of his power, because we cannot exert the like? Or question the wisdom which we cannot comprehend, merely because we cannot comprehend it? Were God pleased to open the stores of his wisdom to our eyes, but not to open our eyes to look upon them with more extended faculties than we now enjoy, is it to be imagined that we should comprehend them? Surely not; and wherefore should we reject the belief of that wonderful exertion of his power for our redemption, which he has laid open to us? It is a way of God, and not of man; and is its being wonderful a cause? It is a way of God, and not of man; and is its exceeding the limited comprehension of our faculties a cause? It is not to comprehend that we are required, but to believe; and to yield that degree of assent which we call belief, is certainly the best, nay the only exertion of our reason in the case before us; for, having granted that God is true, and that he has spoken, the inference is, that what he has spoken is true; and as his power is adequate to all things, no exercise of it can oppose the conclusion drawn; as his wisdom is infinite, no dictate of it is referred to our judgment; and therefore our judgment must retire from giving any decision upon other premises than those laid down; and consequently, instead of opposing, must abet the conclusion that follows from those which are stated. If our blessed Saviour himself, though in union with Godhead, was humble, and referred all to God, I should conceive that, instead of arrogantly opposing,

posing, we should cultivate in ourselves that mind which was in Christ Jesus, and humbly submit to his will, who has in part revealed, and in part reserved for future revelation, the mystery of our redemption, for a mystery I must agree with St. Paul in calling it, rather than with any mere human authority in denying it to be such.

Mr. Lindsey says, That, in a multitude of passages to which he refers, " Jesus Christ formally professes his inferiority and dependence, that he received his being and all his powers from God." It is of no consequence whether the passages referred to prove it or not, for I readily grant him this position, " There is one God, and one mediator between God and Men, the man Christ Jesus," 1 Tim. ii. 5. And when I have granted it, what will he infer more than I have already laid down, that, as Man, the man Jesus Christ (evidently intended here to be distinguished from God by that name only, and therefore in other respects implied to be one with the father, God) was inferior to God; that is, that having two natures, one was greater, and consequently one less than the other. Were I in the midst of an argument, proving the immortality of the soul of man, to declare, that I laboured under a lingering disease of which I feared that I should die, would even Mr. Lindsey say, that I had confuted my own doctrine of the soul's immortality? Would he pronounce that I meant my soul should die? And yet he might as well, as in the case before us, declare, that when Jesus Christ speaks as Man he denies his Godhead.

I do not mean to say, that there exists any analogy between the union of spirit and flesh in man, and the union of God and Man in Christ; for I do not at all
understand

understand how the union of soul and body exists, and consequently cannot compare it with that which I as little understand, for I cannot say that I understand it less; and how, if I am absolutely unacquainted with an union, which not only subsists in every person I hourly converse with, but even in myself, how, I say, am I to declare that an union between God and Man, of which but one instance has ever offered itself to human observation, is impossible? And I refer it to Mr. Lindsey, or any of his disciples, to explain the nature of Spirit, and to shew its compatibility with Flesh; or that of Flesh, and to shew its compatibility with Spirit; and if my request be not complied with, from their absolute and entire ignorance, I must then request farther that they will desist from denying the compatibility of Natures, which they must allow they as little understand. They yield their assent in the one case, because daily observation confirms the existence of an animal in which spirit and flesh are conjoined, and they take their assent to be a conclusion from premises supplied by reason; but because Christ is but one, they have not had an opportunity of analysing him, as they think they have done by their own nature, and so deny what they could never have understood, had there been as many Christs as Men. Would they desire such an intimacy? would they desire such a multiplication? see where the impious tenet ends, " Jesus Christ once crucified is not a sufficient atonement for the sins of mankind." I shall make no farther comment than to declare, that whensoever reason withholds belief in that which it comprehends not, merely because it is beyond the reach and comprehension of reason, the union of the body and soul in man must be denied; for it never can be proved by reason, which must understand the compatibility of both before the union can be declared to exist. I would then advise every man not determined to be a

sceptic,

sceptic, whom I will not hesitate to pronounce a fool, to look upon a revelation of one, the sufficiency of which precludes the necessity, and consequently the existence of more, to be adequate to a fuller view of that which admits of a fuller view. In short, my recommendation amounts to no more, nor less, than the old established maxim, that proofs, and consequently our credit, are to be deduced from the best evidence the nature of the case admits of.

The best evidence then, which the nature of the case before us admits of, is the revelation of God, allowed to have been made by him, and admitted incontrovertibly true. Whatsoever is related therein, is advanced upon authority sufficient to warrant our assent; but as the revelation is not itself supported by an equally strong evidence as that which, upon admittance, it affords to whatsoever it testifies, we are not required to yield more than belief to the assertions contained in it; were it as certainly the word of God, as the word of God is certainly true, we should possess little less than certainty of the facts revealed therein; but being allowed, upon that evidence which is unquestionably sufficient to induce credit, it remains to be enquired into, whether it bears testimony to the divinity of our blessed Reedeemer Jesus Christ, or not?

As I have now reached the threshold, and am just entering into the proofs, and the nature of the proofs, which the scriptures afford of the truth of this great mystery, once more let me warn, and deeply inculcate the warning, to beware of the delusions of natural religion, if such a religion there be, and if that which we conceive to have been derived from nature, be not rather a residuum, after our pride has rejected whatsoever is revealed beyond its reach.

The

The Chinese philosopher believes, that the earth stands upon the back of an elephant, which stands upon the back of a tortoise, which stands upon the back of, &c. &c. &c. Now, suppose this same philosopher to be instructed in the Copernican system, and that he had, upon full consideration, yielded his assent to the great probability of its truth; would it not rather seem absurd in him, after a time, to recur to his old tenets, because the sufficiency of the sun's attractive power to support this world, was inconsistent with the occupation of his old elephant and tortoise, and that he could not see how it should be possible for animals so loaded, and of themselves none of the swiftest, to carry the earth, whirling through its orbit with such astonishing velocity? Just so absurd shall we be, if, after our assent to the truth of God, and admission that he has revealed himself, we suffer any one previous persuasion to recur, and require that scripture should be consonant to it, after we have admitted that the word of God is true, whether it be consonant to any previous persuasion or not. The sensible Chinese would surely reject his ancient tenets upon the admission of that which he had assented to, because of the value of those arguments which had induced his assent; let us then, upon the admission of the scriptures as the ultimate boundary of argument, reject whatsoever seems to make against their ceded truth; howsoever we may persuade ourselves that reason had supplied it to us, we must have expatiated beyond her limits to seek for the tenet, for within her proper province it is not to be found.

CHAP.

CHAP. II.

Of the Nature of the Evidence of our Saviour's Divinity afforded by the Scripture.

THE full effulgence of the Gospel did not burst suddenly upon mankind. That sun of righteousness, by the light of which we are enabled to walk, did not at once reach its meridian height; so exceedingly gradual was its progress, that, when first it dawned upon the world, its rays were not discernible; "it shone in darkness, and the darkness comprehended it not;" it encreased in splendor, but was not sufficient to be the "light of those who come into the world; at length the day-star arose, and a light shone forth to lighten the Gentiles, and the day-spring from on high hath visited us, to give light to them that sit in darkness, and in the shadow of death, to guide our feet into the way of peace."

To drop the metaphor. We find the prophecies of our blessed Saviour, from great obscurity, become more and more explicit as they approach the great event: At the first they were extreamly indefinite, and such only as were adapted to the purposes for which they were pronounced. The first hope of redemption to mankind accompanied the sentence of condemnation, and was graciously conveyed by God himself, who comforted the forlorn state of our fallen parents with a promise conceived in general terms, that the seed of the woman should bruise the head of the serpent which had beguiled her.

Noah is afterwards taught by the Spirit to hope, and to exclaim, "blessed be the Lord God of Shem." To shew that this blessing is a prophecy, it is enough to say, that Noah spoke it in a train of prophecy concerning the future state of his own sons and their posterity. From Shem descended Abraham, to Abraham was the promise made, and from Abraham, as concerning the flesh, Christ came. From the manner in which the blessing upon Shem is pronounced, I incline greatly to believe that this descent was the object of Noah's prophetic vision; it seems to have been the result of his having foreseen, that, in the progeny of Shem, all the families of the earth should be blessed: and let it be remembered, that Noah was no unconcerned prophet in whatsoever should happen to any future inhabitants of the earth; for all were then equally to descend from him as their common parent; and well might he rejoice and bless the God of Shem, by one of whose line he foresaw that all his posterity should be blessed.

To Abraham, because he had obeyed the voice of the Lord, it is foretold, (and this is by the New Testament declared to be spoken of Jesus Christ) that in his seed all the nations of the earth should be blessed; and this promise is from time to time renewed in that line of which our Saviour was to be born; to Isaac, in preference to Ishmael; to Jacob, in preference to Esau; and to Judah, in preference to his eleven brothers. To Judah, indeed, there is somewhat of more particular revelation made, for the length of time during which he shall bear the sceptre (that is, continue a tribe) is made commensurate with the coming of Shiloh, upon which the sceptre is to depart from him. Judah alone continued to be a tribe after the Assyrian Captivity, and then only ceased when Christ came; whence, however difficult it may be to explain this passage with certainty, it is to be presumed that the prophecy of Jacob, concerning the sceptre of Judah and its time

of

of departure, bears reference to the coming of the Meffiah.

Mofes, who is the relater of what was fpoken before his day, in his own perfon alfo often fpeaks of a future prophet: And in the compelled prophecies of Balaam, when he poured forth bleffings from a heart replete with curfes, and in fpight of that indignation with which he afcended the rock to denounce evil, forefhewed the future brightnefs of the ftar that fhall come forth out of Jacob, there is fomething which, however obfcure it may be, is certainly referable to our Lord.

David hoped for one of his feed to fit upon his throne; and though he looked for a defcendent from himfelf, he has neverthelefs " in fpirit called him Lord." That our Saviour was the object of David's expectation, though he knew not why he called him Lord, and only trufted that fome great good was promifed to him, the declaration of the angel to the Virgin Mary evinces, who fays to her of the child which fhe is to bear, and whom fhe is to call Jefus, " He fhall be great, and fhall be called the Son of the Higheft; and the Lord fhall give unto him the throne of his Father David, and he fhall reign over the houfe of Jacob for ever, and of his kingdom there fhall be no end," Luke i. 32, 33.

Every fucceeding prophet throughout the Old Teftament found a confolation to the feveral troubles of Judea, in looking forward to that which was revealed to them in a general way by the fpirit of Chrift; but the full declaration of that which was fo revealed was withheld from them; they underftood it not themfelves, and even when they fpoke of the divinity of our Saviour, like Balaam, they spoke it constrainedly; they uttered only the word which the Lord had put into their mouths. If they who spoke it were ignorant of its meaning, it is no great wonder that they who heard did not understand the full force of the prophecy of the Godhead of him who was to come; nor is their misapprehension a reason why we should doubt that the prophets foretold it. The purpose of prophecy is " to tell before it come to pass, that when it come to pass we may believe," John xiv. 29. And the object of the prophecy of the Old Testament is the coming of a great deliverer, of whom such seeming contrarieties are declared, that it is not possible the Jews could ever have formed a definite idea of the expected Messiah. It is foreshewn of our Saviour, (whom all allow to be the Christ) that he was to be a King of the seed of David, and to sit upon his throne; that he was to be cut off, but not for himself; that he was to be exalted and extolled, and to be very high; oppressed, afflicted, bruised and put to grief, numbered with the transgressors, taken from prison, and from judgment, and cut off out of the land of the living; ruling the nations, &c. Isaiah lii. and liii. With such irreconcileable declarations were the hopes of the Jews kept alive; but in all this there is nothing that could have suggested an expectation that God himself would come; for how should the idea of his infinite majesty unite itself with that of a man of sorrows and acquainted with grief, having a cheek turned to the scorner? and how, indeed, could even such an idea as this agree with the expectation of a great King, to overcome all their enemies? It cannot, therefore, be admitted in argument against the divinity of Jesus Christ, that it was not understood by the Jews; for how should they understand it, when the prophets, who prophesied of the grace that should come unto us, have enquired and

searched

searched diligently of this salvation, " searching what, or what manner of time, the spirit of Christ which was within them did signify, when it testified beforehand the sufferings of Christ, and the glory that should follow. Unto whom it was revealed, that, not unto themselves, but unto us, they did minister the things which are now reported unto you by them that have preached the gospel unto you, with the Holy Ghost sent down from heaven; which things the angels desire to look into, 1 Pet. i. 10, 11, 12. and that many prophets have desired to see these things which our Saviour shewed forth, and have not seen them."

To us then, who have come after the event, it belongs to explain the prophecy, as that which is foretold is come to pass; and therefore we must cease to look for such testimony from the prophets as should have explained the fact, to such as had never seen it: of the sufferings of Christ, and the glory that should follow, they could form no certain idea whatsoever, nor did the prophecy put things into that order, as to impart a notion that the glory was to be subsequent to the sufferings; and this I assert, notwithstanding that Isaiah had said " he shall divide the spoil with the strong: because he hath poured out his soul unto death," Isa. liii. 12. For even the expectation of a man to arise from the dead, never seems, by the history of the Jews, throughout the Old Testament, in the least degree to have suggested itself to them; for if it had, Christ crucified could not have been to the Jews a stumbling block; and it is even probable, that such a fact, clearly understood, might have withheld their hands from inflicting that death whereby " Christ was perfected."

Still nearer to the manifestation of Christ the Angel has declared, that the Prophet, who should be the preparer of the ways of the Lord, should be filled with the Holy Ghost, even from his mother's womb; and Zacharias, upon the birth of John, breaks that silence which had been imposed upon him because of his unbelief, and, being filled with the Holy Ghost, cried out, "Blessed be the Lord God of Israel, for he hath visited and redeemed his people, and hath raised up an horn of salvation for us, in the house of his servant David; as he spake by the mouth of the holy prophets, which have been since the world began," Luke i. 67, 68, 69; and then speaking of his own son, who was the appointed harbinger of the Christ, whom he has already called the Lord God of Israel, he says, " and thou child shall be called the Prophet of the Highest; for thou shalt go before the face of the Lord to prepare his ways," Luke i. 76. The angel said also to the Virgin Mary, when he gave her assurance of the birth of her son to be called Jesus, " He shall be great, and shall be called the Son of the Highest; and the Lord God shall give him the throne of his father David;" and " that Holy Thing which shall be born of thee, shall be called the Son of God," Luke i. 32, 33, 35. The babe leapt in the womb of Elizabeth for joy upon the salutation of Mary, and Elizabeth asks this remarkable question, similar in expression to the prophecy of David already cited, " whence is this to me, that the mother of my Lord should come to me?" Luke i. 43. The shepherds are told by an angel, " unto you is born this day, in the city of David, a Saviour, which is Christ the Lord," Luke ii. 11. At the presentation of the infant Redeemer in the temple, Simeon, to whom it was revealed by the Holy Ghost, that he should not see death before he had seen the Lord's Christ, taking the babe in his arms " blessed God, and expressed his contentment to depart then, his eyes having seen the promised source of salvation,"

Luke

Luke i. 28, 29. And subsequent to these mysterious predictions concerning the supposed child of a carpenter, came forth a prophet, cotemporary in birth with Jesus Christ, appointed to be his immediate forerunner, to prepare the way of the Lord, and to make his paths straight, and he declared of him that "he that cometh from above, is above all;" and that "he that believeth on the Son, hath everlasting life," John iii. 31, 36.

Thus, from the first obscure hint of salvation to our first parents, do the prophecies gradually approximate to an explanation of the great glory which should in the end be revealed; but by no means have they become so explicit yet, as to render a revelation unnecessary; nay, there is yet to proceed a new species of previous intimation to makind of "the salvation of God which all flesh shall see," Luke iii. 6; and accordingly now came forth the great subject of all that had been testified, but not yet to be declared, nor yet indeed the full subject of the prophecy, nor of the subsequent testimony of the spirit, having before him that mighty work to do, toward which the hopes of the prophets looked as the source of deliverance, in vain searching into what the manner of it was to be; a work by which we have received the atonement, and obtained reconciliation, the word and ministry of which was afterwards to be committed by God to those who were to be the appointed witnesses of our Lord: and this ministry of reconciliation is that which alone can be, according to the scriptures, pronounced the manifestation of Jesus Christ; and therefore I consider himself, even the Lord of glory, who was crucified, who arose from the grave, and ascended into heaven, as only bearing, by his miracles, a practical testimony during his stay on earth, to that which should be revealed

vealed of him when his work should be finished. This, indeed, I admit to be a much closer evidence of the Godhead than any given before; and that, perhaps, by which the minds of men should be led to look upon the expected King of the Jews in a much more exalted light than the former prophecies had instructed them to do. It is such an evidence as, when referred to, might well provide credit, when it should come to pass, for that which before it came to pass it had foreshewn. Our Saviour himself, for the most part, declines bearing witness to himself, but refers both to the scriptures which had now begun to be fulfilled, and which he desires to have diligently sought into as about to receive their full completion, and to the testimony of the Holy Ghost hereafter to be given for the purpose of manifesting him; and whenever he does bear record, it is rather such as he would have second to that which should follow the finishing of his work here, thence to derive its explanation, than such as he would have principal in the line of evidence.

Had our blessed Lord and Saviour borne any ultimate testimony to the Jews that he was God, they would have known this hidden mystery; and, "had they known it," says St. Paul, "they would not have crucified the Lord of glory," 1 Cor. ii. 8; and so the very end of his coming in the flesh would have been defeated; mankind must still have remained due to the justice of God, without the atonement which we have received by the death of Christ. The blood of our gracious Redeemer was to be the price of our salvation, and would it have been consistent with wisdom to take measures to prevent the shedding of it? It was enough that his miracles should testify of him to those who were afterwards to preach him, and offer them to mankind as marks of a life consistent with what they should relate

relate concerning his death, resurrection, and ascension, which were the great persuasives to believe in his Godhead, and in that mighty work which he came in the flesh to do for our sake.

Our Saviour, I say, did not frequently bear record to himself; but continuing the train of prophecy of that by which we also have become the children of Abraham, the Israel of God, even of that which all the prophets had in view, the redemption of makind, he very frequently foretells his own sufferings, that " the Son of man shall be lifted up as Moses lifted up the serpent in the wilderness;" that " he will raise the temple in three days, and this he spake of his body;" and " that he will go before us into heaven." That this great event, attended by such mighty consequences to us, consolatory in every woe of Israel, and making all men heirs of salvation, should be the object of prophecy, and of the subsequent testimony of the Holy Ghost, no man surely can doubt, when, in order to enable us to become partakers of the benefits thence derived to mankind, it is necessary that we believe in Christ, " who gave himself a ransom for all, to be testified in due time," 1 Tim. ii. 6. " How beautiful then upon the mountains are the feet of those who bring good tidings of good!" A preacher, even the Holy Spirit, has instructed us in the salvation which is of God, and " said unto Zion, thy God reigneth."

This then is the line of testimony; this the object of revelation, namely, that " Christ, by being made perfect, has become the author of eternal salvation unto all them that obey him;" that he hath been the Redeemer of mankind by the full accomplishment of all that he came to do for us; and not, according to Mr. Lindsey, that he has merely come into the world as a
teacher,

teacher, the truth of whose doctrines were to be witnessed by his death. And let not this be considered as an unsupported suggestion of my own, it is authorised by St. Luke in the first chapter of the Acts; where, speaking of that history which he had before set forth of the life of our Saviour, he is so far from considering it as the manifestation of Christ, that he says, " The former treatise have I made, O Theophilus, of all that Jesus *began* both to do and to teach, until the day in which he was taken up:" so that all the life of our Lord in the flesh was but a commencement of that which was afterwards to be revealed. In the moment of his ascent too, the same apostle presents Christ telling his disciples that " ye shall receive power after that the Holy Ghost is come upon you: and ye shall be witnesses unto me, both in Jerusalem, and in all Judea, and in Samaria, and unto the uttermost part of the earth," Acts i. 8. Of what were they to be witnesses unto him? of that which he had already died to testify? Was his death then so defective a testimony to those who had seen it in Jerusalem, and who had also seen his resurrection? If these were intended but as a mere testimony that he had lived, wrought miracles, and taught among them, we must declare that they have come very short of answering the purpose, if there still remained a necessity of appointing farther witnesses to concur in proving their object. Was it ever before heard of, that the breathless corpse of a man is a better evidence of his having been born into the world than his living and active body, that our Saviour's death should be considered only as a proof of his life? Did a continued series of miracles, performed before the eyes of the multitude, stand in need of one more, to prove, to those who had seen them, that they had been performed? or are those moral doctrines, which our blessed Redeemer delivered to mankind, of such a dubious

nature,

nature, that any man should entertain a doubt of their justice, requiring so strong an engine as the death and resurrection of the preacher, in order to remove it? No, but on the contrary, so obvious is their rectitude, so far from requiring any testimony whatsoever to their indisputable truth, that many who never became Christians allowed their value; and even Trajan, who persecuted those " who called upon Christ as God," adopted from his sermons that charitable doctrine of returning good for evil. But of what were they to be witnesses unto him? of his death and resurrection? What? to Jerusalem, and all Judea, and to Samaria? did Christ hang invisible on a cross at Jerusalem, that a witness shall be wanting to testify it? or was his death and resurrection a transaction carried on in secret? On the contrary, at the very time when he was dragged " from judgment to pour out his soul unto death; when he was numbered with the transgressors, and made intercession for the transgressors," Isaiah liii. all Judea were eye-witnesses of the fact; for it was at the time of the passover, when all Judea had come up to Jerusalem, the scene of the transaction, to celebrate that feast: nay, farther, where all Judea, as if to fill up the measure of her rebellions, and justify her approaching desolation, had, with one voice, cried out, "crucify him, crucify him." Of this then they were not to be witnesses unto him; but of that which the prophets had not made manifest, of that which the life and lessons of our Saviour himself had not made manifest, without farther explanation. They were to be witnesses unto him, that he was the expected Christ, and that the Christ was the " mighty God, the everlasting Father, the Prince of peace;" that the Godhead of him, whom their own eyes had seen, so far from being a great king, that he was actually in " the form of a servant," and an ignominious sufferer, was the royalty

F which

which they had looked for in the expected king of Israel; that he was indeed a "king who had all things put under his feet, who had led captivity captive, and hath given to us the victory over death and the grave; a king, whose throne endureth for ever, and the sceptre of whose kingdom is a right sceptre." To these witnesses of Jesus Christ the Holy Ghost was given, even the spirit of truth, to shew forth the means of our redemption, by which his infinite mercy had reconciled mankind to his infinite justice: whatsoever the prophets had said was given to them to understand, to open, and to reconcile: and whatsoever our Lord had done and said in the flesh, was given to their remembrance to corroborate that which they should themselves declare; and these they have accordingly called upon, and shewed to be a testimony bearing toward the truth, which it was their appointment to render fully manifest, even this great truth, that the blood which streamed from a supposed malefactor, dying for imputed blasphemy upon a cross, was the blood of God himself, Acts xx. 28. "poured out for our transgressions," and "by which we have received the atonement." This is the full manifestation of Christ to mankind; till the work was finished it could not be related, and, when done, so portentous was the deed in itself, so above the reach of all human intellect, that it required and obtained a miraculous testimony; a testimony precisely adequate to that which is required of those who receive it, our belief, which alone is called for as the terms upon which this great salvation is offered to us, "that eternal salvation of which, by being made perfect, he became the author unto all them that obey him," Heb. v. 9.

The prophecies waited for their explanation till all which they had predicted should have come to pass,

and

and therefore were not evidence to those who lived before the event. The four gospels relate, that a man had come into the world endowed with a power of working miracles, which he was perpetually exerting in acts of benevolence; instructing mankind in virtue, by lessons superior to those of any other man; speaking of the kingdom of God, and saying, that he was the door by which it was to be entered; inculcating faith in God, and the hope in his mercies, arising from the cultivation of piety toward him, and goodwill toward man; testifying that he was the object of former prophecy; foreshewing things which the hearers remembered, when they came to pass, to have heard of, but not to have understood before; dying upon a cross, arising from the grave, and ascending into heaven; that is, the gospels relate the history of Jesus Christ in the flesh, but have by no means revealed him, nor declared finally who or what he is, wherefore he died, arose, and ascended. They tell us that he did the work for which he came, but the full import of this work, and why undertaken by this man who finished it, was not the object of the historian to reveal; and till it was finished it could not be revealed to what end it had been done. From our Saviour we are not to expect this revelation, for his ascension into heaven being a part, the final part of his work, he continued not among men to declare its end. Another testimony then must be found, and that such as must be very powerful; we accordingly now find the apostolic body come forth in the strength of the Lord, endowed with miraculous powers to be exerted before all hearers, and blessed with elocution in every language, that all hearers might understand and believe; and thus the end of all that has been done is declared; that our salvation was the object is revealed; that for our sins Christ died, and that for our justification he rose again;

that he has taken our nature into heaven, " having appeared to put away sin, by the sacrifice of himself," Heb. ix. 26. and, " by his own blood entered in once into the holy place, having obtained eternal redemption for us," Heb. ix. 12. that, because he can have a feeling of our infirmities, having been in all points tempted like as we are, he is now our high-priest and intercessor; and that, for the same gracious reason, he is to be our judge, when, in the last day, he shall come forth in his glory, and all nations shall be gathered before him, even before their God.

I hope and believe now that I have pointed out the degrees of proof which have been afforded to the world, that the Lord of life, Jesus Christ, who redeemed it, is the God of our salvation; and having shewn by what light he has been manifested, even that which has come from himself after his ascension and resumption of his former glory, it is easy to see that the prophets and evangelists are to be read by that light only: by this alone the expectations of Israel are to be reconciled, and the prophets found to have spoken consistently; and what other circumstances could have reduced their predictions to good sense, but a revelation of the glory that has followed the sufferings of our Lord and Saviour Jesus Christ? what other circumstances than the death, burial, resurrection, and ascension of a man revealed to be the " King of kings, and Lord of lords," Rev. xix. 16; " who has become the captain of our salvation, who shall come once again with power and great glory, sitting upon the throne of his glory, bringing his reward with him, to judge all men, could reconcile the expectations which the prophets had imparted, that the Messiah should be a King, sitting on the throne of David for ever; that he should be a great deliverer, subduing

all

all nations under them; and also, that he should be a man despised and rejected of men, wounded for our transgressions, and bruised for our iniquities, upon whom was the chastisement of our peace, and by whose stripes we are healed?" Isa. liii. 5. for such were the indefinite hopes of the Jews, and therefore their ignorance is never to be considered as of any weight in argument against the Godhead of Christ, nor a defect of testimony in the Old Testament taken by itself, and not explained by the subsequent revelation, as any ground for denying that which it was never written with a view of ultimately proving. The same thing may be asserted of the four evangelical histories of our Lord and Saviour Jesus Christ, they were not intended to have been ultimate; and, consequently, if partial quotations do not evince his divinity to partial enquirers, it is not in the least degree an argument that he was not one with the Father and the Holy Ghost, God. Those histories, I have said already, were written with a view of setting before all men the works which our blessed Redeemer did, in evidence of a power concerning which he withheld his own testimony, but for the promulgation of which he refers to the scriptures already written, and to the testimony of the Holy Ghost hereafter to be afforded, the truth of which, he foresaw, would be less liable to doubt than that of his own record, which he therefore declined bearing, saying, that it would not be received as true. Had our Lord therefore been wholly silent upon this head, not even his absolute silence would have derogated from the evidence of his divinity. "He came not to bear witness of himself," "but to be testified in due time;" and he even saw that his testimony, had he attempted to have borne it, would be rejected, as an evil interpretation was put upon the most benevolent exertion of his power; that the faith

of

of even his perpetual hearers was defective, and that they had fallen from him, because they could not comprehend him. He therefore looked for the belief of mankind from a miraculous declaration and testimony of his Godhead, to be borne, not after a partial, but a full execution of that great work which he took our nature upon him to do; and saw that Godhead would be more readily acquiesced in, as in union with a man who should be testified to have risen from the dead, and ascended into heaven, than with one, the course of whose innocent life was seemingly unable to resist persecutions and sorrows, nay the infliction of an ignominious death. An acquaintance with grief, a cheek turned to the scorner, the grave and the shadow of death, which he had often (and even with agonies which certified his feeling of our infirmities) predicted to be all before him, were so far from conveying an idea of divinity, that they afforded but a very humiliating picture of humanity. The belief of mankind was not required from such circumstances, and they who inflicted those miseries upon him were forgiven, for they knew not what they did. It is at the same time true, that Jesus Christ has not left us without a record of himself, as I shall hereafter have occasion to shew, but it was carried only so far as to become a testimony, when explained afterwards, otherwise they who crucified him must have known what they did. On the day on which our Lord was betrayed, knowing that his hour was come, he says to his disciples "I have yet many things to say unto you, but ye cannot bear them now. Howbeit, when he the spirit of truth is come, he will guide you into all truth: for he shall not speak of himself; but whatsoever he shall hear, that shall he speak: and he will shew you things to come. He shall glorify me: for he shall receive of mine, and shall shew it unto you.

you. "All things that the Father hath, are mine: therefore said I, that he shall take of mine, and shall shew it unto you," John xvi. 12, 13, 14, 15. What is this but saying, that as they are as yet unable to bear the full revelation of his nature, he will in a future time shew it to them by the spirit who shall speak as he shall receive of Christ. And that it is the full declaration of the Godhead, which, he says, they are as yet unable to bear, and which he will reveal by the spirit who shall testify of the truth, is evident from the testimony which he proceeds to say this spirit shall bear to him; for " he shall glorify him," having received that which he is to shew from Christ, whose it is, and from the Father, whose it is, equal possessors of the glory which shall be revealed. A triumph over death, and an ascent into heaven, were first to intervene; and these, added to every miracle performed in the presence of multitudes, were facts, which, when referred to, were fully sufficient to shew forth a power that none could doubt to be the power of God; and if the Holy Ghost, by miracles subsequent to such an act as that of rising from the darkness of the grave to the mansions of light, should testify of him who had so acted, that he was God, I see not how a more proper line of evidence could have been adopted, or a more certain means of spreading information among men, not hardened against the receipt of it, devised; nor do I see it to be less than an impious presumption to deny the attested fact, because we have not ourselves had the conduct of the evidence, and therefore do not find it where it is not reasonably to be expected.

The doctrine of Christ's godhead then may be considered as imparted to us by four different sorts of revelation; first, by the prophecies and the law, or in general terms that which was called the scriptures, before

fore the writing of the New Testament, to which we are referred, and told that " they are they which testify of me;" secondly, by the testimony of our blessed Saviour himself, whether by words or works, throughout the writings of the evangelists; thirdly, by the testimony of the apostles, confirmed by the Holy Ghost, to which our Saviour usually referred enquirers into his nature, whether delivered by them in the gospels, which were written after the Holy Ghost had been given to the writers, or by their explanation of the nature and the purposes of his having come and suffered in the flesh, in their sermons throughout the Acts, and in their epistles; and fourthly, by the testimony of Christ himself, after his ascension and reassumption of that glory wherewith he had been glorified before the world was, delivered by his having sent the comforter according to his frequent promises that he, and that the father (promiscuously named) would send him, by his compliance with the prayers of the apostles, his appearance in divers circumstances, and by the vision shewed to St. John in the revelation, in which he speaks of himself in the same terms, as God, before his incarnation, had spoken to the prophets.

This is the order in which the evidence is placed before us, and in which I shall therefore produce it in the following chapter. Were it to be stated according to the degree of its strength, it ought to be reversed.

There is yet another species of testimony borne to the divinity of our gracious Redeemer, resulting from the reconcileableness of the whole of sacred writ, upon the adopting this proposition as a datum, namely, that Christ is God. Were a subject to be treated so enigmatically by a man of sense, as that it should escape the understanding of all his readers, and yet leave them

con-

convinced upon the credit of the author, that the book itself was worth study and labour; were there scarce an intelligible sentence contained in the book, and yet a certainty that it contained much matter; and were there at length to arise a man whose ready faculties should alight upon one proposition by which that whole book should be explained, to which every obscure assertion should be referred, and by the reference to which they should become clear and perspicuous; and therefore it should appear, that this proposition was the object of every sentence, the darkness of which it dispelled; could any man pretend that this was not the object of the writer; or conceive that any one point, thus borne down upon by every argument, was not the point intended to be illustrated and proved? certainly not. And if, on the other hand, the contradictory of that proposition was a point to which the process of the argument so little referred, as that it should still continue obscure when referred to it; would any man say that this was the writer's object? certainly not. Exactly such is the state of the Bible; every position falls into sense, the tenour of it becomes a course of argument the instant that the divinity of our Saviour in union with manhood is acknowledged to be its object; whereas, upon a denial of this proposition, there is not on earth a book so fraught with contradictions and irreconcilable absurdities, as that which is acknowledged to be the word of the God of truth. Partial quotations therefore, and passages taken from the whole consistent word of God, are to be considered as of no value whatsoever in argument; they cannot afford any proof of any thing: and nothing contained in the sacred writings is to be explained but as it stands in context with the whole. Nothing less therefore than the whole of the Bible is to be considered as the gospel of Christ; and from the whole, taken together, his almighty Godhead is to be deduced.

CHAP. III.

The Evidence of our Saviour's Divinity afforded by the Scriptures.

AS I have already said that the Old Testament affords but a very small part of the testimony of the Godhead of Jesus Christ, I shall produce but few separate passages from it, under the head of prophecy: such as receive their explanation from the New Testament, being better brought under that head. It is not to shew that the prophets have foretold our Lord and Saviour that I am engaged, for that were an easy office; but to shew that they have foretold his divinity; and that the expected Messiah was, though ignorantly, by them declared to be God himself.

From the prophecies of the Old Testament I take the following proofs of the Godhead of Jesus Christ.

I.

" Therefore the Lord himself shall give you a sign, behold a virgin shall conceive, and bear a Son, and shall call his name Immanuel," Isaiah vii. 14. This prophecy is referred to by St. Matthew, declared to be of our Saviour, and the name interpreted to be " God with us."

II.

" For unto us a child is born, unto us a Son is given, and the government shall be upon his shoulder: and his name shall be called, Wonderful, Counsellor, the mighty God, the Everlasting Father, the Prince of Peace," Isai. ix. 6.

III.

" Thus saith the Lord the King of Israel, and his Redeemer the Lord of Hosts, I am the first, and I am the

the laſt, and beſides me there is no God," Iſai. xliv. 6. This aſſertion is made by God to Iſaiah, and by Jeſus Chriſt (verbatim) to St. John, Rev. ii. 8. God, in the ſubſequent verſes, declares his prerogatives to the prophet; the ſame are applicable to the ſame firſt and laſt, " is there a God beſides me? yea there is no God, I know not any." This God then is Jeſus Chriſt.

IV.

"Awake, awake, put on ſtrength, O arm of the Lord; awake, as in the antient days, in the generations of old. Art thou not it which hath dried the ſea, the waters of the great deep, that hath made the depths of the ſea a way for the ranſomed to paſs over?" Iſai. li. 9. 10. The anſwer to this call has the following words in it, " But I am the Lord thy God, that divided the ſea, whoſe waves roared: the Lord of Hoſts in his name," Iſai. li. 15. To this entire chapter, and the two following, I refer for the explanation of theſe texts which I have brought to evince the divinity of Jeſus Chriſt, and which I take to be even of themſelves ſufficient for that purpoſe. The arm of the Lord is here invoked, and in making anſwer, the arm of the Lord declares " I am the Lord thy God." The arm of the Lord, and the Lord God, are then with Iſaiah ſynonimous terms; but he afterwards ſays " the Lord hath made bare his holy arm in the eyes of all the nations, and all the ends of the earth ſhall ſee the ſalvation of our God," Iſai. lii. 10: and again, " Who hath believed our report? and to whom is the arm of the Lord revealed?" Iſai. liii. 1. To the former of theſe two texts St. Luke refers, and declares expreſsly that it is ſpoken of Jeſus Chriſt, for he relates that they were uttered by St. John the Baptiſt, whoſe office was to be the forerunner of our Saviour, Luke iii. 6. To the latter St. John refers, chap. xii. verſe 38, where he quotes the verſe at large concerning the unbelief in

Christ, and says, "these things said Esaias, when he saw his glory, and spake of him," John xii. 41. Here then is the same arm of the Lord, which is synonimous with God, declared to be Jesus Christ, whose name is therefore synonimous with God, one with him who is the " Lord thy God." St. Paul also intimates, that Christ was the leader of the Israelites through the wilderness, saying, " neither let us tempt Christ, as some of them also tempted," 1 Cor. x. 9; to which I refer.

V.

The arm of the Lord is thus foretold again, " behold, the Lord God will come with strong hand, and his arm shall rule for him: behold, his reward is with him, and his work before him. He shall feed his flock like a shepherd," Isa. xl. 10, 11. In the Revelation, our Saviour says to St. John, " behold, I come quickly; and my reward is with me," Rev. xxii. 12. And in the gospel he says, " I am the good shepherd," John x. 11. St. Paul says of him, " now the God of peace that brought again from the dead our Lord Jesus, that great shepherd of the sheep, through the blood of the everlasting covenant, make you perfect in every good work to do his will, working in you that which is well-pleasing in his sight, through Jesus Christ; to whom be glory for ever and ever. Amen." Heb. xiii. 20, 21. Here we find Isaiah's words concerning the arm of the Lord (the same as God) pronounced by our Saviour concerning himself, both in earth and in heaven, and also testified of him by St. Paul, whose doxology assists us to pronounce of Jesus Christ, in the words of Isaiah immediately preceding the text before us, " behold your God."

VI.

" How beautiful upon the mountains are the feet of him that bringeth good tidings, that publisheth peace, that bringeth good tidings of good, that publisheth salvation,

salvation, that saith unto Zion, thy God reigneth!" Isai. lii. 7. St. Paul, speaking of the necessity of a preacher to instruct men in the belief on Christ, that they may call upon him and be saved, directly applies these words of Isaiah, as being prophetick of a preacher who should publish salvation, and say unto Zion, "thy God reigneth," Rom. x. 15. If then the promulgation of the gospel of our blessed Lord and Saviour be correspondent to this prophecy, the preacher of Christ is surely he who says "thy God reigneth."

VII.

"Out of the mouth of babes and sucklings hast thou ordained strength," or "perfected praise," (which is the interpretation of the New Testament) Psa. viii. 2. These words David directs to God, whose name he declares to be excellent. When children in the temple cried "Hosanna to the Son of David," and the Chief Priests and Scribes were displeased at them for it, our Saviour himself justified the children by assuming the direction of these words to himself, and declaring them a prophecy of his praise, to be perfected by the mouths of babes and sucklings; so that we find a prophecy, that the praise of the Lord, "who had set his glory above the heavens," Psa. viii. 1. is declared to be fulfilled by the direction of praise and hosannas to the Son of David, who must therefore be one with the Father, God, Mat. xxi. 16.

VIII.

"For thy sake are we killed all the day long; we are counted as sheep for the slaughter," Psa. xliv. 22. These words directly addressed to God, by David, are by St. Paul declared to be a prophecy of the perseverance of the apostles in the love of Christ, of which he says, "Who shall separate us from the love of Christ? shall tribulation, or distress, or persecution, or famine, or nakedness, or peril, or sword?" As it is written,
"for

" for thy fake, &c." Rom. viii. 35. For whofe fake? certainly Chrift's, one with the Father, God.

The prophecies afforded by the New Teftament, I have already ftated in the preceding chapter, and fhall not trouble my reader with a repetition of them.

The following proofs are taken from the teftimony borne to our blefled Lord's divinity in the writings of the four evangelifts.

IX.

" Thy kingdom come," Matth. vi. 10. " Thine is the kingdom, and the power, and the glory, for ever and ever. Amen." Matth. vi. 13. That our Saviour's command to the difciples, is to addrefs thefe words, and the prayer in which they occur, directly to God, is not only granted but contended for: but let us fee now who is this God, who is this king of glory. " Then (in the laft day) fhall all the tribes of the earth mourn, and they fhall fee the Son of man coming in the clouds of heaven, with power and great glory. And he fhall fend his angels, &c." Matth. xxiv. 30, 31. " When the Son of man fhall come in his glory, and all the holy angels with him, then fhall he fit upon the throne of his glory. And before him fhall be gathered all nations; and he fhall feparate them one from another, as a fhepherd divideth his fheep from the goats; and he fhall fet the fheep on his right hand, but the goats on the left. Then fhall the King fay unto them on his right hand, come, ye blefled of my Father, &c." Mat. xxv. 31, 32, 33, 34. Here we fee the coming of the kingdom, and we fee alfo whofe is the kingdom, and the power, and the glory. Wherefore then fhould we fay that Jefus Chrift, in prefcribing this form of prayer, forbad worfhip and application to be made to him, whom we find to be the very being

defcribed

described and pointed out as the proper object of our adoration? It is manifestly his command that we should worship him; and hence it follows, that he is one with the Father, God Almighty. He says in another place, "whosoever shall be ashamed of me, and of my words, in this adulterous and sinful generation, of him also shall the Son of man be ashamed, when he cometh in the glory of his Father, with the holy angels," Mark viii. 38. On which I remark, that the glory of the Father, and of the Son, is but one glory, one Godhead; for we see our blessed Lord coming in his own glory, and in the parallel passage, in the glory of his Father. The following texts evince this, and also ascribe the kingdom and the glory to Jesus Christ. "The Son of man shall send forth his angels, and they shall gather out of his kingdom all things that offend, and them which do iniquity," Mat. xiii. 41. "The Son of man shall come in the glory of his Father, with his angels; and then he shall reward every man according to his works," Mat. xvi. 27. "Whosoever shall be ashamed of me and of my words, of him shall the Son of man be ashamed, when he shall come in his own glory, and in his Father's, and all the holy angels," Luke ix. 26. "No whoremonger, &c. hath any inheritance in the kingdom of Christ, and of God," Ephes. v. 5. "Jesus Christ, who shall judge the quick and the dead at his appearing, and his kingdom," 2 Tim. iv. 1. "The everlasting kingdom of our Lord and Saviour Jesus Christ," 2 Pet i. 11. Our Saviour, in answer to the demand of the Pharisees, (Luke xvii. 20 to 30) "when the kingdom of God should come," tells them, "the kingdom of God cometh not with observation;" or as it is translated in the margin of the Bible, "with outward show;" and then, addressing himself to his disciples, continues to declare, that no prognosticks shall foreshew his day; but that, as the flood was not preceded by any figns that it was at hand, but found men eating and drinking, and altogether unprepared, fo fhould it be " in the day when the Son of man is revealed." From the continuance of the difcourfe, and applying ftill the coming without obfervation, to the coming of the kingdom of God, and to his own day, which is often fpoken of as fynonimous with the day in which the Son of man fhall come in power and glory, fitting on the throne of his glory to judge the world, we may, without in the leaft ftraining for an inference, fay, that the day of which he fpeaks to the difciples as coming unobferved, and the kingdom of God, of which he afferts the fame thing to the Pharifees in the fame converfation, are one and the fame thing; and if the day of Chrift be the fame as the kingdom of Chrift, the kingdom of God is here declared to be the kingdom of Chrift; therefore one with the Father, on that day, on the coming of that kingdom to be fully revealed to be God.

X.

The incomprehenfibility of the Father and the Son, except to each other, is a mark of equality of Godhead, which alone can be the fubject of the following words of our Saviour himfelf. " No man knoweth the Son but the Father: neither knoweth any man the Father, fave the Son, and he to whomfoever the Son will reveal him," Matth. xi. 27. Many a man had known Jefus Chrift as Man; but as God, he was known then to the Father only, with whom he was one God. The parallel paffage fays, " No man knoweth who the Son is, but the Father, &c." Luke x. 22. Mr. Lindfey fays he does, but I cannot think it. How fhall he, who is known by all his difciples to be a man, fay he is unknown to all but the Father, if he fpeak not of a nature not human, and of fo high a rank as to be comprehenfible to the Father only, even his Godhead?

When

XI.

When our blessed Lord, just before he ascended into heaven, was sending forth his disciples to baptize all nations in the name of the Father, and of the Son, and of the Holy Ghost, and to teach them to observe all things which he had commanded them, he gives them a promise of his own assistance in the performance of their mission, saying, "And, lo! I am with you alway even unto the end of the world," Matth. xxviii. 20. We accordingly find that, upon his ascent, "they went forth, and preached every where, the Lord working with them, and confirming the word with signs following," Mark xvi. 20. "How then shall we escape if we neglect so great salvation, which at the first began to be spoken by the Lord, and was confirmed unto us by them that heard him; God also bearing them witness, both with signs and wonders, and with divers miracles, and gifts of the Holy Ghost, according to his own will?" Heb. ii. 3, 4. Here we find that the testimony of signs and miracles wrought to confirm what is preached by the apostles, is borne by God, and by the Lord Christ, therefore one, with the Father, God.

XII.

It is evident what was the faith of the father of the sick child, who "cried out, and said with tears, Lord, I believe; help thou mine unbelief," Mark ix. 24. So strong was his faith already, that he looked upon our Lord as possessed of power to assist his spirit, and supply whatsoever was defective in his belief. This application was approved and confirmed to be right by our blessed Saviour himself, who granted the distressed father's prayer, and healed his sick child.

XIII.

Upon hearing Jesus Christ say to the sick of the palsy, "Man, thy sins are forgiven thee," I cannot wonder at the remark of the Scribes, who said, "Who can forgive sins but God alone? For their law had shewed them that God had made an exclusive claim to the forgiveness of sins, saying, "I, even I am he that blotteth out thy transgressions for mine own sake, and will not remember thy sins," Isai. xliii. 25. But our Saviour perceived their thoughts, and healed the sick man, in order to shew "that the Son of man hath power upon earth to forgive sins," Luke v. 20, 25. But God, whom Nehemiah, ix. 17, beautifully, calls "a God of pardons," has an exclusive right in the forgiveness of sins; the Son of man who exercises that right, even Jesus Christ, is therefore one with the Father; God.

XIV.

"Blessed are ye when men shall hate you, and when they shall separate you from their company, and shall reproach you, and cast out your name as evil, for the Son of man's sake. Rejoice ye in that day, and leap for joy: for behold your reward is great in heaven: for in the like manner did their fathers unto the prophets," Luke vi. 22, 23. If the happiness of the disciples, to whom our Saviour addresses the words above, be not to proceed from the reproach, but from the cause wherefore they are to undergo it, there is no similitude between their case and that of the prophets, unless the prophets also suffered for the sake of the Son of man, and for the testimony which they bore to him; and that this was really the intention of our Lord's words, the following text, spoken by St. Stephen, will evince, "Which of the prophets have not your fathers persecuted? And they have slain them which shewed before of the coming of the just one; of whom ye have now been the betrayers and murderers," Acts vii. 52. Stephen was, at the time when he uttered these words, under the persecution which our Saviour had foretold to his disciples that they should sustain for his sake; he therefore reflected on the circumstance pointed out by him,

him, as a means of happiness and blessing, in their afflictions, and considered that, with the prophets, he was "a partaker of Christ's sufferings; that when his glory shall be revealed, he might be glad also with exceeding joy. If ye be reproached for the name of Christ, happy are ye; for the Spirit of glory, and of God resteth upon you: on their part he is evil spoken of, but on your part he is glorified," 1 Pet. iv. 13, 14. Let us just turn then to the relation of the sufferings of this authentic martyr of Christ, and see whether, upon the reproach incurred for his sake, the glory of God, and of Jesus sitting at his right hand, was not revealed to him; and whether the Spirit, which proceeds from the one glory, the one Godhead of the Father and the Son, did not rest upon him, even the Holy Ghost, with which he was comforted, and by which he cried, "Lord Jesus receive my spirit," Acts vii. 51 to 59.

XV.

"Jesus sent him away, saying, Return to thine own house, and shew how great things God hath done unto thee. And he went his way, and published throughout the whole city, how great things Jesus had done unto him," Luke viii. 38, 39. According to a command, to shew what God had done, the man who had been healed testified what Jesus had done. I do not look upon the evidence of this man as of any great weight in the argument; but there is certainly some testimony borne to our Saviour's divinity, by the manner in which the fact is related by an apostle filled with the Holy Ghost, for the purpose of preaching Christ with precision, and who has, nevertheless, repeated the same words concerning the name of God and of Jesus Christ. It is somewhat remarkable also, that in the relation of the same fact made by St. Mark, the command to the man is said to have been, " go home to thy friends, and tell them how great things the Lord hath done for thee," Mark v. 19; and the man's publication is exactly as related by St. Luke, " how great things Jesus had done for him." The title of Lord is so very often, nay, so almost peculiarly ascribed to our Saviour, throughout the New Testament, that the use of it here seems an argument for looking upon our blessed Redeemer to have been intended by it: if Jesus Christ then be the Lord intended here, and that the title of Lord be of the same import as the name of " God," for which it is used by St. Mark, then we must acknowledge, that Christ is the Lord, and the Lord he is God. There is a farther circumstance favouring the position that Jesus Christ is the person named here by the appellations of Lord and God, which is, that the man whom he had healed is desired to add to a declaration of what the Lord had done for him, " that he had compassion on him," which certainly must bear reference to that tenderness with which he felt our infirmities, that sympathy with which " Jesus wept," John xi. 35, for the afflictions of those who called upon him even at the moment that he was in act to wipe away the tears from their eyes.

XVI.

I should not look upon the application of the dying thief to our Saviour, hanging also upon a cross, to be any proof that Jesus Christ is the object of prayer, but for the answer made by him, who immediately granted that which was asked, and by admission into paradise, in consequence of a petition preferred to him in an hour, when, of all others, he seemed least able to assist in the time of trouble, exalted the last words of this poor penitent into an incontrovertible testimony that his is the kingdom, that " by suffering he was about to enter into his glory," and that

that he is therefore the Lord, one with the Father, God, Luke xxiii. 42, 43, and xxiv. 26.

XVII.

"Jesus answered and said unto them, destroy this temple, and in three days I will raise it up," in saying which "he spake of the temple of his body," John ii. 19, 21. Here Jesus Christ declares that he will himself raise his body from the grave; but in the grave that body lay truly dead and incapable of any agency: but here he says, that he will act, he must therefore speak of some very extraordinary power remaining to him. But we are often told, that God raised the body of our Saviour from the grave. "This Jesus hath God raised up," says St. Peter, Acts ii. 32; wherein it is observable, that the union of the two natures being suspended during the death of the body, God is spoken of as distinct from Jesus, whose body only is intended by that name: this distinction Peter seems to have had in view throughout the Acts. That which Christ engaged to do, most assuredly he did. He engaged to raise his own body, therefore he did raise his own body. But "this Jesus hath God raised up." Jesus Christ is therefore one with the Father, God.

XVIII.

"Jesus answered and said unto her, If thou knewest the gift of God, and who it is that saith to thee, give me to drink; then wouldest thou have asked of him, and he would have given thee living water," John iv. 10. "Whosoever drinketh of the water which I shall give him, shall never thirst," John iv. 14. Here Jesus Christ gives the gift of God, more properly the gift of Jesus Christ, who gives it, and only reconcilable to sense, by acknowledging him to be one with the Father, God. "They have forsaken the Lord, the fountain of living waters," Jer. xvii. 13.

"And

"And he shewed me a pure river of water of life, clear as chrystal, proceeding out of the throne of God, and of the Lamb," Rev. xxii. 1. "Let him that is athirst, come: and whosoever will, let him take of the water of life freely," Rev. xxii. 17. This invitation so mercifully made to all mankind, and in the power of all to accept, is made by Jesus Christ; he therefore who gives such " water springing up into everlasting life," John iv. 14, is assuredly the " Lord, the fountain of living waters;" which Jeremiah declares God to be. " Ho! every one that thirsteth, come ye to the waters," Isai. lv. 1; " for I will pour water upon him that is thirsty, and floods upon the dry ground: I will pour my spirit upon thy seed, and my blessing upon thine offspring," Isai. xliv. 3. " Jesus stood and cried, saying, If any man thirst, let him come unto me, and drink. He that believeth on me, as the scripture hath said, out of his belly shall flow rivers of living water. (But this he spake of the spirit, which they that believe on him should receive,") John vii. 37, 38. This last text clears up and explains the figure, and shews what is all along meant by living waters. But " God shall pour his spirit upon him that is thirsty;" and according to this prophecy, Jesus Christ is to give this water springing up into life, which is the spirit. But these waters are said to proceed from God; Jesus Christ therefore, from whom they proceed, is one with the Father, God. Let us then with gratitude come upon the invitation to believe; let us confess that the blood which was shed for us is the blood of God himself, Acts xx. 28, shed for our redemption; acknowledge " Christ the Saviour of the world," John iv. 42, and " with joy draw water out of the wells of salvation," Isai. xii. 3.

"My

XIX.

"My Father worketh hitherto, and I work. Therefore the Jews fought the more to kill him, because he not only had broken the sabbath, but said also that God was his Father, making himself equal with God, John v. 17, 18. As the Hebrew idiom of the scripture language is urged as a reason for doubting of our common acceptation of the assertions made in the New Testament, we must certainly admit the Jews to be the best verbal interpreters of such phrases as were peculiar to themselves, and here they have taught us to understand that whensoever our Saviour, or any witness of his gospel, declares him to be the Son of God, they intended thereby to convey an assurance that Jesus Christ is equal with the Father, and with him one God. The subsequent verses say that " what thing soever the Father doeth, these also doeth the Son likewise." " As the Father hath life in himself: so hath he given to the Son to have life in himself; and hath given him authority to execute judgment also, because he is the Son of man," John v. 26, 27. Here he speaks of himself both as God and man; he declares the self-existing life equal with that of the Father; declares the derivation of that to his manhood, with which it was united by the will of God and the Father; and he declares also the reason wherefore the second person of the Godhead is to have the execution of judgment to be, " because he is the Son of man." And St. Paul has explained the force of this reason, " for that he himself hath suffered, being tempted, he is able to succour them that are tempted," Heb. ii. 18. " That he can be touched with a feeling of our infirmities; having been in all points tempted like as we are," Heb. iv. 15; and in the next verse we are

are called upon to approach the throne of grace boldly, becaufe that Chrift is the Son of man, having taken on him the feed of Abraham, and has called us brethren, and can have compaffion upon fuch infirmities as he was himfelf fubject to in the flefh: fo that whenfoever we hear our gracious Lord and Saviour call himfelf the Son of man, we may look upon it as an inftance of tendernefs, and that he ufes that name, in order to infpire a confidence in mankind, his brethren, to approach his throne without diftruft in his mercy. Whenfoever he fpeaks of coming to judgment, he qualifies the terrors of that dreadful day by faying, that it is before the Son of man that all nations are to be gathered; and in the paffage before us, declares the reafon wherefore all judgment is committed to the Son to be, becaufe he is the Son of man. Our Saviour, after having faid that "the Father quickeneth the dead," John v. 21, proceeds to tell us, that on that day "the dead fhall hear the voice of the Son of God: and they that hear fhall live," John v. 25. And farther, that "the hour is coming, in the which all that are in their graves fhall hear his (the Son of man's) voice," John v. 28: fo that here, they that are in their graves, live, being called upon by the Son of man, becaufe they have heard the voice of the Son of God, the Father being he who quickeneth the dead. Can this be reconciled to any fenfe, if it be not granted that Jefus Chrift, the Son of God, and alfo the Son of man, is equal to, and one with the Father, God? And this once granted, is any pofition more reconcilable to reafon? Refift this who can, for my part I am unable to ftand againft it; but verily "believe, and am fure that thou art that Chrift, the Son of the living God," John vi. 69; words, which I am bold to ufe, as expreffive of an equality between

tween the Son and the Father: nay farther, of an identity and unity of Godhead. As poffeffed of this Godhead "I believe on him, and I worfhip him," John ix. 38.

XX.

"He that believeth on him that fent me, hath everlafting life, and fhall not come into condemnation," John v. 24. "He that believeth on him, (the Son) is not condemned; but he that believeth not, is condemned already, becaufe he hath not believed in the name of the only begotten Son of God," John iii. 18. If there be no condemnation for thofe who believe in the Father, how is it neceffary to believe in the Son in order to indemnify? It can only be fo, becaufe that the Son is one with the Father, God; and the two paffages then convey the fame inftruction. In context with the laft affertion, our Saviour, fpeaking of himfelf, ufes the following very remarkable words, "the Son of man which is in heaven," John iii. 13. This is a very exprefs declaration of his Godhead, the ubiquity of which was by no means affected by its union with the Son of man; for whilft he was fpeaking to Nicodemus he could be on earth only as a man, and as God only filling immenfity could he at that moment of time have been in heaven. He declares alfo, that " he came down from heaven," in the fame verfe; and St. John Baptift, fpeaking of Jefus Chrift, teftifies, that " he that cometh from above is above all," John iii. 31. The pre-exiftence of our Lord in heaven is exprefsly declared by himfelf in the following words alfo, "What and if ye fhall fee the Son of man afcend up where he was before?" John vi. 62. This muft refer to his Godhead, as it is no where afferted that his flefhly body had ever been in heaven before his final afcent. But when he declares, "I came forth from the Father, and am come into the world: again, I leave the world, and go to the Father," " his difciples faid unto him, lo, now fpeakeft thou plainly, and fpeakeft no proverb," John xvi. 28, 29.

XXI.

" Jefus faid unto them, verily verily I fay unto you, before Abraham was, I am," John viii. 58. There is a very remarkable diftinction in this paffage between the words *was* and *am*. By the former, the exiftence of Abraham is marked to have had a commencement, and to have been finite; whereas, by the latter, the eternity of Jefus Chrift, as God, is ftrongly pointed out. The word *am* bears reference to a life in every moment extended to all eternity; which, as the prefence of the Almighty fills infinite fpace, ftretches itfelf at once through all duration, and is at all periods to be fpoken of in the prefent tenfe, as all periods are prefent to it at once; a life " which is, and which was, and which is to come," Rev. i. 4. Jefus Chrift here makes ufe of the fame expreffion which God had declared to be his name to Mofes, and given to him as a token whereby he fhould make himfelf known to the children of Ifrael, to have come from God, Exod. iii. 14; and it can hardly be conceived that he does fo without an intention of marking his divinity, and declaring himfelf to be that God, and that he it was who led the forefathers of thofe with whom he fpoke, out of the land of Egypt by the hand of Mofes. In fome paffages, ending in a declaration, " *I am* " in the original, the tranflation has fupplied the word *he*; becaufe a relative pronoun, the expreffion of which the Greek tongue can difpenfe with, is neceffarily to be expreffed in ours, in order to make good fenfe of the paffage in Englifh, which is good fenfe in Greek without it. For inftance: the woman of Samaria tells our Saviour, that

that "when Chrift comes, he will tell us all things:" to which he anfwered, "I that fpeak unto thee, am," John iv. 26; fo it ftands in the original, and requires no more words to convey the idea that he was Chrift of whom fhe fpake; whereas it is indifpenfibly requifite that the tranflator fhall add a pronoun referring to what had been faid before, and turn the paffage, as our Bible has it, "I that fpeak unto thee am *he*." From this circumftance it is urged, that no inference, favouring our Saviour's divinity, is to be drawn from the paffage before us, becaufe (as is alledged) it is only of the fame ftamp of the others. Without going farther into grammatical difquifitions, let us try the experiment upon it, and write it accordingly, "Jefus faid unto them, verily verily I fay unto you, before Abraham was, I am *he*." Who? Abraham? Will any man infift on this? The word *am* in this verfe fignifies, I exift, in a neuter fenfe, and fo cannot require a relative pronoun to follow it. The context alfo requires the interpretation which I have put upon thefe words; our Saviour declares to the Jews, "I am," in anfwer to their objection to the poffibility of his having feen Abraham, not being yet fifty years old: Upon the whole, I look upon this to be a very explicit declaration of his Godhead and pre-exiftence to the time of his having come into the world, a teftimony borne to it by the author of our falvation himfelf, and therefore I muft yield my affent to his word, that he is one with the Father, God.

XXII.

"I and my Father are one," John x. 30. When our Saviour made this very literal declaration, the Jews ftoned him, and gave as a reafon, "becaufe that thou, being a man, makeft thyfelf God," John x. 33. This fhews how they underftood him; and the answer of our Saviour to their charge shews also that they were right, for, instead of retracting, he refers them to the testimony of his works; "that ye may know and believe that the Father is in me, and I in him," John x. 38: words, which, however they might admit of a figurative interpretation in any other passage, being here spoke to confirm what he had before declared, must be interpreted by that declaration, and mark a mutual relation, resulting only from the possession of one Godhead with the Father.

XXIII.

" Philip saith unto him, Lord, shew us the Father, and it sufficeth us. Jesus saith unto him, have I been so long with you, and yet hast thou not known me, Philip? He that hath seen me, hath seen the Father: and how sayest thou then, shew us the Father? Believest thou not, that I am in the Father, and the Father in me? The words that I speak unto you, I speak not of myself: but the Father that dwelleth in me, he doeth the works. Believe me that I am in the Father, and the Father in me: or else believe me for the very works sake," John xiv. 8, 9, 10, 11. The interpretation of this passage may be drawn from the remark made upon the texts last cited, for our Saviour testifies, that he is in the Father, and the Father in him, in order to evince, that Philip, in having known him, had known the Father. As our Lord could not mean that Philip's acquaintance with the Father was the same as his acquaintance with himself, in the flesh, he has pointed out, that the means whereby he had known the Father, in having known him, was by his knowledge of those words which he had spoken, and those works which he had done by the operation of his Godhead,

head, one with that of the Father. These had been often cognizable by Philip; he therefore in having known the Son, who had said and done such things in testimony of what he was, might well be said to have known the Father, with whom our Lord and Saviour was, in that respect which was pointed out, one and the same God.

XXIV.

"I go unto my Father. And whatsoever ye shall ask in my name, that will I do, that the Father may be glorified in the Son. If ye shall ask any thing in my name, I will do it," John xiv. 12, 13, 14. I believe no man will deny that a petition is to be made to him who is to grant it. Jesus Christ here declares to his disciples, that he will fulfil their prayers, and do that which they shall ask in his name; who then can hesitate to pronounce this doctrine of our Saviour a command to ask of him, a declaration that he is the God of our salvation, from whom cometh help? "With Melancthon, (as quoted by Mr. Lindsey, but for what purpose I cannot comprehend) I take refuge in those plain declarations of scripture, which injoin prayer to Christ, which is to ascribe the proper honour of divinity to him, and is full of consolation." And with Mr. Lindsey himself I observe, 1st, that this eminent person thought, and justly as it should seem, that prayer is the highest act of worship, the proper honour of God, and peculiar to him alone. And, 2dly, that the principal argument for Christ's divinity was to be fetched from religious worship, and prayer being addressed to him." Apology, p. 135. Mr. Lindsey's candour is such that I rely upon his not starting from this conclusion, which he admits as necessarily following from Christ's being proved the object of prayer and religious worship. I shall therefore, if the above texts afford a

proof,

proof, or many others, which I shall call up in evidence of this fact, testify that Christ is properly to be adored, demand and peremptorily insist upon Mr. Lindsey's acquiescence in this position, that Jesus Christ is one with the Father, God. It is a certain fact, even upon a supposition that our Saviour was no more than man, that he was " without sin," and, consequently, that he did not in any instance contradict himself, whereby he must have once spoken that which was not true; but he says to his disciples, " And in that day ye shall ask me nothing; verily verily I say unto you, whatsoever ye shall ask the Father in my name, he will give it you;" John xvi. 23. As our blessed Redeemer cannot mean here to say that he had before spoken an untruth, these words must have exactly the same meaning as those before us; for, if not, they flatly contradict them. That I will grant your prayers, and that the Father will grant your prayers, must therefore signify that the one Godhead of the Father and the Son will grant them; and therefore it follows, that the Father and the Son are one God. " If ye shall ask any thing, in my name, I will do it," says our Saviour; whence I have inferred, that he it is of whom the demand is to be made: But I foresee a possible objection to be made to this inference, which I shall endeavour to obviate. It is, that in this case Jesus Christ has commanded prayer to be preferred to himself in his own name; to which I answer, that so to have done is exactly correspondent to the conduct of God, so long as he had a selected nation his worshippers, and dealt by them as a peculiar people to call upon his name; and that therefore, when they were to cease to be peculiar, and that a whole world was to be adopted, there is no force in the objection, which only shews God governing his additional adorers, as he had governed their predecessors.

Before

Before God was to be adored through Chrift, he was to be adored through thofe benefits which he had conferred upon the children of Ifrael; before the name of Chrift was given, through which he was to be invoked, his innumerable mercies were commanded to be held in remembrance, and in the name of them he was to be called upon; and accordingly we find the Hebrews adored him as the God of Abraham, the God of Ifaac, and the God of Jacob, the God of their fathers, to whom he had promifed, and frequently renewed the promife of a bleffing to proceed from them to all nations of the earth. They adored him as the God of their fathers, who had led them out of the houfe of bondage into a land flowing with milk and honey; and, as the God who had dealt thus gracioufly by them, he prefcribed to them, and prefaced the decalogue with a claim to their obedience, and to their worfhipping him only, grounded, upon that debt of gratitude, which they owed for the protection and deliverance that he had vouchfafed them; and he has exprefsly commanded them to call upon him as the God of their fathers, and made this "his name for ever, and his memorial unto all generations," Exod. iii. 15. But he has fince been pleafed to hold out a light to lighten the Gentiles, and, remembering his mercies, hath holpen his fervant Ifrael, according to his promifes; wherefore then fhall we refrain from offering up the facrifice of praife and thankfgiving to God, in the name of his mercies vouchfafed to us by his having taken our nature upon him? in the name of that man in whofe flefh he was manifefted *, and in which our eyes have feen, and our hands have handled the word of † life, even that word which is ‡ God? Wherefore, in remembrance of fo great benefits, fhould we not
say,

* 1 Tim. iii. 16.   † 1 John i. 1.   ‡ John i. 1.

say, "by thine agony and bloody sweat, by thy cross and passion, by thy precious death and burial, by thy glorious resurrection and ascension, good Lord deliver us?" The sense, in which I understand the words calling upon God in the name of Christ, is calling upon God to assist us, whom he had already thought worthy of so great benefits, in memory of those benefits which he suffered in the flesh, in order to confer. And surely in this sense, it is perfectly conformable to the course of God's government, that our Saviour should desire us to call upon his Godhead in memory of what he has done for us as man, having already declared that he had, in remembrance of his former mercies, holpen us.

XXV.

"It is expedient for you that I go away: for if I go not away, the Comforter will not come unto you; but if I depart, I will send him unto you," John xvi. 7. "The Comforter, which is the Holy Ghost, whom the Father will send in my name, he shall teach you all things, and bring all things to your remembrance, whatsoever I have said unto you," John xiv. 26. Here Jesus Christ sends the Holy Ghost, and the Father at the same time sends the Holy Ghost; therefore the Father and the Son are one God, from whom the spirit is to proceed. He says in another passage, "but when the Comforter is come, whom I will send unto you from the Father, even the Spirit of Truth, which proceedeth from the Father, he shall testify of me," John xv. 26. The Holy Ghost here proceedeth from the Father only; we find that the same witness of Christ preceded his coming, and testified of him beforehand, as well as after his ascent; "For the prophecy came not in old time by the will of man: but holy men of God spake as they were moved by the Holy Ghost," 2 Peter i. 21. But we find the prophets themselves, who spake as they were

were moved by the Holy Ghoſt, "ſearching what, or what manner of time the ſpirit of Chriſt which was in them did ſignify, when it teſtified beforehand the ſufferings of Chriſt, and the glory that ſhould follow," 1 Pet. i. 11; ſo that the apoſtles, filled with the Holy Ghoſt, have here expreſsly declared what glory that is which ſhould be teſtified after the ſufferings of Chriſt, even that the ſpirit which proceedeth from the Father is the ſpirit of Chriſt, therefore one with the Father, God. But our Saviour himſelf, as if determined to put the matter out of doubt, by preparing the ears of his audience to hear the teſtimony of the Holy Ghoſt concerning him, declares that "he ſhall glorify me: for he ſhall receive of mine, and ſhall ſhew it unto you. All things that the Father hath, are mine: therefore ſaid I, that he ſhall take of mine, and ſhew it unto you," John xvi. 14, 15.

XXVI.

Our bleſſed Lord and Saviour, having taken our nature upon him, and having been in all points tempted like as we are, on the approach of that hour in which he was to be made perfect by ſuffering death for all men, and in which he was to finiſh the great end of his having come in the fleſh, conſoles himſelf by looking beyond his grave, and contemplating the glory that ſhould follow; and as a man about to endure great afflictions, and, ſurmounting them, to take our nature "into heaven itſelf, now to appear in the preſence of God for us," Heb. ix. 24. addreſſes himſelf to that Being to which, as Man, he was inferior, ſaying, "Father, the hour is come; glorify thy Son, that thy Son alſo may glorify thee," John xvii. 1. "And now, O Father, glorify thou me with thine own ſelf, with the glory which I had with thee before the world was," John xvii. 5. "For thou lovedſt me before the foundations of the world," John xvii. 24. The pre-exiſtence of our Saviour is exprefsly declared here, and the identity of that Godhead with which he and the Father are mutually to glorify each other; that glory which the Son had in all refpects equal with the Father, before he had, for the fake of mankind, taken upon him that nature whereby he was, upon earth, inferior to him.

XXVII.

"Pilate therefore faid unto him, art thou a king then? Jefus anfwered, thou fayeft that I am a king. To this end was I born, and for this caufe came I into the world, that I fhould bear witnefs unto the truth. Every one that is of the truth, heareth my voice," John xviii. 37. Thefe words are preceded by a declaration made by our Saviour, that, "my kingdom is not of this world;" and the whole together is faid by St. Paul to be " a good confeffion witneffed before Pilate," 1 Tim. vi. 13. That Nathanael, an Ifraelite indeed, in whom was no guile, underftood the prophecies of our Saviour's kingdom in this fenfe is evident, for, upon feeing him an unattended man, he pronounced him " the King of Ifrael," which he muft have feen that he was not in any other acceptation of the terms than as he was the " Son of God," John i. 49. and this interpretation he put upon the prophecies, upon feeing our Saviour poffeffed of an extraordinary knowledge. Greater things have been referved for us to fee than Nathanael faw; why then fhall we hefitate to fay, according to the teftimony which this great witnefs of the truth bore to himfelf, " thy kingdom is not of this world," and with Nathanael, " thou art the King of Ifrael, the Son of God;" words which I have already fhewed, when fpoken by a Jew, to mean, thou haft equality of Godhead with the Father.

" And

XXVIII.

"And Thomas answered and said unto him, my Lord, and my God. Jesus saith unto him, Thomas, because thou hast seen me, thou hast believed," John xx. 28, 29. To call this saying of Thomas an exclamation, is a poor and disingenuous evasion of the Bishop, quoted by Mr. Lindsey; for it is declared to be *an answer* and *an address* to our Saviour, who had convinced him that he was the same Jesus who had been dead and was alive again; an argument which I should conceive sufficient to evince the truth of doctrines which Thomas had heard before, but through a defective faith did not understand; and to induce that confession which he now makes, saying unto him, "my Lord and my God." When Mary, ver. 16, saw and knew our Lord after his resurrection, she made no exclamation, but directly addressed herself to him, saying, "Master," acknowledging him to whom she spoke. Mary had not been a witness of all the declarations of his own nature which he had made to his apostles, who were to be witnesses unto him; she acknowledges him as she had known him before; but Thomas, who considered a resurrection from the dead to be a conclusive proof of the truth of what he had often heard, instantly draws the natural inference, and acknowledges him to be his Lord and his God. If the works of this bishop of *Mopsuestia*, which have not reached us, be of the same stamp as the fragment quoted by Mr. Lindsey, we have no great reason to regret the loss, or condemn our ancestors for having consigned the rest of them to oblivion. The poor bishop himself must also be obliged to those who have redeemed him from our censure.———

Next in order follows the testimony borne to the divinity of Jesus Christ by the apostles, men appointed to be his witnesses, on whom "he breathed and said," "receive

"receive ye the Holy Ghoft," "the fpirit of truth, he will guide you into all truth;" "he fhall teach you all things, and bring all things to your remembrance, whatfoever I have faid unto you;" "he will fhew you things to come; he fhall glorify me." Men, "whofe underftanding he opened that they might underftand the fcriptures," "holy men of God who have made known unto us the power and coming of our Lord Jefus Chrift, for they were eye-witneffes of his Majefty." To perfons thus qualified, fpeaking as they were moved by the Holy Ghoft, coming in due time to fpeak of him who had given himfelf a ranfom for all, "underftanding the myftery of Chrift, which in other ages was not made known unto men, as it is now revealed unto his holy apoftles and prophets by the Spirit;" taking the prophecies from a dark place to fpread abroad their radiance, and render their fure word a light to us; to fuch men we fhall do well that we take heed; to their teftimony it is effential to our own eternal happinefs that we give credit, and not that we look upon all fuch things as occur in their writings, which are "hard to be underftood, as given to our ignorance and inftability to wreft to our own deftruction;" they have pointed out the way to a bleffed immortality; it is our duty to fearch into what they have faid, and where we cannot underftand to confide. From the apoftles we are to expect the manifeftation of fpiritual things, and as fuch are certainly beyond the reach of our farther enquiry, it is but reafonable to truft thofe who were permitted to look into them, and to promulgate fo much as concerns us to know.

XXIX.

"And they prayed, and faid, thou Lord, which knoweft the hearts of all men, fhew whether of thefe two thou haft chofen, that he may take part of this miniftry and apoftlefhip," Acts i. 24. This prayer

is

is preferred to the Lord who had sent forth his disciples, saying, " ye shall bear witness, because ye have been with me from the beginning," John xv. 27. " Go ye into all the world, and preach the gospel to every creature," Mark xvi. 15; and by whom, St. Paul says, " we have received the apostleship," Rom. i. 5; to that Lord, who knew to whom he should commit himself, " because he knew all men, and needed not that any should testify of man; for he knew what was in man," John ii. 25. And the petition is that out of two men, namely, Justus and Matthias, selected from those " who had been with our Saviour from the beginning," " which have companied with us, all the time that the Lord Jesus went in and out among us, beginning from the baptism of John, unto that same day that he was taken up from us," Acts i. 21, 22; he should ordain one to be a witness of his resurrection in the place of Judas, who had fallen by transgression. That it is addressed to Jesus Christ, not only the context, but the following circumstance may thoroughly demonstrate: The very same call being to be made of another apostle, as the Lord is now desired to make, a light shone from heaven round about Saul, and of the voice which spoke it is thus declared: " the Lord said, I am Jesus whom thou persecutest:" " and the Lord said, arise, and go into the city, and it shall be told thee what thou must do," Acts ix. 5, 6. But when Saul, according to this commandment, came into Damascus, " he is met and received by a certain disciple named Ananias, to whom said the Lord in a vision, Ananias. And he said, behold I am here, Lord. I have heard by many of this man, how much evil he hath done to thy saints at Jerusalem: and here he hath authority from the Chief Priests, to bind all *that call upon thy name.* But the Lord said unto him, go thy way:

way: for he is a *chosen* vessel unto me, to bear my name before the Gentiles and Kings, and the children of Israel," Acts ix. 13, 14, 15. That the vessel which was to bear the name of Christ before the Gentiles, &c. was to be chosen by him is here evident; and St. Paul himself farther says, " Christ sent me (not to baptize, but) to preach the gospel," 1 Cor. i. 17. To him who was to *choose*, it is therefore to be concluded the petition was preferred that he would shew whether of these two he had *chosen* to preach his gospel, and take part of that ministry to which " the wisdom of God," Luke xi. 49, even " Christ," Mat. xxiii. 34; said, " I will send them prophets and apostles:" so that here is an instance of adoration incontrovertibly offered up to Jesus Christ; therefore one with the Father, God, the proper object of prayer and religious worship.

But, throughout the relation, there is a farther testimony to be found of the adoration of Jesus Christ; for Ananias, himself a disciple, declares, that Saul was a persecutor of those *who called upon the name of Christ*, and " the disciples of our Saviour were therefore afraid of him when he assayed to join himself unto them," Acts ix. 26; for " all that heard him preach Christ in the synagogues were amazed, and said, is not this he that destroyed them which *called on this name* in Jerusalem, and came hither for that intent, that he might bring them bound to the Chief Priests?" Acts ix. 20, 21. We have here direct proof that the disciples of Christ called upon his name, both from those who did, and those who did not call upon it.

I shall in this place take notice of Mr. Lindsey's assertion, (supported by quotations from various authors) that to call upon the name of Jesus is the same as to
be

be called by the name of Jesus, or to have the name of Jesus called upon the subject spoken of. This declaration he has made in his very extraordinary comment upon 1 Cor. i. 2. Apology, p. 132. And he farther declares, that Stephen's calling upon the name of Jesus, is the only passage in which these words mean directly the same as invoking him. Notwithstanding that the name of that great critick in the Greek language, Dr. Clarke, is produced in evidence of this assertion, I own I am not convinced of its truth; nor can I see a reason why the identical word, signifying an invocation in one place, shall be denied to have the same signification in another, where the context is exactly similar to that in which it is allowed to have that meaning, and indeed in which it requires to be so interpreted, in order to its bearing any meaning at all. But, with respect to the passage before us, it is a little remarkable that the name of Christ had not yet been called upon his disciples, and that for want of a name to comprehend them all, the commission to Saul is couched in the following aukward terms: "that if he found *any of this way*, he might bring them bound unto Jerusalem," Acts ix. 2. In the execution of this warrant from the priests it was, that Saul was chosen to bear *the name* of Jesus Christ to the Gentiles; and this happened exactly two years after the ascension of our Saviour, whereas it was not till ten years after that event that the disciples were first called christians at Antioch. How disingenuously then do men deal, not only with the world, but with themselves also, in wresting words from their true meaning, to the support of their own suggestions. If one man, filled with the Holy Ghost for the purpose of " guiding him into all truth," has invoked Jesus Christ, is not such an act, once so performed, sufficient to evince the propriety of the invocation, and to establish the right of Jesus

sus Christ to be invoked? And if adoration then be the due of Christ, why should we deny a literal interpretation to words by which it is asserted, that the disciples of our Lord rendered him that praise and adoration to which he is entitled? Is it meant that the disciples contradict the testimony of the Holy Ghost by which Stephen called upon the Lord Jesus? They were themselves filled with the Holy Ghost; and is the Spirit of Truth divided against himself? If this be the assertion, either Stephen, or the disciples, or Dr. Clarke, or Mr. Lindsey, are guilty of an impious and absurd blasphemy, and I leave it to my reader to choose the blasphemer. " He is a chosen vessel unto me," says Jesus Christ to Ananias, Acts ix. 15. " The God of our Fathers hath chosen thee," says Ananias to Saul, Acts xxii. 14. Who can now withhold the application of the following address to the Lord Jesus, or his concurrence with me in saying to him, " Lord thou art God."

There is yet another circumstance in the passage before us, which proves that the prayer was addressed to Jesus Christ. Peter, (who had, upon his own appointment to the ministry, taken our Lord to witness that he loved him, and would with fidelity discharge the trust of feeding his sheep committed to his keeping, saying, " Lord, thou knowest all things; thou knowest that I love thee," John xxi. 17.) was certainly the chief speaker, and the person who preferred the prayer of this venerable assembly. It is therefore highly probable, that he who had accepted of his own apostleship with such an acknowledgment of our Saviour's omnisciencc, repeated the like acknowledgment when calling upon him to choose another to associate with them, who should also love him, and faithfully acquit himself of a part in the same apostleship. When Peter spoke

those

those words to Jesus Christ in his own case, he certainly alluded to his knowledge of the heart, for "he was grieved;" and well he might upon recollection of the event which induced the declaration, for he had an aching memory of our Lord's more intimate knowledge of his own heart than he was himself possessed of, when upon his confidence of his own faith, saying, "I will lay down my life for thy sake, Jesus answered him, wilt thou lay down thy life for my sake? verily verily I say unto thee, the cock shall not crow, till thou hast denied me thrice," John xiii. 37, 38. This he knew to have been truly spoken by his Master, and for him, whose own particular experience had taught him that Jesus Christ was acquainted with man, and needed not that any should testify of man, it is exceedingly natural that he should on such an occasion say to him "who knew all things," "Lord which knowest the hearts of all men, &c."

XXX.

When Peter and John had, "in the name of Jesus Christ of Nazareth," healed the lame man at the gate of the temple, the people who saw it ran together greatly wondering; "and when Peter saw it, he answered unto the people, ye men of Israel, why marvel ye at this? or why look ye so earnestly on us, as though by our own power or holiness we had made this man walk?" Acts iii. 12. "Be it known unto you all, and to all the people of Israel, that, by the name of Jesus Christ of Nazareth, whom ye crucified, whom God raised from the dead, even by him doth this man stand here before you whole," Acts iv. 10. Upon which, the Rulers, having threatened Peter and John, were obliged to let them go, "for all men *glorified God* for that which was done," Acts iv. 21. Peter, when he restored Eneas to health at Lydda, called him from his bed in the following remarkable terms: " Eneas, Jesus Christ maketh thee whole: arise, and make thy bed," Acts ix. 34. He arose immediately, and the consequence was, that " all that dwelt at Lydda, and Saron, saw him, and *turned to the Lord*," ver. 35.

XXXI.

" When they heard these things, they were cut to the heart, and they gnashed on him (Stephen) with their teeth. But he being full of the Holy Ghost looked up stedfastly into heaven, and saw the glory of God, and Jesus standing on the right hand of God, and said, behold, I see the heavens opened, and the Son of man standing on the right hand of God. Then they cried out with a loud voice, and stopped their ears, and ran upon him with one accord, and cast him out of the city, and stoned him: And the witnesses laid down their clothes at a young man's feet, whose name was Saul. And they stoned Stephen, calling upon *God*, and saying, Lord Jesus receive my spirit. And he kneeled down, and cried with a loud voice, Lord, lay not this sin to their charge," Acts vii. 54, 55, 56, 57, 58, 59, 60.

Mr. Lindsey's remark upon this passage is so very particular, that I will give it at large, and then proceed to shew its futility to the very few of my readers, who shall not have found it out of themselves. " There is no doubt but Stephen made this request, addressed this prayer to the Lord Jesus. But this can be no precedent for directing prayer to him *unseen*, or addressing him as God, whom the blessed Martyr declares *he saw with his eyes*, and calls him " the Son of man standing on the right hand of God." Calls him *the Son of man*, in this his highest state of exaltation. *Son of man, and God most high: what a space*

space between?" Apology, p. 129. Does this gentleman conceive that the actions of an almighty God are circumscribed by the limits appointed to his comprehension, that the space beyond which his imagination cannot pass, is equally an obstruction to the will of him to whom "all things are possible," and that the Omnipotent is to pause in his progress, till Mr. Lindsey shall have leisure to come up with him and mark his footsteps? I hope I have already evinced the absurdity of this appeal from the written word to natural religion, and shewed that the scriptures only are the fountain from whence the course of our argument is to flow; they are granted to be true, and to be ultimate, and if from them I find that God has put his own nature into union with that of man, I will believe that he has done so; that he has formed us a creature, with whom it was possible for him who had "put all things into his own power" to come into union, notwithstanding that neither Mr. Lindsey nor I know any thing of the manner. The space between God and man may be utterly unsurmountable to our conceptions, but shall it therefore impede the Almighty? It is not reason which stands in the way of our belief, but the impious pride of ignorance, "speaking evil of that which it understands not," "beguiling unstable souls," "withdrawing from the knowledge of the Lord and Saviour Jesus Christ, by which we had before escaped the pollutions of the world," 2 Peter. ii. Mr. Lindsey having allowed that "the principal argument for Christ's divinity is to be fetched from religious worship and prayer being addressed to him," Apology, p. 135, is most exceedingly distressed at the passage before us, and accordingly uses his utmost diligence to extricate himself from the melancholy necessity of yielding up his spirit into the hands of his Redeemer, his Mediator, and his Judge; and left it sho follow that he who " bought us with the price of his own blood," " and so loved us that he gave himself a ransom for all," has any right in his purchase, or should " in due time be testified," by the invocation of St. Stephen, to be one with the Father, God, recourse is had to an expedient, the most singular perhaps that ever was made use of to any purpose whatsoever, and it is asserted that this first Martyr of our Saviour having *seen* the Lord Jesus *with his eyes* when he prayed, affords no precedent for directing prayer to him *unseen*. The very fact, as stated by Mr. Lindsey, is disputable; for although it be said that Stephen, while before the council, and under their displeasure, so long as he looked up stedfastly into heaven saw Jesus Christ, it by no means follows that the vision continued, or that he could conveniently keep his eyes fixed stedfastly upon it at the time when they ran upon him, cast him out of the city, and stoned him; that is, at the time when he called upon the Lord Jesus. But I will, for argument's sake, admit that Stephen still continued to have his eyes upon him, and that, " being filled with the Holy Ghost, he *still* saw the glory of God, and Jesus Christ standing at the right hand of God." Is not God himself here equally before the eyes of the blessed Martyr as the Son of man? why then should his view of the one induce prayer more than his view of the other? Nay, wherefore should he pass down from God most high through that immense space which lay between him and the Son of man, unless that, conducted by the Holy Ghost, sent " to guide him into all truth," John xvi. 13. he saw that Father and Son were not one and another, but one and the same God, and that there was no space between the Son of man and God most high? unless indeed he saw the Lord Jesus, into whose hands he commended his spirit, to be the almighty God to whom David had said " into thine

hand

hand I commit my spirit: thou hast redeemed me, O Lord God of truth?" Psalm xxxi. 5. Will Mr. Lindsey persist to say that the Holy Ghost had led him into error? and yet into an error he has led him, if Jesus Christ, even in this his highest state of exaltation, be but his fellow creature. But because Jesus was in sight he was to be worshipped; and there is nothing wrong in worshipping a visible creature. If the command be, and if the duty of a christian therefore be to worship God only, I own myself too blind to discern how the visibility of any Creature should supersede the commandment, and alter the unalterable law of God. The Angel was visible to St. John, Rev. xxii. 9. yet restrained him from worship, which Christ did not do by his adorer; but he, who was equally visible to Stephen as the Son of man, winked at the disrespect with which he passed by his own glory, and addressed himself to the Lord Jesus; and by a display of that glory testified in the highest his approbation of that address which was preferred to the Son of man by this holy Martyr, " with the Spirit of Truth," as being consistent with the command, as a direct obedience to his will declared in these words, " Thou shalt worship the Lord thy God, and him only shalt thou worship." " Worship God," said the Angel to St. John; our Saviour said no such thing to Stephen, nor referred him to that God whose glory was before his eyes. I therefore think it evident, that God, and God only, Stephen did worship, in the person of Jesus Christ, one with the Father, God. I grant Mr. Lindsey's assertion, that the word " God" is supplied in the 59th verse, " calling upon *God*, and saying Lord Jesus receive my spirit." It is of no consequence if it be omitted, for then the invocation is made directly to Christ, and remains a proof that he is God, though he be not addressed by that name. The word " God" being inserted by the translators,

lators, shews how they understood the passage before us, and though I do not choose to make use of human authority, I cannot help this once saying that I look upon this conclusion, drawn by men of great abilities, and employed in the most diligent perusal of the whole Bible, as more than a balance to every quotation produced by Mr. Lindsey from men pursuing systems, and wresting half sentences to their own particular purposes. Upon the whole, unless it be admitted that being visible is a reason for addressing prayer to any thing we are looking at, here is an instance of adoration, a precedent of religious worship preferred to our Lord and Saviour, and, if " religious worship and prayer be a proof of Godhead," I demand Mr. Lindsey's acquiescence in this conclusion, that Jesus Christ is one with the Father, God; who has said, " am I a God at hand, and not a God afar off?" Jer. xxiii. 23.

I mean now to resume what for a time I admitted, that Stephen had Jesus Christ before his eyes when he was cast out of the city and stoned. The scriptures are seldom so vague as to require our belief of that which is not particularly revealed. The star which appeared to the wise men is never withdrawn from before their eyes till it stood over the house where the young child was. The evangelist has constantly kept it in view, whereas there is no mention made that the heavens continued open to Stephen, from the time he was taken from before the council; and therefore we have no reason to affirm that they did. The very prayers which our Lord and Saviour, suffering in the flesh, preferred, are preferred by Stephen, who therefore must be aware of the force of example; or, if not so acute himself, must have known by the Spirit of Truth that future times would refer themselves to the conduct of this martyr; and that men, like him, in articulo mortis,
would

would commend their spirit to the Lord Jesus. Did the spirit mean to deceive? It surely has not guided to all truth, if it did not, and that Mr. Lindsey's hypothesis be true; and therefore even the Holy Ghost comes under this gentleman's charge of incompetency to be a witness to the great preserver of all spirits.

Before I dismiss this subject I shall add one more remark, which, if it do not afford conclusive proof of what has been advanced already, must be allowed greatly to corroborate the force of it.

"Behold," says Stephen, "I see the heavens opened, and the Son of man standing on the right hand of God; then they cried out with a loud voice, and stopped their ears, and ran upon him with one accord, &c." Acts vii. 56, 57. "Hereafter," says our Lord, "shall ye see the Son of man sitting on the right hand of power, and coming in the clouds of heaven: then the high priest rent his clothes, saying, he hath spoken blasphemy," "then did they spit in his face, and buffeted him, &c." Matth. xxvi. 64, 65, 67. "Art thou the Christ, the Son of the blessed? and Jesus said, I am. And ye shall see the Son of man sitting on the right hand of power, and coming in the clouds of heaven. Then the high priest rent his clothes, and saith, What need we any farther witnesses, ye have heard the blasphemy? what think ye? and they all condemned him to be guilty of death, and some began to spit on him, &c." Matth. xiv. 61 to 65. When Jesus said, "before Abraham was, I am," "the Jews took up stones to cast at him;" when he said, "I and my Father are one, they took up stones again to stone him," saying, "because that thou being a man makest thyself God." The Jews also sought to kill him, "because he said that God was his Father, making himself

equal

equal with God." Here the ground of the Jewish resentment appears, they were Unitarians, and looked upon an equality or unity of Godhead between the Father and Son as the greatest indignity to the God of their fathers. To the words for which our Saviour was condemned by the high priest and his council, we may therefore ascribe the same meaning, and conclude that they were designed to convey the same idea of our Lord's equal and one Godhead with the Father. The very same thing which Jesus here says they shall hereafter see, St. Stephen declares to the very same tribunal to be now before his eyes; and the very same consequence attends his declaration; so that we may consider Stephen as having in this respect also borne his testimony to the one Godhead of the Father and of the Son of man.

XXXII.

After Peter had healed Eneas at Lydda, saying, "Jesus Christ maketh thee whole, arise," the friends of Tabitha, who was sick, and had died at Joppa, in the neighbourhood of the town where he had wrought this miracle, solicited his immediate attendance; upon which he arose and went with them, and coming into the chamber where they had laid her body, and having put forth all those who stood weeping by, "he kneeled down and prayed, and turning him to the body, said, Tabitha, arise. And she opened her eyes: and when she saw Peter, she sat up," Acts ix. 40. "And it was known throughout all Joppa; and many believed in the Lord," verse 42. The words which Peter spoke to Eneas were addressed to him in order to induce his faith, and that of those who saw the work which he had done, in the Lord. But in the case of Tabitha, where he had put forth those whose clamorous grief might interrupt the fervour of his devotion, and remained alone with the dead body,

such

such language being absolutely unnecessary, it is very probable that Peter did not use it on that account; but as there is no doubt that the same Jesus Christ, who had made Eneas whole, now called Tabitha back to life, it is surely to be inferred that the prayer of Peter was preferred to him; and this is the more probable, when we see that the consequence of her revival on the call of Peter was, that " many believed on the Lord," for many who saw what had been done to Eneas " turned to the Lord."

XXXIII.

" When God had to the Gentiles also granted repentance unto life," " some of the disciples which were come to Antioch, spake unto the Grecians preaching the Lord Jesus. And the hand of the Lord was with them: and a great number believed, and turned unto the Lord:" upon which, when the church at Jerusalem heard it, " they sent forth Barnabas, that he should go as far as Antioch. Who, when he came, and had seen the grace of God, was glad, and exhorted them all, that with purpose of heart they would cleave unto the Lord," Acts xi. 18, 20, 21, 22, 23. Upon the hand of the Lord being with them, Barnabas is glad to have seen the grace of God; or, he was glad upon having seen the " grace of God, who hath to the Gentiles also granted repentance unto life:" " but we believe that through the grace of the Lord Jesus Christ, we shall be saved even as they," Acts xv. 11. Here the grace of the Lord Jesus, and of God, are one and the same, the same also is the one Godhead of the Father and of the Son.

XXXIV.

That our Saviour was not intended " to be a light to lighten the Gentiles," and consequently, that the full manifestation of his Godhead was delayed till after his ascension, as I have already shewed, is evident from the following words of St. Paul to the Jews at Antioch, who were contradicting and blaspheming, because he gratified the request of the Gentiles, and on the sabbath day preached to them also " the word of God." " It was necessary," said he and Barnabas, " that the word of God should first have been spoken to you: but seeing ye put it from you, and judge yourselves unworthy of everlasting life, lo! we turn to the Gentiles. For so hath the Lord commanded us, saying, I have set thee to be a light of the Gentiles, that thou shouldest be for salvation unto the ends of the earth," Acts xiii. 45, 46, 47. These words were spoken by the Lord to Isaiah, when he asked him, was it a light thing that he appointed him to be his servant, and " for a light to the Gentiles, that thou mayest be my salvation unto the end of the earth?" Isa. xlix. 6. These words evidently spoken by God to Isaiah, and as evidently alluded to by St. Paul, who declares them a prophecy of the appointment made by the Lord Jesus Christ to his Apostles, whom he had commanded " to go forth and preach his name to all nations, and to be his witnesses unto the uttermost parts of the earth," to teach repentance and remission of sins among all nations in his name, " and to bear his name to the Gentiles," are an uncontrovertible evidence that the Lord, who commanded the apostles, saying, " I have set, &c." is the same God who had before spoken by his holy prophet. It is farther remarkable, that our Saviour then first " opened their understanding that they might understand the scriptures, and see the necessity there was that Christ should suffer and rise from the dead the third day, when he was about to commission them to go forth and preach him to the Gentiles, which was not till after his resurrection, not indeed till the moment preceding his ascension.

fion. "He was not fent but to the loft fheep of the houfe of Ifrael," Matth. xv. 24. ".for it was neceffary that the word of God fhould firft have been fpoken to them;" "but when they had put it from them," and offered up this great facrifice for the fins of the whole world, hanging upon a crofs "the Lord of glory," we find that, after he was made perfect by fuffering death, and, by his fuffering, had atoned for and adopted all nations, he was to be preached to the Gentiles, fo that the whole which he came to do according to the fcriptures, by which it was feen that it behoved him to die and rife again from the dead, could not have preceded his death, for fo the profit had been only to Ifrael; to them were his life and leffons, but to the whole world his falvation, which was to be promulgated after he had died for it; he therefore now fent out the apoftles to hold forth this great light to lighten the Gentiles alfo, according to the prophecy before, certifying to them, "that they fhould be for falvation unto the ends of the earth." Paul and Barnabas continued fome time at Antioch, preaching the "word of God," "and when the Gentiles heard this, they were glad, and glorified the word of the Lord: and as many as were ordained to eternal life, believed. And the word of the Lord was publifhed throughout all the region," Acts xiii. 48, 49. The Jews having ftirred up the honourable women, and raifed a perfecution againft them, they proceeded to Iconium, where they "fo fpake, that a great multitude," both of the Jews, and alfo of the Greeks, believed," "long time therefore abode they, fpeaking boldly in the Lord, which gave teftimony unto the word of his Grace, and granted figns and wonders to be done by their hands," Acts xiv. 1, 3. What Paul and Barnabas preached is to be collected from its being faid, that both Jews and Greeks believed. The God of the Jew and of the Unitarian is the fame; it was not therefore the God of the Jews, that the Jews were now firſt induced to believe; the Jews preached not their Jehovah, they fought not to make profelytes, it was not therefore in the God of the Jews that the Greeks believed; but Paul was fent " to bear the name of Chriſt to the Gentiles, and to all nations, beginning from Jerufalem;" that the fecond perfon of the Godhead was then the object of Paul's doctrine to thofe who needed not a teacher of the one Godhead, but knew nothing before of the three Perfons in that Godhead, is evident hence; and therefore we may, with thofe believing Jews, lay afide the Unitarian fyftems of Mr. Lindfey, and believe, that Jefus Chriſt, who, according to his promife that " he would be with them alway, even unto the end of the world," Matth. xxviii. 20. " continued working with them, and confirming the word with figns following," Mark xvi. 20. " and who now gave teſtimony unto the word of his grace, and granted figns and wonders to be done by their hands," Acts xiv. 3. is one with the Father, that " God who bore them witnefs, both with figns and wonders, and with divers miracles, and gifts of the Holy Ghoſt, according to his own will," Heb. ii. 4. " that God who wrought fpecial miracles by the hands of Paul" before thofe " who heard him preach the word of the Lord Jefus, both Jews and Greeks," Acts xix. 11, 10.

XXXV.

When the fame Lord, who, juſt before his afcenſion, had " opened the underſtanding of his difciples, that they might underſtand the fcriptures," Luke xxiv. 45. had opened the heart of Lydia, a feller of purple, at Thyatira, that fhe attended unto the things which were fpoken of Paul, and conſtrained him to abide with her; a damfel, pofleffed with a fpirit of divination, " followed Paul, and us, and cried, faying,

thefe

these men are the servants of the most high God, which shew unto us the way of salvation," Acts xvi. 14, 15, 16, 17. Jesus Christ, when veiled in the flesh, "suffered not the devils to speak, because they knew him," Mark i. 34; even the testimony of this spirit of divination then is to be admitted, and it has called Paul, who declares himself to the Romans i. 1. to be "a servant of Jesus Christ," "a servant of the most high God." The space contracts itself exceedingly between Son of man and God most high. Paul has himself addressed not the Romans only, but the Philippians, under the title of the servant of Jesus Christ," Philip. i. 1. and to Titus he commences his epistle by the name of "Paul, a servant of God," Titus i. 1. These terms are therefore synonimous.

XXXVI.

The doctrine of Paul and Silas to the Keeper of the prison at Philippi, and the consequence of it, are remarkable. The keeper said to Paul and Silas, his prisoners, "Sirs, what must I do to be saved? and they said, believe on the Lord Jesus Christ, and thou shalt be saved, and thy house. And they spake unto him the word of the Lord, and to all that were in his house. And he took them the same hour of the night, and washed their stripes; and was baptized, he, and all his, straightway. And when he had brought them into his house, he set meat before them, and rejoiced, believing in God with all his house," Acts xvi. 30 to 34. Here is a very rapid transaction. Paul and Silas being at prayer, and singing hymns at midnight, the foundations of the prison are shaken, the doors fly open, and the bands of the prisoners are loosed; the keeper, terrified at the probability of their escape, falls into despair; and, about to take away his own life, is restrained by Paul, who, to his astonishment, shewed himself and the rest undismayed, without chains, and yet not making use

of

of so favourable an opportunity. Convinced that some power controlled the ordinary course of nature, and had interfered in behalf of his prisoners, the man immediately applies to them to know what he should do to be saved: and here the apostles preach to a heathen, that his salvation is to be the consequence of his belief in the Lord Jesus Christ; and accordingly we find him, even at the same hour of the night, rejoice, and indeed believe in the Lord Jesus Christ, one with the Father, God.

XXXVII.

In the Acts, St. Luke says, that "because Paul preached Jesus to the Athenians, they said he seemed to be a setter forth of strange gods," Acts xvii. 18. On this they questioned him, and his answer was, that having seen among them an altar inscribed To THE UNKNOWN GOD, "whom therefore ye ignorantly worship, him declare I unto you," ver. 23. Here, upon a call to explain himself, and answer the charge of setting forth strange gods, in having preached Jesus, he avows, that he whom he had preached was that God whom they knew not, but worshipped ignorantly: but he had preached Jesus; therefore Jesus Christ was that God hitherto unknown to them, and one with the Father. The attributes with which the apostle proceeds to characterize the God, to whose worship he is persuading the Athenians, are as follow, and, in apposition to them, I will put those attributes which are by the same preacher ascribed to Jesus Christ; and if upon comparison it be found that he has arrayed him with the same power and glory as he proposes to the Athenians to invite their adoration to God, we may, we must say, that he is that God, and that honour and religious worship are his due who is possessed of the same glory to excite them.

Of God whom he preached at Athens, even Jesus, he says,	Of Jesus Christ, expressly so named, he says,
"God that made the world, and all things therein, seeing that he is the Lord of heaven and earth," ver. 24; "for in him we live, and move, and have our being," ver. 28.	"By him were all things created that are in heaven, and that are in earth, visible and invisible, whether they be thrones, or dominions, or principalities, or powers, all things were created by him, and for him. And he is before all things, and by him all things consist," Coloss. i. 16, 17.

If then the exclusive prerogatives of God be in Jesus Christ, and that we see him clothed in that glory of which God has spoken, saying, "I am the Lord, that is my name, and my glory will I not give to another," Isaiah xlii. 8. we must surely say of him who wears it, that he is one with the Father God. That which is but one, even the glory, and which the declaration of God had made incommunicable, must be a distinguishing mark of him who has declared that he will not impart it. Jesus Christ has this glory: the declaration therefore came from that Godhead which is his equally as the Father's.

XXXVIII.

"And Crispus, the chief ruler of the synagogue, believed on the Lord with all his house: and many of the Corinthians, hearing, believed, and were baptized. Then spake the Lord to Paul in the night by a vision, be not afraid, but speak, and hold not thy peace: for I am with thee, and no man shall set on thee,

thee, to hurt thee: for I have much people in this city. And he continued there a year and six months, teaching the word of God among them," Acts xviii. 8, 9, 10, 11. That they who were baptized believed upon Jesus Christ, on hearing him preached, is evident from the necessity of that belief to baptism: that it was Jesus Christ whom Paul preached, is therefore evident also, for " how should they believe without a preacher." But Paul is in a vision called upon by the Lord to persevere without apprehension of danger, and accordingly we find him continue to teach the word of God among them, the same doctrine that he had before held forth that they might believe and be baptized. Lest it should be doubted who the Lord was who spake to him, I will remind my reader of a similar vision, wherein " in the night." " the Lord stood by him, and said, be of good chear, Paul: for as thou hast testified of me in Jerusalem, so must thou bear witness also at Rome," Acts xxiii. 11. As we know well whose name Paul was chosen to bear before the Gentiles, and that he was the Lord who spake to him now, we have no reason to doubt that it was the same Lord Jesus Christ who cheared him in the instance before us, and allayed the apprehensions which a man, who had undergone such persecutions for the sake of Christ, might reasonably entertain, if he persevered in the maintenance of his testimony.

XXXIX.

That the prophecies were in themselves insufficient to make a perfect revelation of Christ, nay, that the baptism of John was not sufficient to make him known, is evident from the case of Apollos, " a man mighty in the scriptures, fervent in spirit, who spake and taught diligently the things of the Lord, at Ephesus;" but that these were a strong assistant testimony to the manifestation of his Godhead, afterwards by the spirit

of

of truth, is evident alfo from the doctrines of the fame man, who, "knowing only the baptifm of John, was inftructed by Aquila and Prifcilla, who expounded unto him the way of God more perfectly," upon which " he helped them much which had believed through grace; for he mightily convinced the Jews, and that publickly, fhewing by the fcriptures, that Jefus was Chrift," Acts xviii. 24 to 28.

XL.

Paul having continued, by the fpace of two years, daily difputing in the fchool of one Tyrannus, " all they which dwelt in Afia, heard the word of the Lord Jefus, both Jews and Greeks," Acts xix. 10. And having manifefted that God bore witnefs to that which he teftified by fpecial miracles wrought by his hands, " fear fell on them all, and the name of the Lord Jefus was magnified. Many alfo of them which ufed curious arts, brought their books together, and burned them before all men: and they counted the price of them, and found it fifty thoufand pieces of filver. So mightily grew the word of God, and prevailed," Acts xix. 17, 18, 19, 20. But it was the word of the Lord Jefus which they had heard; therefore it was his word that grew and prevailed; his name therefore is worthily magnified, being one with the Father, God.

XLI.

When Agabus foretold to Paul, that he fhould be bound at Jerufalem, and delivered into the hands of the Gentiles, the difciples " befought him not to go up to Jerufalem. Then Paul anfwered, what mean ye to weep, and to break mine heart? for I am ready, not to be bound only, but alfo to die at Jerufalem for the name of the Lord Jefus. And when he would not be perfuaded, we ceafed, faying, the will of the Lord be done," Acts xxi. 11, 12, 13, 14. The context here fhews, that the Lord, to whofe will the apoftles resigned themselves, was the Lord Jesus, for whose name Paul was ready to resign himself, not to bonds only, but to death. This example therefore authorises us to address to the Lord Jesus that expression of our submissiveness to his pleasure in the Lord's prayer, "thy will be done in earth," Matth. vi. 10.

XLII.

" Arise, and be baptized, and wash away thy sins, calling on the name of the Lord," Acts xxii. 16. Belief in the Lord Jesus Christ is throughout the scriptures made necessary to baptism; and the testimony of Saul's belief, which is required by Ananias here, in order to his being baptized, is nothing less than invocation itself.

XLIII.

" And it came to pass, that when I was come again to Jerusalem, even while I prayed in the temple, I was in a trance: and saw him saying unto me," Acts xxii. 17, 18. Whom did Paul see? the pronoun *him* has no antecedent substantive to which it should be referred, though it be made the subject of a long subsequent detail; the antecedent then must be sought for from the meaning of the sentence altogether; but it is therein declared that Paul prayed. The object of his adoration then is the subject of the proposition, and this subject is then found to be the antecedent to this pronoun. But of this object of Paul's religious worship, it is said, that he " saw *him* saying unto him, Make haste, and get thee quickly out of Jerusalem: for they will not receive thy testimony concerning me. And I said, Lord, they know that I imprisoned, and beat in every synagogue them that believed on thee. And when the blood of thy martyr Stephen was shed, I also was standing by, and consenting unto his death, and kept the raiment of them that slew him," Acts xxii. 18, 19, 20. That it was of Jesus Christ Paul was to bear testimony, ny, is a well-established fact; and that it was of Jesus Christ that the Jews would not receive Paul's testimony, is clear from this, that they were very ready to receive an Unitarian doctrine. That Stephen, at whose blood-shedding Paul stood by, consenting to his death, was the martyr of Christ, is also certain; for the word martyr signifies no more than witness, and it was for the testimony of Christ that he died. That Jesus Christ, upon the whole, was the object of Paul's religious worship in the temple, is evident; and therefore Mr. Lindsey himself must conclude him, one with the Father, God.

XLIV.

Paul charged before Felix with "having gone about to profane the temple," and being "a ringleader of the sect of the Nazarenes," Acts xxiv. 5. declares himself not guilty of any profanation of the temple; but to the other part of the accusation he answers, "But this I confess unto thee, that, after the way which they call heresy, so worship I the God of my Fathers, believing all things that are written in the law and the prophets," Acts xxiv. 14. The scriptures, that is, the law and the prophets, "are they which testified of Christ," John v. 39. according to that testimony, which Paul's "understanding was opened that he might understand," this bold apostle of our Lord declares himself a worshipper of the God of his Fathers; but this he acknowledges he is, according to the charge before Felix, that he was a ringleader of the sect of the Nazarenes. Jesus Christ of Nazareth is here therefore pronounced by Paul to be the God of his Fathers, even one in Godhead with Jehovah, the Father.———

XLV.

St. Paul commences his epistle to the Romans thus, "Paul, a servant of Jesus Christ, called to be an apostle, and separated unto the gospel of God," Rom. i. 1.

and then making a declaration of his great good-will towards them, he says, " For God is my witness, whom I serve with my spirit in the gospel of his Son, that without ceasing I make mention of you always in my prayers," Romans i. 9. So that here, in the same breath, this great apostle of our Lord and Saviour declares himself the servant of Jesus Christ, the preacher of the gospel of God, and the servant of God, the preacher of the gospel of Jesus Christ. One only is the Master whom Paul served, and he, whose gospel Paul preached, but one, even Jesus Christ one with the Father, God.

XLVI.

" Thinkest thou that thou shalt escape the judgment of God?" Rom. ii. 3; but " the Father judgeth no man, but hath committed all judgment unto the Son," John v. 22. who " shall reward every man according to his works," Matth. xvi. 27. Who then is that God whose judgment is inevitable? certainly Jesus Christ one with the Father, that " God, who will render to every man according to his deeds," Rom. ii. 6.

XLVII.

" Or despisest thou the riches of his goodness, and forbearance, and long-suffering; not knowing that the goodness of God leadeth thee to repentance," Rom. ii. 4. to " repentance unto life," Acts xi. 18. " Howbeit," says the same apostle, " for this cause I obtained mercy, that in me first Jesus Christ might shew forth all long-suffering, for a pattern to them which should hereafter believe on him to life everlasting," 1 Tim. i. 16. We must then " account that the long-suffering of our Lord is salvation; even as our beloved brother Paul also, according to the wisdom given unto him, hath written," 2 Pet. iii. 15. Who then is this Lord, who, " is long-suffering to us-ward?" " not willing that any

any should perish, but that all should come to repentance," 2 Pet. iii. 9. Certainly he is the same Lord Jesus Christ who mercifully shewed all long-suffering to Paul, for a pattern to them who should hereafter believe on him to everlasting life; one, with the Father, God, the riches of whose goodness, and forbearance, and long-suffering, leadeth to repentance unto life.

XLVIII.

The argument carried on through the latter part of the third, and the whole of the fourth chapter of St. Paul's epistle to the Romans, affords a strong proof of the Godhead of Christ. Abraham was faithful in God, his faith was imputed to him for righteousness, and the promise was therefore made to him; he believed in God, and was justified by his belief; but God is declared to be the "justifier of him that believeth in Jesus," Rom. iii. 26. The faith of Abraham, and the fruits of it are set forth as a pattern and persuasive to us to have faith in Jesus; but the faith of Abraham, whereby he was justified, was in God. Were Jesus Christ therefore other than God, he could not have been held out to us by this eloquent preacher of his gospel, as an object of faith after the example of Abraham. The same mode of argument is carried through the 11th chapter of Hebrews, and in the 12th we are told that Jesus Christ is the object of faith.

XLIX.

"Ye are not in the flesh, but in the spirit, if so be that the spirit of God dwelleth in you. Now, if any man have not the spirit of Christ, he is none of his," Rom. viii. 9. Here the context, and the course of St. Paul's argument, put it out of controversy, that the spirit of God and the spirit of Christ are synonimous terms; but of him, whose this spirit is, it is said, that "he raised up Jesus from the dead," Rom. viii. 11.

which

which affords an apostolical expression of that which I have already laid down, that the one Godhead of the Father, and of the Son, was indeed the power which raised up the man Jesus from the dead; for though I assert that Christ is God, I never yet denied that he was also a Man, and that his manhood was inferior to that Godhead which was in the flesh, and upon which the state of man is necessarily dependent.

L.

" Whose are the Fathers, and of whom as concerning the flesh Christ came, who is over all, God blessed for ever. Amen," Rom. ix. 5. As it is not a very common case for men to come of their fathers as concerning any thing else than the flesh, St. Paul has used an expression concerning Christ, which implies, that he had come of some other origin than of the Jews, and in some other manner than as concerning the flesh, and therefore has rendered an explanation necessary, which he accordingly proceeds to make; and in order to shew what that nature of Christ was, from which he had distinguished his flesh, he directly asserts in so many express words, that " he is over all, God blessed for ever. Amen."

LI.

" For the same Lord over all, is rich unto all that call upon him. For whosoever shall call upon the name of the Lord, shall be saved. How then shall they call on him in whom they have not believed? and how shall they believe in him of whom they have not heard? and how shall they hear without a preacher?" Rom. x. 12, 13. St. Paul is here preaching Jesus, of the confession of whom cometh salvation, and in whom, he says, whosoever believeth shall not be ashamed: and, as a reason for what he had said, declares him rich to all that call upon him, and that salvation is the fruit of invoking him. Here Mr. Lindsey must confess him

one

one with the Father, God. He is here preaching to the Jew as well as the Greek; and to the Jew a preacher was surely not wanting to induce his belief in Jehovah, the God of the Unitarians.

LII.

"He that eateth, eateth to the Lord, for he giveth God thanks; and he that eateth not, to the Lord he eateth not, and giveth God thanks. For none of us liveth to himself, and no man dieth to himself. For whether we live, we live unto the Lord; and whether we die, we die unto the Lord: whether we live therefore or die, we are the Lord's. For to this end Christ both died, and rose, and revived, that he might be Lord both of the dead and living," Rom. xiv. 6, 7, 8, 9. St. Paul here makes our eating " to the Lord" depend upon our giving God thanks, which are therefore a dedication of the act; but this dedication of the act is to God, whereas the act itself is, in consequence of it, " to the Lord:" the Lord therefore to whom we find it to be done must be the same God, to whom by thanksgiving it had been addressed. But who that Lord is to whom we eat or eat not, to whom we live or die, and whose we are, the following verses render very certain; and he it is who died, and rose, and revived, even Jesus Christ, over all, one with the Father, God, blessed for ever, the proper object of our gratitude and thanksgiving, " to whose glory, whether we eat, or drink, or whatsoever we do, we should do all," 1 Cor. x. 31: " for the earth is the Lord's, and the fullness thereof," 1 Cor. x. 28.

LIII.

" For we shall all stand before the judgment-seat of Christ. For it is written, As I live, saith the Lord, every knee shall bow to me, and every tongue shall confess to God. So then every one of us shall give account of himself to God," Rom. xiv. 10, 11, 12. Here, in bowing

bowing the knee to Jesus Christ, we fulfil the prophecy that is expressly spoken to Isaiah, by God, of himself, "I have sworn by myself, the word is gone out of my mouth in righteousness, and shall not return, that unto me every knee shall bow, every tongue shall swear," Isaiah xlv. 23. If this then be fulfilled by the bowing the knee to Christ, Christ is that God who spoke this prophecy. I must then refer to the whole chapter, every declaration in which is made of him who has so spoken, even Jesus Christ: "there is no God else beside me, a just God, and a Saviour, there is none beside me. Look unto me, and be ye saved, all the ends of the earth: for I am God, and there is none else," Isaiah xlv. 21, 22. Besides this circumstance, every man is here confessing to God before the judgment-seat of Christ, therefore that God, (one with the Father) before whom they are confessing, " for we must all appear before the judgment-seat of Christ; that every one may receive the things done in his body, according to that he hath done, whether it be good or bad. Knowing therefore the terror of the Lord, we persuade men," 2 Cor. v. 10; and surely when arrayed in all the terrors with which he will come to judgment, " it is a fearful thing to fall into the hands of the living God," Heb. x. 31.

LIV.

"I know, and am persuaded by the Lord Jesus, that there is nothing unclean of itself," Rom. xiv. 14. We do not find any particular revelation made to Paul that there is nothing unclean: he must then have had it from Peter, to whom it was revealed, and who says, "God hath shewed me, that I should not call any man common or unclean;" and this the Lord had shewed him by a vision in which Peter is called upon to eat things heretofore common and unclean, but now cleansed by God. If Paul therefore was persuaded by Jesus Christ,

through

through the relation made by Peter, we find him look upon our Lord to be the God which had shewed the vision to him; or, if Paul had a like vision, it is very probable that it was presented to him and to Peter by the same agent: but as Paul is not said to have had such a revelation himself, the former supposition is most to be relied on. But if it be insisted on that Paul was persuaded by the Spirit, with which he was full, it must follow, that the Holy Ghost, proceeding from the Father, proceeds equally from the Son, by whom Paul declares himself to be persuaded.

LV.

" That I should be the minister of Jesus Christ to the Gentiles, ministering the gospel of God," Rom. xv. 16. He goes on to say, that, according to this appointment, " from Jerusalem and round about unto Illyricum, I have fully preached the gospel of Christ," Rom. xv. 19; but he declines boasting of the mighty signs and wonders which he did in confirmation of this gospel by the power of the spirit of God. The grace which was given to him, that he should be a minister of Christ, is that wherein he says he may glory, and not in the miracles he had wrought, which, however, he declares to be the work of Christ by the hands of those who do them. The gospel of God is here the gospel of Christ, that which is God's is not another's: Jesus Christ is therefore one with the Father, God.

LVI.

" The churches of Christ salute you," Rom. xvi. 16. " Paul called to be an apostle of Jesus Christ, through the will of God, and Sosthenes our brother, unto the church of God which is at Corinth," 1 Cor. i. 1, 2. It is remarkable that St. Paul wrote from Corinth to Rome, and in his epistle thence calls the churches there the churches of Christ; and that when he is at another time writing to the very same churches which he had so denominated, he addresses himself " to the church of God which is at Corinth," and describes the members of this church to be " sanctified in Christ Jesus, called to be saints, and calling upon the name of the Lord Jesus, both theirs and ours." There is but one church of God, and that is of Christ who is called upon in it: Jesus Christ is therefore one with the Father, God. " Grace be unto you," says St. Paul, immediately after addressing the church which called upon the Lord Jesus, whom he professes to be his Lord and theirs, " and peace from God our Father, and from the Lord Jesus Christ;" and then he proceeds, " I thank my God always on your behalf, for the grace of God which is given you by Jesus Christ," 1 Cor. i. 3, 4. This is a very extraordinary gift for our Saviour to make if it was not his to give; but he has given it. The grace of God is therefore the grace of our Lord Jesus Christ, with the Father, one God.

LVII.

" So that ye come behind in no gift; waiting for the coming of our Lord Jesus Christ: who shall also confirm you unto the end, that ye may be blameless in the day of our Lord Jesus Christ," 1 Cor. i. 7, 8. " He that judgeth me is the Lord. Therefore judge nothing before the time, until the Lord come, who both will bring to light the hidden things of darkness, and will make manifest the counsels of the hearts. and then shall every man have praise of God," 1 Cor. iv. 4, 5. That God, for whose praise Paul is contented to wait, rather than seek the praise of men, is certainly the Lord who will come to judge, and to make manifest the counsels of the hearts. But that the Lord who " judgeth Paul" is the Lord Jesus, whose coming he desires the Corinthians to wait for, that in his day they may be found blameless, is also certain: the conclusion is, that the Lord Jesus is the Lord, and that " the Lord

he

he is God;" and if this needed farther proof, it will appear from the following texts to be the Lord Jesus Christ whose praise he desireth: " we are come as far as to you also, in preaching the gospel of Christ: having hope, when your faith is encreased, that we shall be enlarged by you according to our rule abundantly, to preach the gospel in the regions beyond you, and not to boast in another man's line of things made ready to our hand. But he that glorieth, let him glory in the Lord. For not he that commendeth himself is approved, but whom the Lord commendeth," 2 Cor. x. 14 to 18.

LVIII.

" For it hath been declared unto me, that there are contentions among you. Now this I say, that every one of you saith, I am of Paul, and I of Apollos, and I of Cephas, and I of Christ. Is Christ divided? was Paul crucified for you? or were ye baptized in the name of Paul?" 1 Cor. i. 11, 12, 13 From Christ's not being divided, he dissuades them from divisions, ver. 10. " Who then is Paul, and who is Apollos, but ministers by whom ye believed, even as the Lord gave to every man? I have planted, Apollos watered: but God gave the encrease," 1 Cor. iii. 5, 6. So that God who gave to every man the encrease, that is, assisted them in receiving the gospel, which was planted and watered by Paul and Apollos, is the Lord, according to whose gift they believed. Of Jesus Christ it is said, that " he shall confirm them unto the end," 1 Cor. i. 8. That which was given to every man, confirmation in faith, is then the gift of Jesus Christ the Lord; but God gave the encrease: therefore Jesus Christ, the Lord who gave it, is one with the Father, God.

LIX.

"I thank God, that I baptized none of you, but Crispus and Gaius: left any should say, that I had baptized in my own name," 1 Cor. i. 14, 15. As Jesus Christ had given command to his disciples to baptize "in the name of the Father, the Son, and the Holy Ghost," one God; and as they, in obedience to this command, went forth into all nations, baptizing in the name of Jesus Christ, one with the Father and the Holy Ghost, God, (for I dare not suppose them disobedient to the voice of their ascending Lord) Paul, having reprehended the Corinthians for looking upon him, Apollos, and Cephas, as equally objects of their adherence as Christ, who alone was crucified for them, proceeds to return thanks to God that he had not led such unstable souls into farther errour, and by the exercise of that duty which was to be performed in the name of God, brought them to transfer that divinity to himself which belonged to Christ only: for if their preaching Christ crucified could bring his hearers to conceive the preachers as Christ, he easily saw that baptism in his name would have induced them to look upon them as baptizing in their own name, and assuming to themselves that Godhead, to the belief in which baptism was administered in the name of Christ; an errour of so great magnitude, that the apostle is very happy in not having afforded occasion for it to men, whom he saw so ready to misinterpret the ministry and apostleship of the gospel, which he had preached among them. Mr. Lindsey draws a very extraordinary conclusion from the passage before us, and says, it affords a proof that "baptizing in the name of any one does not of itself imply any divinity in the person in whose name baptism is made." I request that this chapter may be turned to, and refer it to the meanest reader, who shall honour me with a perusal, whether Mr. Lindsey has not fallen into the very

very errour which St. Paul is here cenfuring in the Corinthians; for at the leaft it muft be admitted that Paul's thankfgiving is made, either that they did not account him as Chrift, or Chrift as him.

LX.

As I have already proved that it was Jefus Chrift who fent forth the apoftles to preach him, and who had chofen thofe veffels which fhould bear his name before the Gentiles, I fhall not now repeat the arguments already made ufe of, but defire my reader may compare the paffages brought together to that purpofe, with the following declaration of St. Paul, " that not many wife men after the flefh, not many mighty, not many noble are called. But God hath chofen the foolifh things of the world, to confound the wife; and God hath chofen the weak things of the world, to confound the things which are mighty; that no flefh fhould glory in his prefence," 1 Cor. i. 26, 27, 28, 29. This he fpeaks of the preachers of the gofpel who had been fent by Jefus Chrift; for he fays, " it pleafed God by the foolifhnefs of preaching to fave them that believe," 1 Cor. i. 21. Jefus Chrift therefore, who chofe them, and " whofe ftrength is perfected in weaknefs," is one with the Father, God; who hath chofen the weak things to confound the mighty. " He that glorieth, let him glory in the Lord," 1 Cor. i. 31, and 2 Cor. x. 17; in which latter place it is evidently fpoken of Jefus Chrift. It is reafonably to be concluded then that he is the Lord, in whom Paul defires us to glory; " as it is written," by Jeremiah, to whom God fpeaks, " let him that glorieth, glory in this; that he underftandeth and knoweth me, that I am the Lord, which exercife loving-kindnefs, judgement and righteoufnefs in the earth: for in thefe things I delight, faith the Lord," Jer. ix. 24.

" Had

LXI.

"Had they known it, they would not have crucified the Lord of glory," 1 Cor. ii. 8. "Ye killed the Prince of Life," or, as it stands in the margin of the Bible, "the Author of Life." And now, brethren, I wot that through ignorance ye did it, as did also your rulers," Acts iii. 15, 17. "My brethren, have not the faith of our Lord Jesus Christ *the Lord* of glory, with respect of persons," James ii. 1. In this last text the translation has supplied the words "*the Lord*," but the following words "of glory," which express the whole meaning in the Greek, require them, or others to the same purpose, to express it in English; and St. Paul's having used the whole phrase is a sufficient warrant to the translators for preferring that which they have used. And the Lord of glory is a title not very applicable to a creature; for God has said, "I am the Lord, that is my name, and my glory will I not give to another." "Who is this King of glory? the Lord of Hosts, he is the King of glory," Psa. xxiv. 10. Who is this Prince and Author of life? "The Lord God who formed man of the dust of the ground, and breathed into his nostrils the breath of life," Gen. ii. 7.

LXII.

"We speak the wisdom of God in a mystery." "The things of God knoweth no man, but the spirit of God." "But God has revealed them unto us by his spirit:" "we have received, not the spirit of the world, but the spirit which is of God:" "but the natural man receiveth not the things of the spirit of God;" "for who hath known the mind of the Lord, that he may instruct him? but we have the mind of Christ," 1 Cor. ii. 7, to the end, This needs no comment.

LXIII.

That Christ himself spoke by the apostles, is evident from what follows. Paul says to the Corinthians, "Now,

"Now, concerning virgins, I have no commandment of the Lord: yet I give my judgement as one that hath obtained mercy of the Lord to be faithful," 1 Cor. vii. 25. Here the preacher makes a distinction between that effect which the immediate dictate of the spirit had on him, with the authority of speech derived from thence, and the improvement of his natural judgement by the means of habitual faith, through which indeed he became a wiser and a better man, but not more authorized to prescribe. St. Paul often speaks of his having obtained mercy of Jesus Christ, whence it is evident that Christ is the Lord meant here. "To the Lord our God belong mercies, and forgivenesses." Dan. ix. 9. Let him then who extends them be acknowledged to be the God of our salvation.

LXIV.

St. Paul says to the Corinthians, "We know that an idol is nothing in the world, and that there is none other God but one," 1 Cor. viii. 4. This unity of the God, of whom, and by whom he declares all things to be, is opposed to the multitude of idols to which the Corinthians offered sacrifice. These he is about to put down, and in their place to establish the worship of the true God; and now, if ever accuracy of expression be necessary, it was incumbent upon St. Paul to distinguish between the Father and the Son, in terms never to be confounded, to ascribe such attributes to each as must perfectly distinguish him from the other; nay, perhaps he should have gone farther, and have absolutely omitted the name of him, who was not to be considered as a proper object of worship, lest his idolatrous hearers, to whom a multitude of gods would not have been exceptionable, should interpret his words into an implication, that he, who was described to them with attributes the very same as those bestowed upon God, was pointed out as an object of adoration, instead of the idols which they heard him object to, and instead of which he was about to substitute a God for them. Has this been the conduct of the apostle? has he diligently withheld the name of Jesus Christ, while he recommends a new worship? If not, I think it reasonably to be concluded, that he did recommend the worship of Jesus Christ to them, to whom he says, "though there be that are called Gods, whether in heaven or in earth, (as there be Gods many, and Lords many) but to us there is but one God, the Father, of whom are all things, and we in him; and one Lord Jesus Christ, by whom are all things, and we by him," 1 Cor. viii. 6. To me this text appears conclusive for the one Godhead of the Father and of the Son. In the same manner Paul and Barnabas, after they had at Lystra "preached the gospel," and, by a miracle of healing, confirmed the testimony which they bore to the truth of their doctrines, and had received divine honours from the idolaters of the country, dissuade them from doing sacrifice unto them, but " preached unto them, that they should turn from these vanities unto the living God, which made heaven and earth, and the sea, and all things that are therein," Acts xiv. 7, 15. I shall here take occasion to observe, upon a very particular mode of argument made use of by Mr. Lindsey, in order to get rid of the conclusion, which naturally follows from the application of the same attributes to the name of the Father, and of the Son, so frequently made by the disciples of our Lord. " The apostles," says this gentleman, Apology, p. 132, " were not so exact in the use of the words, Lord, Saviour, *and the like*, which they indifferently give both to God and to Christ, never supposing that any would mistake their Lord and Master so lately born, and living amongst men, to be the supreme God and object of worship." If the apostles, who, it is allowed, foresaw that men

would

would in future time depart from the truth, and, as Mr. Lindſey ſays, adopt a trinity from Plato, never conceived the poſſibility of ſuch a miſtake; they were, of all men, not only the moſt careleſs and inattentive, but the moſt heinouſly ſinful; for they ſinned againſt the Holy Ghoſt, whoſe inſpiration had given them a view into futurity, and that for the purpoſe of making them inſtrumental to the propagation and ſupport of truth only; but they have moſt wickedly neglected this firſt cauſe of their appointment; and miſrepreſentation, inſtead of being the fault of our perverſe wills, muſt hereafter be aſcribed to the inſufficiency of revelation, to the incompetency of thoſe whom God's choice had pronounced competent, or to their wilful omiſſion of that duty, to which God had been pleaſed to call them, and aſſiſt them with a " guide to all truth", for our inſtruction. I refer it to reaſon, whether common attributes do not imply, nay more, do not demonſtrate a common nature, and if to be our Lord, and our Saviour, *and the like*, be equally the attributes of God, and of the Son, whether the Son be not therefore God?

But theſe ſame apoſtles, according to Mr. Lindſey, not endowed with a prophetick view, but not even ſuppoſing a miſtake poſſible, muſt have been very extraordinary reaſoners, though they even derived their confidence, that, from the circumſtances of his having been born, and ſo lately living amongſt men, we ſhould not conclude the Godhead of Chriſt from their application of the divine attributes to his name. Will any man pretend that the birth and life of our Saviour were ſuch as ſhould mark his nature to be no more than that of the reſt of mankind? his death, his reſurrection from the dead, and his aſcenſion into heaven, followed immediately by the gift of the Holy Ghoſt,

Ghoſt, according to his promiſe, might alſo lead the apoſtles to conſider, and preach him as ſomething more than an ordinary man; nay, that very birth which Mr. Lindſey thinks a proof that he was a meer man, the apoſtles, who have related it to us, knew to have been of a Virgin found with child of the Holy Ghoſt, and overſhadowed by the power of the Higheſt, and that the Holy Thing, which was born of that Virgin, was declared to be the Son of God. They alſo knew that life, which he paſt amongſt men, to have been ſpent in daily miracles, to have been ſo interrupted, and ſo reſumed, that it is aſtoniſhing to hear the birth and life of our Saviour made uſe of as a reaſon why we ſhould doubt the veracity of the apoſtles, when they declare him to be God, and why they ſhould not have conceived it neceſſary to mark ſuch a diſtinction as ſhould preclude the poſſibility of ſo momentous an errour, if an errour it be to aſcribe divinity to him, inſtead of uſing an inaccurate expreſſion, whereby we ſhould be led into an opinion that he is God. From that very birth and life, teſtifying whence, and with what endowments he came, I am led to interpret even ambiguous expreſſions as atteſtations of his Godhead, much more to yield my aſſent to ſuch as are perfectly explicit, and declare it without any ambiguity at all; of the latter ſort there are multitudes, from which the former derive their explanation; for if it be in one inſtance declared expreſsly, that " Chriſt is over all, God bleſſed for ever," it will be no difficulty to redeem the names of the diſciples of our Lord from the cruel charge of having lied to the Holy Ghoſt, or neglectingly rejected the conduct of this " guide to all truth;" and when they have uſed the words, Lord, and Saviour, *and the like*, and indifferently given them both to God, and to Chriſt, to declare that they have intentionally done it, in order to inculcate the doctrine of

our

our blessed Redeemer's divinity, instead of imputing to these inspired men a criminal inaccuracy, the consequence of which could not escape the foresight of the meanest human understanding. "Ye know that ye were Gentiles carried away unto these dumb idols, even as ye were led. Wherefore I give you to understand, that no man speaking by the spirit of God, calleth Jesus accursed, and that no man can say that Jesus is the Lord, but by the Holy Ghost," 1 Cor. xii. 2, 3. "God is not the author of confusion," 1 Cor. xiv. 33. I shall therefore rely upon the identity of expression used in speaking of God and of Christ, as evidence of the identity of the Godhead of the Father and of the Son; and as the passages occur, in which such language is used, I shall quote them as testimonies of it.

LXV.

Speaking of the sacrifices of the Gentiles, which he says were offered not to God but to devils, St. Paul says, "Ye cannot drink the cup of the Lord, and the cup of devils: ye cannot be partakers of the Lord's table, and of the table of devils," 1 Cor. x. 20, 21. Here is manifestly a declaration made, that the taking the cup of blessing, and the bread which we break, as the communion of the blood and body of Christ, is an act of worship to him, adequate to that of the Gentiles' sacrifices to their idols. He does not indeed call it a sacrifice, nor intimate that it is one, but says, that it is an ascribing of honour to him, inconsistent with honour being paid to devils. In the same manner as our Saviour himself has said, "Ye cannot serve God and mammon," St. Paul shews, that they cannot, consistently with the worship of the true God, ascribe honour to idols. "What concord hath Christ with Belial? or what part hath he that believeth, with an infidel? and what agreement hath the temple of God with idols? for ye are the temple of the living God, &c." 2 Cor. vi. 15, 16.

LXVI.

"We preach not ourselves, but Christ Jesus the Lord," 2 Cor. iv. 5. These words I produce only to shew the object of the apostle's preaching, a circumstance to which I am frequently obliged to refer. Paul has also defined the gospel to be "the testimony of our Lord Jesus Christ," 2 Tim. i. 8. The preaching of the gospel is therefore the bearing testimony to him, which I wish to have remembered and carried on in the mind of my reader.

LXVII.

Were I to quote every passage in the second epistle of St. Paul to the Corinthians that affords a proof of our Saviour's Godhead, I should be under a necessity of transcribing the whole epistle, to which I therefore choose to refer my reader. One passage however I must select, and shew its weight in the argument, because Mr. Lindsey has taken some pains to extricate himself from the necessity of bending under it. It is indeed surprizing, that a man who has shewed so evidently his attachment to what he believes the truth, should not be more circumspect in the pursuit of her, but allow himself to be deceived by every painted fallacy that shall appear ever so little like the original. I am at a loss to conceive how the following daubed mask should be taken for the native and unadorned simplicity of truth, by one who professes himself enamoured of that simplicity. But upon the 12th chap. and 8, 9 ver. of 2 Cor. a Mr. Beausobre has afforded the following comment, to which Mr. Lindsey accedes with the most supine facility. "For this thing I besought the Lord thrice, that it might depart from me," 2 Cor. xii. 8, 9. "Paul appears here to have directed his prayer to God, the Father, and to have had in his
thoughts

thoughts and to have imitated our Lord's prayer in the garden, the night before his suffering, when he prayed to God, that, if it pleafed him, the cup of affliction might pafs away from him without his drinking it." *Beaufobre* on the place. Apology, p. 132. Let us take the whole paffage together, and examine it with the context, and then fee whether the apoftle had any fuch ftuff in his thoughts as the dreams of Mr. Beaufobre are made of. St. Paul having faid, " of myfelf I will not glory, but in mine infirmities," proceeds to give an account of thofe infirmities, and to affign the reafon why they are an object of glory to him, faying, " left I fhould be exalted above meafure through the abundance of the revelations, there was given to me a thorn in the flefh, the meffenger of Satan to buffet me, left I fhould be exalted above meafure. For this thing I befought the Lord thrice, that it might depart from me. And he faid unto me, my grace is fufficient for thee: for my ftrength is made perfect in weaknefs. Moft gladly therefore will I rather glory in mine infirmities, that the power of Chrift may reft upon me. Therefore I take pleafure in infirmities, in reproaches, in neceffities, in perfecutions, in diftreffes for Chrift's fake: for when I am weak, then am I ftrong," 2 Cor. xii. 5, 7, 8, 9, 10. Wherefore does St. Paul glory? wherefore take pleafure in his infirmities? that the power of Chrift may reft upon him; for, by fuffering fuch infirmities as contribute to perfect the ftrength of the Lord, (to whom he prayed) in weaknefs, he is then ftrong when he is weak: but he glories in his infirmities for Chrift's fake; it is the ftrength of Chrift then that is perfected in his weaknefs: but it is the Lord who faid, my ftrength is made perfect in weaknefs; the Lord therefore who fo fpoke, is Chrift: but of the Lord who fo fpoke, Paul thrice befought the departure of " this thing." The Lord then being

Chrift,

Chrift, and Paul having thrice preferred his fupplications to him, it neceffarily follows, that the Lord Jefus Chrift is a proper object of prayer and religious worfhip, and therefore that he is one with the Father, God. Such is the conclufion from the context; whereas a delufive affertion is inferred by a Mr. Beaufobre, from a partial quotation of but one fmall part of the paffage, in itfelf proving nothing, but made the fubject of the weakeft comment that ever obtained the acquiefcence of a man of virtue; a man, whofe errours afflict me, as I honour his worth. I cannot fee him turn afide from the ftudy of the word of God itfelf, to the ftudy of the manner in which partial vifionaries have interpreted it, without fenfible regret. I do not defire that even my comment fhould fupplant a fingle inference drawn by a fenfible and candid man, from a perufal of the fcriptures themfelves; it cannot therefore be expected that I fhall indulge Mr. Lindfey in laying afide the ufe of his own better underftanding, that he may adopt the doctrines of a multitude of defigning or filly men and women upon whom he places fuch implicit reliance. I only afk of him, and every other reader, that they will take the uncorrupted word of God itfelf into their own confideration, and with diligence fearch the fcriptures only, and thence infer, for their own ufe, fuch tenets as the Holy Spirit fhall be found to have teftified.

LXVIII.

St. Paul, in his epiftle to the Galatians, commences with a declaration that he is " an apoftle (not of men, neither by man, but by Jefus Chrift, and God the Father,") Gal. i. 1. Here the Father and the Son are put into oppofition to man, and declared to be the Being from whom the apoftle had his authority; and he declares farther, that " the gofpel which was preached of me, is not after man. For I neither received it of man, neither

neither was I taught it, but by the revelation of Jesus Christ," Gal. i. 11, 12. Who then is Jesus Christ who has thus revealed the gospel to Paul, and whose authority is so very high above that of men? One with the Father, God.

LXIX.

"For do I now persuade men, or God? or do I seek to please men? for if I yet pleased men, I should not be the servant of Christ," Gal. i. 10. This is in context with the last cited passages, and the apostle, still preserving the distinction between God and man, shews the Galatians the authority with which he is about to reprove them, and that they may not expect too great lenity, he shews that he does not seek to please them, but Christ, whose servant he should not be if he neglected to maintain that gospel which some among them had perverted. He distinguishes himself from those who "desire to make a fair shew in the flesh, left they should suffer persecution for the cross of Christ," Gal. vi. 12; whereas he bore in his body the marks of the Lord Jesus, ver. 17.

LXX.

"God hath sent forth the spirit of his Son into your hearts, crying, Abba, Father," Gal. iv. 6. There is something very remarkable in the course of St. Paul's argument here, and the manner in which he has ascended to the assertion before us. He is shewing that the law was given as "a schoolmaster to bring us unto Christ, that we might be justified by faith," that it was given in the interval of time, between the promise and the time of fulfilling it; but by no means with a view of supplying the place of that which was promised, for it was impossible that a law could be given by which righteousness could come; he farther says, that, being justified by faith, the tuition of the law became unnecessary, and that being therefore emancipated from the

bondage

bondage of the law, " we are made the children of God, by faith in Christ Jesus:" and now he says, that the fullness of time being come, " God sent forth his Son, made of a woman, made under the law, to redeem them that were under the law, that we might receive the adoption of sons." Is not this assigning a reason wherefore Christ took manhood, and particularly why he was sent to the lost sheep of the house of Israel? But he has, according to "the gospel, preached before to Abraham," Gal. iii. 8, suffered, and redeemed them, whereby they have been justified by faith, and by faith to justification become Children of God; and what is now the process? After we have received the adoption of sons, the spirit is sent forth into our hearts to make us acknowledge him to be God, whom, till he had so redeemed us to faith, we had only seen to be a man, " made of a woman, under the law." In the passage before us, we are told, that God sent forth the spirit of his Son; and by the same preacher it is declared to the Romans, that it is by " the spirit of him that raised Jesus from the dead, that we are led, in order to be the sons of God, and that by this spirit of adoption we cry, Abba, Father," Rom. viii. 11, 14, 15. That spirit, which raised Jesus from the dead, is therefore that eternal, and invisible, and incomprehensible God, who was in union with him, while he was living, and who again resumed our nature upon its resurrection from the grave. " No man can say that Jesus is the Lord but by the Holy Ghost," 1 Cor. xii. 3. Through faith then, having received the adoption of sons, and by the spirit of our blessed Redeemer sent forth into our hearts, let us, without hesitation, cry to him, " Abba, Father," and address the Lord's prayer to him, through whom, and by whom only, we have been called sons, and are enabled to say, " that Jesus is the Lord," " our Father." I must observe here, that as St. Paul was
preach-

preaching to men difpofed to Judaifm and the doctrines of the law, the fpirit of adoption, fent after juftification by faith in Chrift Jefus, was by no means neceffary to induce them to cry Abba, Father, to the God of the Unitarians; for this they were difpofed to do before, and not to recede from it. Somewhat not acceded to by the followers of Mofes was then the doctrine of the apoftle of Jefus Chrift; and he therefore teaches, that by faith in him they are juftified, and thereby receive the fpirit by which they cry to him Abba, Father.

LXXI.

"In whom we have redemption through his blood, the forgivenefs of fins, according to the riches of his grace," Eph. i. 7. "Unto me who am lefs than the leaft of all faints, is this grace given, that I fhould preach among the Gentiles the unfearchable riches of Chrift," Eph. iii. 8. "For this caufe I bow my knees unto the Father of our Lord Jefus Chrift, of whom the whole family in heaven and earth is named, that he would grant you according to the riches of his glory," Eph iii. 14, 15, 16. "Or defpifeft thou the riches of his goodnefs, and forbearance, and long-fuffering; not knowing that the goodnefs of God leadeth thee to repentance?" Rom. ii. 4. "What if God, &c. that he might make known the riches of his glory," Rom. ix. 23. The riches of God and of Chrift are here made fynonimous terms, and furely the riches of grace, and of glory, and of long-fuffering, can only be the attributes of God. But left it fhould be doubted what are the unfearchable riches of Chrift, St. Paul fays, that he prays that his hearers "may be able to comprehend with all faints, what is the breadth, and length, and depth, and height; and to know the love of Chrift, which paffeth knowledge, that ye may be filled with all the fulnefs of God," Eph. iii. 18, 19; fo that all the fulnefs of God, and the knowledge of the love of Chrift, are again made fynonimous terms. But this fulnefs of God is attained to only by having "Chrift to dwell in our hearts by faith," Eph. iii. 17; and then when we have attained to this, and " come in the unity of the faith, and of the knowledge of the Son of God," what is the confequence? are we then " filled with all the fulnefs of God?" moft certainly we are, for we come " unto a perfect man, unto the meafure of the ftature of the fulnefs of Chrift," Eph. iv. 13. Unto himfelf St. Paul fays this knowledge was given, that he might preach the myftery of Chrift to the Gentiles, that they fhould be partakers of the promife in Chrift by the gofpel, " whereof I was made a minifter, according to the gift of the grace of God given unto me," Eph. iii. 7. " But unto every one of us is given grace according to the meafure of the gift of Chrift," Eph. iv. 7. " O the depth of the riches both of the wifdom and knowledge of God! how unfearchable are his judgments, and his ways paft finding out! for who hath known the mind of the Lord, or who hath been his counfellour?" Rom. xi. 33, 34. Thefe laft words afford at once an argument, and no unufeful leffon to a reader of the word of the God of truth.

LXXII.

" When he afcended up on high, he led captivity captive, and gave gifts unto men. (Now that he afcended, what is it but that he alfo defcended firft into the lower parts of the earth? He that defcended, is the fame alfo that afcended up far above all heavens, that he might fill all things,") Eph. iv. 8, 9, 10. St. Paul feems here to enter into the argument, and by the manner in which he puts the above affertions, to have confronted himfelf to Mr. Lindfey; from which I conclude that he had at leaft an equal forefight of the Lindfeian, as of the Platonick fchifm. He forefaw

that

that our Lord's pre-exiftence would be denied, and has therefore made his afcent a proof that he had before defcended to the earth, (for that is all that is meant by the lower parts of the earth) and had again returned to where he had been before, to heaven. (For that in the fame manner is all that is meant by, far above all heavens; and the two terms are ufed in order ftrongly to contraft his dignity and condefcenfion). He forefaw that his divinity would be denied, and has therefore lifted him far above the heavens, and extended him even that he might fill all things. Let us then " henceforth be no more children, toffed to and fro, and carried about with every wind of doctrine, by the fleight of men, and cunning craftinefs, whereby they lie in wait to deceive. But fpeaking the truth in love, grow up into him in all things, which is the Head, even Chrift," Eph. iv. 14, 15.

LXXIII.

" Servants, be obedient to them that are your mafters according to the flefh, with fear and trembling, in finglenefs of your heart, as unto Chrift: not with eye-fervice, as men pleafers, but as the fervants of Chrift, doing the will of God from the heart; with good will doing fervice, as to the Lord, and not to men: knowing that whatfoever good thing any man doeth, the fame fhall he receive of the Lord, whether he be bond or free," Eph. vi. 5, 6, 7, 8. If words could be found more explicitly declaring that the fervant of Chrift and of God is one, whilft " no man can ferve two mafters;" and alfo that the fervice done as to the Lord, is diftinct from that which is done to pleafe men, I fhould endeavour to paraphrafe this paffage. I fhall only now remark, that, in a parallel paffage to the Coloffian fervants, he fays, inftead of " with fear and trembling, in finglenefs of heart, as unto Chrift;" " not with eye-fervice, as men pleasers, but in singleness of heart, fearing God," Coloss. iii. 22.

LXXIV.

"Who being in the form of God, thought it not robbery to be equal with God: but made himself of no reputation, and took upon him the form of a servant, and was made in the likeness of men: and being found in fashion as a man, he humbled himself, and became obedient unto death, even the death of the cross," Philip. ii. 6, 7. 8. If Mr. Lindsey, who denies not that Jesus Christ was a man, will not deny that he is here declared to be such, I think he cannot deny that he is here declared to be God: for if the words *the form of a servant, the likeness of men, and the fashion of man*, be exactly of the same import as an assertion that he was actually a man, it necessarily follows, that the similar expression, " being in the form of God," must have a similar interpretation, and signify that he is actually God; and from the whole passage our Saviour's pre-existence (in a state of glory) to the time of his being " made man" is so necessarily deducible, that it cannot be avoided; the condescension of Christ, equal with God, in taking on him a nature so inferior as that of man, being the proposed example of humility, by which we are exhorted to be humble. If this text stood without another to support it, it is conclusive for the Godhead of Jesus Christ. Being in the form of God, having the same meaning as the being actually God, we are thereby enabled to interpret St. Paul's assertion that our Saviour " is the image of the invisible God," Coloss. i. 15; and many other passages declaring him to be " in the form of God."

LXXV.

" For our conversation is in heaven, from whence also we look for the Saviour, the Lord Jesus Christ," Philip. iii. 20. St. Paul having declared that his expectation

pectation of the Saviour is from heaven, pronounces the Saviour to be Jesus Christ; but to Timothy he says, that he is " an apostle of Jesus Christ by the commandment of God our Saviour," 1 Tim. i. 1. That prayers and supplications, and giving of thanks for all men, " is good and acceptable in the sight of God our Saviour," 1 Tim. ii. 3. " We trust in the living God, who is the Saviour of all men, specially of those that believe," 1 Tim. iv. 10. And to Titus he says, that God " hath in due times manifested his word through preaching, which is committed unto me, according to the commandment of God our Saviour," Titus i. 3: so that God our Saviour, is the Saviour whose coming from heaven Paul looked for, even Jesus Christ, one with the Father; that God who committed the preaching of his word, and the manifestation of himself to be made in due time, saying, " I am Jesus whom thou persecutest," Acts ix. 5.

LXXVI.

" Who is the first-born of every creature," Col. i. 15. Instead of conceiving that these words in the least degree derogate from the dignity of Christ as God, or in the least point him out to be even *the first and purest Creature of God*, I believe them to have the very reverse tendency; for from the context we may find St. Paul using the benefit of our redemption thro' the blood of Christ, which he declares to be forgiveness of sins, deliverance from the power of darkness, and translation into the kingdom of the Son, by whom he says, " were all things created that are in heaven, and that are in earth, visible and invisible, whether they be thrones, or dominions, or principalities, or powers: all things were created by him, and for him, and he is before all things, and by him all things consist," Col. i. 16, 17. And this redemption, which is afforded to us, the apostle testifies to be by the blood of the Son, who

is

is the " firſt-born of every creature." By the ſacrifice of Chriſt, and by the ſufficiency of his body once offered, we find the daily ſacrifice for the people taken away, and a full atonement made at once: by his daily prophecies, we find the deſtruction of the Jewiſh temple, and conſequently of the Jewiſh ritual at hand; and the event ſoon juſtified the prophecy; we find their altars and offerings aboliſhed, and their nation ceaſe to be a people peculiar to God: but we find alſo the adoption of all mankind to be, as it were, the children of the promiſe through faith. Now, as the entire hiſtory of the Jewiſh nation is a typical prophecy of our bleſſed Saviour's incarnation, ſufferings, and the adoption of all mankind thro' him, and that their peculiar ſanctity was maintained by blood, and by ſacrifices; ſo we find, that this blood, and theſe ſacrifices were a type of the ſacrifice to be made for all mankind in order to their adoption; for, as the ſacrifice was for an atonement for the ſins and errours of the people, ſo is the ſacrifice of Chriſt, once offered, an atonement for the ſins of thoſe who were thereby adopted. But we find alſo, that the Jews were to be ſanctified by the offering up of the firſt-born to God; and among other parts of their ritual, this ſanctification now no longer ſerviceable, was to be ſet aſide; that event, of which it was a type, having taken place, and our ſanctification to God, by the offering up of Jeſus Chriſt to be " the firſt-born of every creature" being accompliſhed. But it may be ſaid, that the offering of the firſt-born child was long before ſet aſide, and a compenſation taken by God, who accepted of the whole tribe of Levi to be ſervitors in the ſervice of the ark, and afterwards of the temple, inſtead of the firſt-born child through Iſrael. But this very compenſation being now to be ſet aſide, the newly adopted world required a firſt-born after the type of Iſrael, and found it accordingly in Chriſt Jeſus,

who

who not only gave himself for the whole of mankind, to be " the first-born of every creature," but also has, instead of the Levitical priesthood, stood forth himself to be an High-priest for us, whom he hath bought with his blood. If this interpretation of the words before us, which is altogether consonant to the doctrine of St. Paul to the Hebrews, by whose rites he declares our Saviour's sacrifice foreshewed, be not accepted, let the " first-born of every creature" be referred to a declaration in a few verses after, that Jesus Christ is " the first-born from the dead," Col. i. 18. Words spoken with respect to his resurrection, whereby our resurrection to life eternal thro' him is obtained, as he has become the Captain of our salvation, our Leader to a triumph over death and the grave, the first-born of a regenerate world. No man who ever read the context, and saw these words joined to a declaration, that by Jesus Christ all things were made, and that by him all things consist, &c. could conceive them intended to convey an idea that " the Creator of all things that are in heaven, and that are in earth, visible and invisible," was no more than a meer Creature, and the work of his own hands. Some other meaning corresponding to the general sense of the apostle must be sought for, and I sincerely think that I have affixed the true one to the words before us, and am certain that, if I have not, I have not deviated farther from it than they who translate " first-born" into " first-made." Compassion for the unhappy Servetus seems altogether to have absorbed Mr. Lindsey's attention; his death is made into a martyrdom, and his martyrdom into an argument sufficient to make any thing St. Paul says on this subject altogether unnecessary to be enquired into. The little passage is taken apart, and an interpretation fastened upon it, which, when it is restored to its original connection, it altogether rejects.

The

LXXVII.

The following is an explicit declaration that Jesus Christ is both God and Man, " for in him dwelleth all the fulness of the Godhead bodily," Col. ii. 9.

LXXVIII.

To forgive sins is the peculiar attribute of him to whom belong mercies and forgiveness; and accordingly we are called upon by St. Paul to " put on (as the elect of God, holy and beloved) bowels of mercy, kindess, humbleness of mind, meekness, long-suffering; forbearing one another, and forgiving one another, if any man have a quarrel against any: even as Christ forgave you, so also do ye," Col. iii. 12, 13. This passage is immediately preceded by a declaration, that " Christ is all in all."

LXXIX.

" Of the Lord ye shall receive the reward of the inheritance: for ye serve the Lord Christ. But he that doeth wrong, shall receive for the wrong which he hath done: and there is no respect of persons," Col. iii. 24, 25. Before whom is there no respect of persons? certainly before him who is to deal out the reward impartially, whom we serve; but we are told that " God will render to every man according to his deeds," " for there is no respect of persons with God," Rom. ii. 5, 11. And in the Ephesians, St. Paul says, having called us first servants of Christ," " your Master also is in heaven, neither is there respect of persons with him," Eph. vi. 6, 9. And accordingly we find St. James say, " My brethren, have not the faith of our Lord Jesus Christ, the Lord of glory, with respect of persons," James ii. 1.

LXXX.

To the Thessalonians, St. Paul says, " We were bold in our God, to speak unto you the gospel of God, with much contention," 1 Thess. ii. 2. " We were willing to have imparted unto you, not the gospel of God

God only, but also our own souls," " for labouring night and day, because we would not be chargeable unto any of you, we preached unto you the gospel of God," 1 Thess. ii. 8, 9. " and sent Timotheus our brother and minister of God, and our fellow labourer in the gospel of Christ, to establish you, and to comfort you concerning your faith," 1 Thess. iii. 2. If Christ be not God, is this the method of establishing their faith? no, but of shaking it to its very foundation, for the idea that he is God is suggested by it. Either St. Paul intended to inculcate that doctrine, or he did not; if he did, we must accede to it; if he did not, he has lied to the Holy Ghost, given " to guide him into all truth," John xvi. 13. or the spirit of truth has, by inaccuracy, deceived and dealt by our faith with duplicity. But as Paul has declared his exhortation to have been " not of deceit, nor of uncleanness, nor in guile," 1 Thess. ii. 3, I will believe that this eloquent apostle spoke the dictate of the spirit without ambiguity; and though Mr. Lindsey has charged the appointed witnesses of our blessed Redeemer with equivocation, I am confident he will not blasphemously dare to impute falsehood to the Spirit of truth himself. If Paul then speaking, with the Holy Ghost, has suggested that Christ is God, we must necessarily believe that he meant to inculcate that doctrine, and therefore that Jesus Christ is one with the Father, God.

LXXXI.

Reminding the Thessalonians of his former lessons, St. Paul says, " For ye know what commandments we gave you by the Lord Jesus. For this is the will of God," 1 Thess. iv. 2, 3. He then proceeds to instruct them in brotherly love, as the will of God, the commandment of the Lord Jesus.

LXXXII.

"It is a righteous thing with God to recompence tribulation to them that trouble you; and to you who are troubled, rest with us, when the Lord Jesus shall be revealed from heaven, with his mighty angels, in flaming fire, taking vengeance on them that know not God, and obey not the gospel of our Lord Jesus Christ: who shall be punished with everlasting destruction from the presence of the Lord, and from the glory of his power; when he shall come to be glorified in his saints, and to be admired in all them that believe (because our testimony among you was believed) in that day," 2 Thess. i. 6, 7, 8, 9, 10. Seeing then that Jesus Christ is revealed from heaven, taking vengeance, and destroying by everlasting expulsion from before the presence of the glory of his power; is not he that God with whom it is a righteous thing to recompence tribulation to them that trouble, to them that know him not to be God in obedience to the gospel of our Lord Jesus Christ, " that the name of our Lord Jesus Christ may be glorified?" See the entire chapter. The glorification of the name of our blessed Lord gives a sanction to our addressing him in these words, "Hallowed be thy name," Matth. vi. 9. "The Lord Jesus shall be revealed, taking vengeance on them that obey not the gospel of our Lord Jesus Christ;" and " what shall the end be of them that obey not the gospel of God?" 1 Pet. iv. 17.

LXXXIII.

"Now our Lord Jesus Christ himself, and God even our Father, which hath loved us, and hath given us everlasting consolation, and good hope thro' grace, comfort your hearts, and establish you in every good word and work," 2 Thess. ii. 16, 17. I am not yet going to enquire into Mr. Lindsey's curious doctrine of pious wishes, but, exclusive of the general sense of this passage,

passage, to make a remark on the great singularity of the expression. Either there are two nominatives joined by the copulative " and," or there is but one preceding the verb in the sentence before us, and in that case, the copulative unites two specific terms put in apposition to the one general nominative; if the former were the case, the verb must necessarily have been put in the plural number, whereas, from its standing in the singular, we must conceive it governed by one nominative only; now, if there be found one term in the sentence including the rest within its general import, that is the nominative case governing the verb: But I have all along asserted, that the Father is God, and that the Son is God, and therefore now say that the word " God," is here that general term comprehending within itself, " our Lord Jesus Christ himself, and even our Father," one God, which *hath* loved us, and *hath* given us everlasting consolation. St. Paul seems to have been diligent to establish this point by the energetick addition of the word " himself" after the name of our Lord; for thus emphatically to dwell upon a word to be dismissed instantly from being of any consequence in the construction of a sentence, is a practice unknown to any writer in any language, and surely not to be imputed to one of the most accurate, concise, and obtrusive speakers that ever forced the meaning of words upon the understanding of mankind; a preacher who gave words only to his ideas, and never sought an expletive to grace, much less to disgrace his language, and distract his argument. After he had thus given them a blessing from his warm and benevolent heart, this excellent man calls upon his hearers for their prayers, and, in consideration of the benediction that he has already bestowed on them, " that God should establish them in every good word and work," he says, " the Lord is faithful, who shall stablish you, and keep you from evil," 2 Thess. iii. 3.

LXXXIV.

"And the Lord direct your hearts into the love of God, and into the patient waiting for Christ;" or, as it stands in the margin of the Bible, "the patience of Christ," 2 Thess. iii. 5. Here is *the Lord*, according to Mr. Lindsey's manner of interpreting, quite neuter, being neither God nor Christ, for, apart from both, he is to lead to the love of the one, and to the patience of the other. But I believe this gentleman will hardly insist upon it that he is not either in this passage; and if not here, I refer it to the candour of every advocate of the Unitarian system, whether a distinction between the Father and Son, as God, is intended to be marked in such passages as the following: " now thanks be to God which always causeth us to triumph in Christ," 2 Cor. ii. 14. " In the sight of God speak we in Christ," 2 Cor. ii. 17; and in a multitude of texts, where the distinction is marked only as in that before us, where the neuter word *Lord* is certainly both that God and Christ from whom he seems to be distinguished by the action appointed to him.

LXXXV.

" There is one God, and one mediator between God and man, the man Christ Jesus; who gave himself a ransom for all, to be testified in due time," 1 Tim. ii. 5, 6. Having already commented on the former part of this passage, I shall not now weary my reader by repetition, but remark that, from a declaration that Christ had given himself a ransom to be testified in due time, and that that time was now come, in which God our Saviour will have all men come to the knowledge of the truth by the testimony of the apostolical preaching, with the Holy Ghost, Paul instantly passes on to say, that having been himself appointed a witness of our Saviour, a preacher, and an apostle, teaching of the Gentiles in faith and verity, " I will therefore that men pray every where, lifting up holy hands,

without

without wrath and doubting," 1 Tim. ii. 7, 8. Wherefore? because he is a witness to testify of Christ who gave himself a ransom for all. And how does this authorize him to will that all men should pray? there can be but one answer given to this, namely, that he, whom he testified, was the proper object of that prayer which he desired should be preferred, even Jesus Christ, one with the Father, God.

LXXXVI.

St. Paul, about to send Timothy to preach "sound doctrine, according to the glorious gospel of the blessed God, which was committed to his trust," 1 Tim. i. 10, 11. gives him the following epitome of what he would have him promulgate and testify; "Now, without controversy, great is the mystery of godliness: God was manifest in the flesh, justified in the spirit, seen of angels, preached unto the Gentiles, believed on in the world, received up into glory," 1 Tim. iii. 16. What can more demonstrate the Godhead of him who, having been manifest in the flesh, was witnessed by the apostles to have ascended into heaven, and who, by them, was now preached unto the Gentiles, than this direct assertion, that he, of whom it was asserted, was, and is God. And shall we now deny that the revelation of godliness is a mystery?

LXXXVII.

Forewarning Timothy of future defection from the truth, and recommending perseverance, St. Paul says, "We both labour, and suffer reproach, because we trust in the living God, who is the Saviour of all men, 1 Tim. iv. 10. "This" he declares to be "a faithful saying, and worthy of all acceptation;" and in so many words he has asserted the same thing of the following fact, that "Jesus Christ came into the world to save sinners," 1 Tim. i. 15. To be the Saviour then is the common attribute of God and of Christ, who is therefore God; for Jesus Christ is not said to have been the means of salvation, which would have better described the instrument of God in our redemption, but he is one and the same Saviour with God. Of the man Christ Jesus of the seed of David, it is indeed said that he was raised from the dead, 2 Tim. ii. 8. But Jesus Christ as God, clothed with eternal glory, is he by whom we have obtained eternal salvation, 2 Tim. ii. 10.

LXXXVIII.

" I give thee charge in the sight of God, who quickeneth all things, and before Christ Jesus, who before Pontius Pilate witnessed a good confession; that thou keep this commandment without spot, unrebukeable, until the appearing of our Lord Jesus Christ: which in his times he shall shew, who is the blessed and only potentate, the King of kings, and Lord of lords; who only hath immortality, dwelling in the light which no man can approach unto, whom no man hath seen, nor can see: to whom be honour and power everlasting. Amen," 1 Tim. vi. 13, 14, 15, 16. Here even the glory of God, unapproachable by man, is ascribed to Jesus Christ; and this is only ascribable to his divinity, as many men had seen the man Jesus; and St. Paul says, " yea, though we have known Christ after the flesh, yet now henceforth know we him no more," 2 Cor. v. 16. That he is the King of kings, and Lord of lords, is not only asserted here, but is in so many terms declared to be the name of Jesus Christ by St. John, Rev. xix. 16. His Godhead is therefore incontrovertibly established here. That St. Paul should speak of the Son only, is an inference naturally resulting from the consideration that he was making out an appointment to Timothy to go and to preach Jesus Christ, of whom he speaks in such terms in the first chapter of this epistle, that I choose to refer to it,

rather

rather than make a partial quotation, and the whole is too long to infert. The *picus* wifh, or rather let me have liberty to call it the benediction of the apoftle, is " grace, mercy, and peace from God our Father, and Jefus Chrift our Lord;" a wifh, which I cannot well imagine how he fhould expect to have gratified by a mere creature; nay, he fays more, that the grace of our Lord was exceeding abundant, fets forth, that to his truft was committed the glorious gofpel of God, and inftantly thanks Jefus for putting him into the miniftry; declares Jefus Chrift to have come into the world (a phrafe extraordinary, if the commencement of our Saviour's life was in the flefh) to fave finners; and having recounted the particular mercy and long-fuffering of Jefus Chrift toward himfelf, his gratitude breaks out into a doxology, the object of which muft evidently appear to be the fame as the Being from whom he received the benefits that invite his praife. "And now" he fays " unto the King eternal, immortal, invifible, the only wife God, be honour and glory, for ever and ever. Amen." He muft be a perverfe interpreter who can underftand thefe words in any other fenfe than that of a declaration that the merciful and long-fuffering Jefus, the abundance of whofe grace had pardoned his multitudinous perfecutions and blafphemies, for a pattern to all who fhould hereafter believe to life everlafting, " is the King eternal, the only wife God, to whom he afcribes honour and glory, in confideration of the exceedingly great benefits which he had received of him, and which were now fo ftrongly impreffed upon his mind, as at once to call forth his acknowledgments and his exulting praife."

LXXXIX.

St. Paul fays to Timothy, whom he is fending to " do the work of an Evangelift," " I charge thee therefore before God and the Lord Jefus Chrift, who fhall judge the quick and the dead at his appearing,

and

and his kingdom: preach the word, &c." 2 Tim. iv. 1. And " unto all them that love his appearing," he says, " the Lord the righteous Judge shall give a crown of righteousness at that day," ver. 8. Here the kingdom, the judgement-seat, and the appearing, are assigned to Jesus Christ, and the crown of righteousness is conferred on all those who love his appearing, according to what he says to Titus, to whom he is giving a like charge: " looking for that blessed hope, and the glorious appearing of the great God, and our Saviour Jesus Christ," Titus ii. 13. That these then are all synonimous terms I shall not affront the understanding of my reader by an attempt to make more evident than it must at once appear; and our Saviour Jesus Christ is therefore one with the Father, God.

XC.

In the charge to Titus last cited, St. Paul holds out " this blessed hope, and glorious appearing of the great God, and our Saviour Jesus Christ," to such as deny worldly lusts, and who, by so doing, " adorn the doctrine of God our Saviour," Titus ii. 10. Jesus Christ was the doctrine committed to Titus, and more particularly " how our salvation arose from his having given himself for us, that he might redeem us from all iniquity;" " that having been disobedient, serving lusts and pleasures, not our merits, but his mercy shone forth in saving us:" that therefore, " Jesus Christ having loved us, and washed us from our sins in his blood," Rev. i. 5. " the kindness and love of *God our Saviour* appeared, by washing of regeneration, and renewing of the Holy Ghost; which was shed on us abundantly, thro' *Jesus Christ our Saviour*," Titus iii. 4, 5, 6. Here, speaking to a man who was to act under him, and whose discharge of the office conferred on him, must in a great measure depend upon the accuracy of St. Paul's expression, this apostle, preaching that which was committed to him, according to the commandment of God our Saviour," falls into a mode of expreſſion, which, if Jeſus Chriſt be not God, muſt perpetually miſlead Titus, keep him wandering in continual errour, and utterly incapacitate him to "exhort and convince by ſound doctrine." That mankind had obtained ſalvation, is the committed doctrine; that God is our Saviour, and that Jeſus Chriſt is our Saviour, are ſentences occurring every where through the epiſtle, nay, in contiguous verſes; for, after declaring himſelf an apoſtle by the commandment of *God our Saviour,* St. Paul proceeds to ſay, " To Titus mine own Son after the common faith: grace, mercy, and peace from God the Father, and the *Lord Jeſus Chriſt our Saviour,*" Titus i. 3, 4. Did he mean to diſtract him? if not, he is very defective in his addreſs; but if he meant to inculcate the divinity of Chriſt, and to ſhew that the Father and the Son are one God, our Saviour, he has ſpoken to the purpoſe, and conſiſtently with the coherent ſtile that ſo exceedingly diſtinguiſhes the writings of St. Paul.

XCI.

" Verily, he took not on him the nature of angels; but he took on him the ſeed of Abraham," Heb. ii. 16. This is urged as a perſuaſive to us to lay hold of and embrace the great ſalvation, afforded to us by ſo wonderful an inſtance of condeſcenſion as that of our Saviour's having taken our nature upon him, which he is declared to have done, that he might, as man, become the Captain of our ſalvation, by ſuffering death for all men. But St. Paul ſays, that he took not on him the nature of angels, but deſcended a little lower: What is this but ſaying, that out of two things equally poſſible to him, he has made a choice? and to that which is not yet uſhered into being, we know that there is not any thing poſſible; therefore Jeſus Chriſt had pre-exiſtence to the time he came in the fleſh: But he verily

rily took not on him the nature of angels; therefore, in his pre-exiftent ftate, he was not an angel. But while the power of making choice among all inferior natures which he would take was his, he affumed that in which a purpofe beneficial to mankind was to be anfwered; and we are accordingly invited to offer up the tribute of our gratitude and confidence to him who had been thus merciful. But who was he to whom fuch a choice belonged? Certainly God, to whom alone all things are fubfervient, " by whom and for whom all things were created, that are in heaven, and that are in earth," Col. i. 16. who can exalt, as well as debafe, the works of his own hands, and take into himfelf whatfoever nature it fhall pleafe him to honour. This ftupendous dignity he has conferred upon ours; and for our advantage has become man, even the man Jefus Chrift. This adopted nature, this progeny of his power and mercy he has declared his Son; and for the fake of this his " holy child Jefus," who, notwithftanding that he was in all points tempted like as we are, continued to the end doing the will of God, fpotlefs, without fin, became obedient to the death for our redemption, and having fuffered, thereby to become the Author and Captain of our falvation, accompanied the * reafcending God into heaven, there for ever to remain our Mediator and Interceffor; for his fake, I fay, has God been pleafed to extend falvation to us; " for this beloved Son, in whom he is well pleafed," and whom therefore he has eternally united with himfelf, has undertaken the caufe of our infirmities, and has gracioufly condefcended to call us brethren; he has even called us fons; and having taken part in that flefh and blood whereof we are partakers, pronounced

us

* " Now, that he afcended, what is it but that he alfo defcended firft into the lower parts of the earth?" Eph. iv. 8.

us his children; and with more than paternal kindness bowed himself down to death for our sanctification, " that he might thereby destroy him that had the power of death, that is the devil, and deliver them that, through fear of death, were all their life time subject to bondage." See Heb. ii. throughout. Let us then, in memory of that fellowship which God himself has with us, having been " partaker of that flesh and blood," through the mercies which he has thereby vouchsafed us, approach the throne of his grace with confidence, " knowing that we have a new and living way consecrated to us, through the vail, that is to say, his flesh," Heb. x. 20. " And having," therefore, "an high priest over the house of God, let us draw near with a true heart, in full assurance of faith," " without wavering;" for if we sin wilfully, after that we have received the knowledge of the truth, " of the offering of the body of Jesus Christ once," " there remaineth no more sacrifice for sin, but a fiery indignation shall devour the adversary, who hath trodden under foot the Son of God, and counted the blood of the covenant wherewith he was sanctified an unholy thing, and hath done despite unto the spirit of grace; for we know him that hath said, vengeance belongeth unto me, I will recompence, saith the Lord. And again the Lord shall judge his people," Heb. x. throughout.

Where now is Mr. Lindsey's analogy between the offering up of prayer and religious worship to Aaron the high priest of the Jews, and to our great high priest Jesus Christ? between the priest " that standeth daily ministering and offering oftentimes the same sacrifices which can never take away sin," and this Man. who, after he had offered one sacrifice for sins, for ever sat down at the right hand of God; who, by one offering, hath perfected for ever them that are sanctified? " For the law maketh men high priefts; but the word of the oath which was fince the law, maketh the Son, who is confecrated for evermore;" " who, having as a prieft, once made facrifice, having offered up himfelf," is fet on the right hand of the throne of the majefty in the heavens, where he has become the mediator of the new covenant; in which he has declared, " I will put my laws into their minds, and write them in their hearts, and I will be to them a God, and they fhall be to me a people," Heb. vii. and viii. chap. And he, who has, by his flefh, broken down the partition wall that divided God and man, and whofe human nature, perfected by fufferings for an atonement to reconcile man to God, is now in eternal union with the divine nature, and clothed with the one glory, is furely a mediator, a high prieft, of a dignity to which the pofterity of Aaron never afpired; " he is a high prieft in things pertaining to God, to make reconciliation for the fins of the people;" and he is an object of our adoration and religious worfhip; " for in that he himfelf hath fuffered, being tempted, he is able to fuccour them that are tempted," Heb. ii. 17, 18. To this high honour the glorified body of Chrift is called, after it had been made perfect, and thence become the author of our falvation: whereas of Aaron's priefthood it is faid, that " the facrifices which were offered year by year continually," under it, " could never make the comers thereunto perfect," Heb x. 1. Are Aaron and Jefus Chrift now equally objects of our adoration? or are we equally to withhold our worfhip from both, him who cannot, and him who can fuccour us? from him who daily fhed the infufficient blood of bulls and goats, for the errours of the people, and from him who abolifhed the facrifice and offering by the one facrifice, the one offering of his own " prepared body, which came and bled for us, that we might be enabled to do

thy

thy will, O God," Heb. x. 5, 6. that we might be a party to the new covenant? The doctrine of the apostle is therefore here manifestly, that, inasmuch as the flesh and blood of the man Jesus is now in union with the eternal Godhead, and that in the world he had suffered so much for us, and had called us brethren, we may entertain great hope in the mercy of him, whose experience of human infirmities and temptations, can cause him to have compassion on us; and therefore we are desired to call upon God through these mercies, through Jesus Christ, his name, as our ransom from death, abolished by the death of his human body. It is not to " the unlearned reader" that I refer what I have now written, for I do not expect it to have any weight with such as have not read the law of Moses, and compared the types of the Jewish ritual with the great event of which it was the shadow; and also attended to the course of the apostle's argument throughout his epistle to the Hebrews. Before I conclude this comment I must insist upon the circumstance of the law having been no more than a shadow of the things to come, and not the exact portraiture; and therefore cannot refrain from expressing my surprize at seeing Aaron and our blessed Lord so closely brought together and assimilated by Mr. Lindsey, who will not admit of even a shadowy representation, throughout the law, of that which was to come, when it happens to typify that which opposes his own system. But as I have the word of God for it, I shall venture to assert, that the government of the Jews, by God, was an epitome of the government of the afterwards adopted world; that the selection of the Jews, for the faith of Abraham their father, was an instance of the value of faith in the pure eyes of God, and an epitome of the adoption " of many sons," to be elected thro' faith in Jesus Christ; that the purifications by blood, and the atonement,

by

by sacrifices for the people, were a type of that great sacrifice of the body of our Lord, offered once for our atonement, by which we are reconciled and restored to that blessed hope of everlasting life, which we had forfeited as heirs to the transgression of Adam; for as in Adam all men died, and as the law was given that sin might abound, so by Jesus Christ are all men made alive, and by the abundance of sin, his grace has the more abounded to us, by faith in our redemption, by the blood of the new covenant, to which the old covenant was a guide, that new covenant, of which the man Jesus perfected by death, and in eternal union with God, is the mediator. Let us then, on our part, declare, that we will be to him a people, as he has, upon his, promised, that he will be to us a God; and let us, when we hear the voice of " the Son of God" from our graves, acknowledge " the God who quickeneth the dead," and " rejoice in the appearing of the Son of man coming in the clouds of heaven;" when we consider that for our sakes he took our nature upon him, that he might have compassion upon our infirmities; and that he is our appointed judge, " because he is the Son of man."

XCII.

As it is already laid down, and, I presume, well remembered, that all are to be judged by our Lord Jesus Christ, when he shall come in his glory on his own day, with the holy angels, bringing his reward with him, and recompensing every man according to his works, I shall not repeat the proofs of it. " Of the Lord then, whose coming draweth nigh," St. James says, " be ye patient therefore brethren unto the coming of the Lord; the judge standeth before the door; we count them happy which endure; ye have heard of the patience of Job, and have seen the end of the Lord: that the Lord is very pitiful and of tender mercy," James v. 8,

8, 9, 10, 11. The patience of Job is here urged as an example to them who were defirous of haftening the day of the Lord; but the patience of Job was in waiting the end of God, whose pity and tender mercy at length amply rewarded his refignation. The pitiful and tenderly merciful Lord, who shall recompenfe them who, after the example of Job, and " the prophets, who spoke in the name of the Lord," with patience wait for his own appointed day, is therefore the fame God who rewarded Job, and for whose coming the prophets waited. But St. James goes on and fays, that with refpect to fick perfons the elders of the church are to be called for, and to pray over them, " and the prayer of faith shall fave the fick, and the Lord shall raife him up," James v. 14, 15. This is in context with the preceding paffage, which renders it manifeft who the Lord is that shall hear the prayer of faith, and heal the fick; even the fame Lord of whom St. Peter faid to Eneas, at Lydda, " Jefus Chrift maketh thee whole, arife," Acts ix. 34; who faid himfelf to her that, with full affurance of his power, touched but his garment, and had her iffue of blood ftaunched, " daughter, be of good comfort: thy faith hath made thee whole," Luke viii. 48; and who, without the intermediate use of any other name, faid to the leper who befought him with a prayer of faith, * " I will; be thou clean," Luke v. 13: of Jefus Chrift then we are to afk and have. He therefore is one with the Father, God.

XCIII.

In the commencement of his epiftle, James calls himfelf " a fervant of God, and of the Lord Jefus Chrift," James i. 1. As a reafon why we should " not have

---

* Quere, How does this ftand in the French? is it *je fouhaite?* or if it be, what does it fignify? See *Apology, note, p, 5.*

have the faith of our Lord Jesus Christ, the Lord of glory, with respect of persons," James ii. 1, he says, " hearken, my beloved brethren, hath not God chosen the poor of this world, rich in faith, and heirs of the kingdom which he hath promised to them that love him?" James ii. 5. " If ye have respect to persons, ye commit sin," James ii. 9. " For he shall have judgement without mercy, that hath shewed no mercy; and mercy rejoiceth against judgement," ii. 13.

XCIV.

In order to avoid repetition of arguments already used, I shall observe upon but one passage in St. Peter's first general epistle in its course.

" The elders which are among you, I exhort, who am also an elder, and a witness of the sufferings of Christ, and also a partaker of the glory that shall be revealed: feed the flock of God which is among you," " neither as being lords over God's heritage, but being ensamples to the flock. And when the chief shepherd shall appear, ye shall receive a crown of glory that fadeth not away," 1 Pet. v. 1, 2, 3, 4. If it be remembered that this charge comes from St. Peter to men engaged in the same occupation as himself, it is but reasonable to suppose that he had in mind those words of our blessed Lord when he conferred the charge of his flock upon him, which were so emphatically spoken, and so affectingly received by him. After his resurrection from the dead, Jesus having on the third time shewed himself to his disciples " when they had dined, saith to Simon Peter, Simon son of Jonas, lovest thou me more than these? he saith unto him, yea, Lord; thou knowest that I love thee. He saith unto him, feed my lambs. He saith to him again the second time, Simon son of Jonas, lovest thou me? he saith unto him, yea, Lord; thou knowest that I love thee. He saith unto him,

him, feed my sheep. He saith unto him the third time, Simon son of Jonas, lovest thou me? Peter was grieved, because he said unto him the third time, lovest thou me? and he said unto him, Lord, thou knowest all things; thou knowest that I love thee. Jesus saith unto him, feed my sheep," John xxi. 14, 15, 16, 17. A charge attended by such circumstances, and repeatedly conveyed in such terms, must necessarily have been deeply impressed on the memory of Peter, who was grieved that he who knew all things should think it necessary to renew it a third time. That Peter should therefore ever afterwards consider the office conferred upon him as that of a shepherd, and those to whom he was sent as the flock of the chief shepherd who had committed them to him, is not to be wondered at; and accordingly we find him in another place say of him, who had declared himself " no hireling, but the shepherd, whose own the sheep are; the good shepherd, who giveth his life for the sheep," John x. 13, 14. " Ye were as sheep going astray; but are now returned unto the shepherd and bishop of your souls," 1 Pet. ii. 25. So that here is that flock of Jesus Christ, the good shepherd, whose own the sheep are, expressly declared to be the flock of God. St. Paul too has called " Jesus Christ, that great shepherd of the sheep, Heb. xiii. 20; and speaking to the Ephesian Elders, he desires them to " take heed to all the flock, over the which the Holy Ghost had made them overseers, to feed the church of God," Acts xx. 28. From the chief shepherd also, when he shall appear, we are to receive a crown of glory which fadeth not away. " Blessed is the man that endureth temptation; for when he is tried, he shall receive the crown of life, which the Lord hath promised to them that love him," James i. 12. This promise is explained; " Hath not God chosen the poor of this world, rich in faith, and heirs of the kingdom,

T which

which he hath promifed to them that love him?" James ii. 5. From whom now are we "* to obtain an incorruptible crown," "a crown of righteoufnefs, which the Lord, the righteous Judge, fhall give at that day, unto all them that love his appearing? †" Certainly from that God who hath promifed the kingdom; that Lord who hath promifed the crown of life to them that love him, fhall we receive a crown of glory which fadeth not away, when the chief fhepherd fhall appear as a righteous judge to give an incorruptible crown of righteoufnefs to all them that love his appearing. This chief fhepherd is therefore that righteous Judge, that Lord, that God who hath promifed, and will give a crown of glory to all that love him, even Jefus Chrift, one with the Father, God; "to whom be praife and dominion for ever and ever. Amen." 1 Pet. iv. 11.

XCV.

The firft verfe of the firft chapter of St. Peter's fecond epiftle general, has thefe remarkable words, as literally tranflated in the margin of our Bible. "Simon Peter, a fervant and apoftle of Jefus Chrift, to them that have obtained like precious faith with us, through the righteoufnefs of our God and Saviour Jefus Chrift," 2 Pet. i. 1. Paul to Timothy, alfo calls himfelf "an apoftle by the commandment of God our Saviour, and Lord Jefus Chrift, which is our hope," 1 Tim i. 1.

XCVI.

"An entrance fhall be miniftered unto you abundantly, into the everlafting kingdom of our Lord and Saviour Jefus Chrift," 2 Pet. i. 11.

XCVII.

"The day of the Lord will come as a thief in the night; in the which the heavens fhall pafs away with a great noife, and the elements fhall melt with fervent heat,

---

* 1 Cor. ix. 25. † 2 Tim. iv. 8.

heat, the earth also and the works that are therein shall be burnt up. Seeing then that all these things shall be dissolved, what manner of persons ought ye to be in all holy conversation and godliness, looking for and hasting unto the coming of the day of God, wherein the heavens being on fire shall be dissolved, and the elements shall melt with fervent heat?" 2 Pet. iii. 10, 11, 12. As there is but one day mentioned in this passage, it is evident that the Lord, whose day it is called in the first, is the same as the God, whose day it is said to be in the last verse; one and the same God. But, that the specified Lord, who is God, is our Lord Jesus Christ, the context, to which I refer, shews beyond contradiction. Besides other circumstances evincing this fact throughout the whole chapter, the apostle says, " the long-suffering of our Lord is to be accounted salvation; even as our beloved brother Paul also hath written unto you," 2 Pet. iii. 15. Now the words of Paul, to which St. Peter here refers, are, " For this cause I obtained mercy, that in me first Jesus Christ might shew forth all long-suffering, for a pattern to them which should hereafter believe on him to life everlasting," 1 Tim. i. 16. Here then, mercy and life everlasting, which are salvation, are preached to all thro' the long-suffering of Jesus Christ, after the pattern of Paul, to which Peter has referred, calling him, who is by Paul called Jesus Christ, Lord; and immediately after calling him, whom he had himself named Lord, God. Let us not therefore " fall from our stedfastness, but grow in grace, and in the knowledge of our Lord and Saviour Jesus Christ: to him be glory both now and for ever. Amen." 2 Pet. iii. 18.

XCVIII.

" He is Antichrist, that denieth the Father and the Son," 1 John ii. 22. How is he who denieth the Father, Antichrist? How is he who denieth Jesus to be the Chrift, and "confeffeth not that he is come in the flefh," to be confidered as denying the Father? For this plain reafon, that the Son is one with the Father, God; and confequently the Father is denied upon the denial of him who is with him, one.

XCIX.

"Every fpirit that confeffeth not that Jefus Chrift is come in the flefh, is not of God," 1 John iv. 3. Though the apoftle's intention in this verfe be to fhew that Jefus Chrift was truly man, yet it is no ftrained inference to fay, that the Being, who came in the flefh, had pre-exiftence to the time of taking it upon him; and this indeed follows the more naturally, when we confider that this denial is made " by the fpirit of Antichrift," which denieth the Father and the Son.

C.

As I do believe the 7th verfe of the 5th chapter of St. John's 1ft epiftle to be at the beft a very dubious text, I refign all advantage that might accrue to my caufe, from its having come from his infpired pen. But I fhall beg leave to exprefs myfelf in the words of it, which very well comprize the conclufion following from the whole of facred writ, and which I hope I have rendered obvious by this time. In my own perfon then I fay that I believe in " the Father, the word, and the Holy Ghoft, and thefe three are one."

CI.

If words could be found more directly enjoining prayer to Jefus Chrift than thofe which follow, I fhould endeavour to enlarge on the fubject; but as the beloved difciple of our Redeemer has given us the precept, I fhall leave it to Mr. Lindfey to draw the conclufion, for which he ftands engaged, and to acknowledge that Jefus Chrift is one with the Father, God. " Thefe things have I written unto you that believe on the name of the Son of God; that ye may know ye have

have eternal life, and that ye may believe on the name of the Son of God. And this is the confidence that we have in him, that if we afk any thing according to his will, he heareth us. And if we know that he hear us, whatfoever we afk, we know that we have the petitions that we defired of him," 1 John v. 13, 14, 15. " Beloved, if our heart condemn us not, then have we confidence towards God. And whatfoever we afk, we receive of him, becaufe we keep his commandments," 1 John iii. 21, 22. Here exactly the fame precept is repeated; but the one Godhead is named in the latter, inftead of the fecond perfon of the Trinity fpecified in the former paffage.

CII.

" And we know that the Son of God is come, and hath given us an underftanding, that we may know him that is true: and we are in him that is true, even in his Son Jefus Chrift. This is the true God and eternal life," 1 John v. 20. It is remarkable that this declaration is followed by a defire to "keep from idols," to the overthrow of whofe worfhip he preaches the Godhead of Jefus Chrift, the Son. But left it fhould be faid that the elder was inattentive to the confequence of fpeaking in ambiguous language to idolaters, concerning the God whom he preached to them, I will produce proofs from the context to teftify that Chrift is here fpoken of, and pointed out for adoration. " He that hath the Son, hath life," and " God hath given us eternal life, and this life is in his Son," and " thefe things have I written unto you that believe on the name of the Son of God; that ye may know that ye have eternal life," 1 John v. 11, 12, 13. Thefe words explain who is the true God in whom we have this eternal life; befides, the gift of underftanding is an act of Godhead, and is here made to us by the Son. Suppofe for a moment with Mr. Lindfey that the prophetick
eyes

eyes of the apoſtles were blinded to the opinion afterwards to be entertained by mankind, who have ſince their day believed Jeſus Chriſt to be God, notwithſtanding that they had ſeen him a man born and living amongſt men, even this abſurd ſuppoſition would not extend to St. John, nor indeed to St. Paul, who were themſelves witneſſes of that early hereſy by which the manhood of Jeſus Chriſt was denied, and had heard that body which he had come in, declared only to have been an appearance; ſo that their own living experience might have given them a hint, that accuracy in the application of the terms Lord, and Saviour, and *the like*, was neceſſary, if they had not been the moſt ſtupid as well as wicked men that ever lived on the earth. They were accurate men, they were honeſt men; and by the application of thoſe terms to both the Father and the Son, they have left us an irrefragable proof that the Father and the Son are one God.

The goodneſs of God, and that gracious indulgence with which he has conſulted the infirmities of our ſtate, is, in this reſpect alſo, very ſtrongly diſplayed, that he took manhood on him, in order to give a ſenſible object of worſhip to mankind, incapable of forming any adequate idea of the abſtract God, whoſe qualities are of a nature incomprehenſible by our minds; and not only our natural incapacity to conceive a God purely ſpiritual was conſidered, but the world, merged in idolatry at the time of his incarnation, was mercifully indulged with an object of ſenſe, to which men could look according to habit alſo, and to whom, even by the exertion of the ſame faculties by which they had adopted and adored idols, they could prefer worſhip without the imputation of idolatry. A reſting place is hereby given to the mind, inſtead of its being continued

nued under the necessity of launching out into vast infinity and eternity, and vainly endeavouring to engage itself in the contemplation of matters, of which it can form no idea at all.

CIII.

" Whosoever transgresseth, and abideth not in the doctrine of Christ, hath not God : he that abideth in the doctrine of Christ, he hath both the Father and the Son," 2 John 9. After having shewed who had not God, the elder goes on to shew of the direct contrary character, that he hath the Father and the Son, who are therefore that God which abideth in him. " Whosoever denieth the Son, the same hath not the Father," 1 John ii. 23. But " whosoever shall confess that Jesus is the Son of God, God dwelleth in him, and he in God," 1 John iv. 15. " If we love one another, God dwelleth in us," 1 John iv. 12. Who now is the Father and the Son, who dwelleth in us if we abide in the doctrine of Christ?

CIV.

" Jude, a servant of Jesus Christ, and brother of James, to them that are sanctified by God the Father," Jude 1. Paul, who has frequently called himself both the servant of God and of Jesus Christ, (see Philip. i. 1, and Titus i. 1.) has in like manner addressed the Corinthians, " to them that are sanctified in Christ Jesus," 1 Cor. i. 1.

CV.

Speaking of the judgement that awaits " ungodly men, turning the grace of God into lasciviousness, and denying the only Lord God, and our Lord Jesus Christ," " who speak evil of those things which they know not," Jude says, that " Enoch also, the seventh from Adam, prophesied of these, saying, behold, the Lord cometh with ten thousands of his saints, to execute judgement upon all, and to convince all that are
un-

ungodly among them, of all their ungodly deeds, which they have ungodly committed, and of all their hard speeches, which ungodly sinners have spoken against him." Now we know very well that Jesus Christ is to come to judgement, with the holy angels; that to those who work iniquity he shall give everlasting punishment, but unto the righteous, eternal life. We must therefore conclude him to have been the object of Enoch's prophecy; and the more so, as the apostle proceeds to recommend the remembrance and observation of what " the apostles of our Lord Jesus Christ had spoken, that in the latter times there should be mockers, sensual, not having the spirit," and to desire that they to whom he writes, " building up themselves in our most holy faith, should pray in the Holy Ghost, keep themselves in the love of God, looking for the mercy of our Lord Jesus Christ, unto eternal life. Now unto him that is able to keep us from falling, to present us faultless before the presence of his glory with exceeding joy; to the only wise God, our Saviour, be glory and majesty, dominion and power, both now and ever. Amen." See Jude throughout. A comment must be unnecessary here.

As I prescribed to myself the order in which the books of the scripture are arranged, and had determined to enquire of the testimony afforded by each in its course; and as I had but one conclusion in view, to the evidence of which alone proofs were to be brought, my intelligent reader will see the impossibility of stepping from proof to proof in a mathematical process, or of producing an encreasing testimony commencing at a partial, and, in the end, resulting in a full demonstration of the truth of that one proposition, which must be rendered equally manifest by the first, as by the last argument in its behalf. That the scriptures have declared

clared the divinity of our Lord, it is my office to show; and that this declaration is true, if made, must necessarily follow, upon the conceſſion that the scriptures are the word of God, and therefore true; and as this conceſſion is made, I am only to produce such declarations as are contained in them: this muſt be at once seen to preclude progreſſive enquiry. I have, however, for the gratification of my reader, reserved a very few paſſages, in which it is more directly and literally aſſerted that Jesus Chriſt is one with the Father, God; and with these I shall close the evidence of the apoſtles, the appointed witneſſes of our bleſſed Redeemer.

CVI.

"Hereby perceive we the love of God, becauſe he laid down his life for us," 1 John iii. 16. The name of " Jesus Chriſt" does not once occur in the preceding part of the chapter, of which this is the 16th verse, so that it cannot poſſibly be referred to by the pronoun " he;" our Lord and Saviour is therefore literally declared to be God. The course of the argument alſo makes a literal interpretation abſolutely neceſſary, for the beloved diſciple is perſuading us to love one another in conſequence of our brotherhood, a motive which God could not have, to love beings so infinitely inferior to him; but that God loved us, is manifeſted by his having rendered himſelf ſubject to death for our ſake; we are therefore deſired to love one another, from the equality and ſympathy of our nature: the love of God is perceived, becauſe he laid down his life for us; and therefore, " we ought to lay down our lives for the brethren," 1 John iii. 16.

CVII.

St. Paul preaches thus to the Epheſians, whom he had called to Miletus, and whom he appointed elders over the church to preach the gospel.

"Take heed therefore unto yourselves, and to all the flock over the which the Holy Ghost hath made you overseers, to feed the church of God, which he hath purchased with his own blood," Acts xx. 28. What can convince if this be unable? Shall we see the blood of God himself streaming for our redemption, and still deny that God and man are one Christ? or shall we not rather seek to be of the fold, "return to the shepherd of our souls," to the "Lord God, who shall feed his flock like a shepherd? who shall gather the lambs with his arm, and carry them in his bosom," Isaiah xl. 11. But St. Paul foresaw that men would look upon this position, which he has laid down, as a difficulty, which would turn aside such as yielded not their faith, but should proceed to enquire of the hidden mystery, and withdraw from the acknowledgment of spiritual things, because they were not in possession of spiritual things to compare with them, whereby they should comprehend the things of God, into which the natural man is unable to enquire; and therefore he has said even to these elders to whom he directs his charge, "For I know this, that after my departing, shall grievous wolves enter in among you, not sparing the flock. Also of yourselves shall men arise, speaking perverse things, to draw away disciples after them," Acts xx. 29, 30. I wish that St. Paul may not have had our present day in view when he spoke thus.

CVIII.

To the Hebrews, St. Paul says, that the address from the Majesty on high to him, "by whom he made the worlds," is, "Thy throne, O God, is for ever and ever; a sceptre of righteousness is the sceptre of thy kingdom: And, thou Lord, in the beginning hast laid the foundation of the earth; and the heavens are the works of thy hands. They shall perish, but thou remainest: and they all shall wax old as doth a garment;
and

and as a vesture shalt thou fold them up, and they shall be changed: but thou art the same, and thy years shall not fail," Heb. i. 8, 10, 11, 12. That the attributes here ascribed, are ascribable only to God, I believe will not be denied; but they are ascribed by God himself, and to whom? To Jesus Christ, after he had laid aside the form of a servant, and again taken upon him the form of God, the express image of his person; when he had by himself purged our sins; and, being the brightness of his glory, sat down on the right-hand of the Majesty on high. They are ascribed to Jesus Christ, upon the reassumption of that glory which he had laid down, when he was made a little lower than the angels, that, by the grace of God, he might taste death for every man; that, by suffering, he might be made perfect, to lead mankind to salvation; to him who had called us brethren, and had now taken up his anointed body, "anointed with the oil of gladness above his fellows;" that body, by which he became our fellow, our brother, and our Saviour; and by the ascent of which he has marshalled our way to his eternal kingdom. To him, I say, who had been partaker of our flesh and blood, and who, having made himself acquainted with our infirmities, has taken into heaven that nature, by which he can be touched with a compassionate feeling of them; and has therefore become our "merciful high priest and intercessor," are these attributes ascribed, this address of exultation is made; it is (if I may so say) the welcome of God to the captain and leader of mankind to glory. And, if I may dare to use the expression, we find, as it were, a passion of joy in the great God of our salvation, at seeing the means of his grace take effect in restoring mankind to that forfeited happiness, from which by transgression he had fallen; in reconciling him to himself; in seeing that a passage is now opened into his own eternal happiness to man, by the taking the manhood into God, as the Godhead had before on earth rendered one man a worthy and sufficient atonement for all men. His grace is now perfected; our nature is seated in heaven; and the glory which Christ had with the Father before the foundations of the world were laid, is now ascribed to him; the Father has glorified him with his own self; he is, by the majesty most high, declared to be one with him, declared to be God, whose throne endureth for ever, and whose years shall never fail; the man was seen to ascend; but the God is acknowledged by him to whom alone the God is comprehensible, "who only knoweth who the Son is." I do not see how it is possible to avoid, or evade, the strength of this proof, resulting from the application of these words of David to the Son, of whose Godhead they are as express a declaration as words can convey. God himself acknowledges and declares the second person in himself; and this in exact conformity with our Lord's own words, upon seeing Judas go out with a resolution to betray him; his hour he knew was now come, and, "therefore, when he (Judas) was gone out, Jesus said, now is the Son of man glorified, and God is glorified in him. If God be glorified in him, God shall also glorify him in himself, and shall straightway glorify him," John xiii. 31, 32. And as such a doxology, according to this prediction, comes from God himself to Christ, I own that to me it appears an impious perverseness to withhold prayer, an impious ingratitude to withhold our praise and thanksgiving from him. When we see our own salvation the source of such joy in heaven; when we see the infinitely great "maker of all things that are in heaven, and that are in the earth," take such an interest in the happiness of us his very little creatures, we have an additional encouragement to approach the throne of his

mercy

mercy with thanfgiving for our redemption; for which he not only fuffered, but rejoiced in his fufferings, and efteemed them glory for our fake. " Of Jefus Chrift, the fame yefterday, and to day, and for ever," Heb. xiii. 8. Let us then acknowledge, that " of the Jews, as concerning the flefh, Chrift came, but that he is over all, God bleffed for ever. Amen." Rom. ix. 5.——

I now come to the fourth kind of teftimony borne to the divinity of our Lord and Saviour Jefus Chrift, that which he has afforded himfelf, by the revelation made to St. John, after his afcenfion, and in which he has, in his glorified ftate, declared his own nature. I do not mean to difcufs the prophecy contained in the apocalypfe, but to produce fuch evidence as the book affords to my point only; fuch other proofs as are referable to this head, I have noted, as they have occurred in the former parts of this enquiry.

CIX.

Jefus Chrift reveals himfelf to St. John in the following words: " thefe things faith the firft and the laft, which was dead, and is alive," Rev ii. 8. God fays to Ifaiah, " I am the firft, and I am the laft, and befides me there is no God," If. xliv. 6. Hence we fee, that befides the firft and the laft, there is no God: but Jefus Chrift fays, " I am the firft, and I am the laft;" the conclufion is, that befides Jefus Chrift, one with the Father, there is no God, and he is the " alpha and omega, the beginning and the ending, which is, and which was, and which is to come, the Almighty," Rev. i. 8, and xxii. 13.

CX.

Jefus Chrift fays, " I am he that fearcheth the reins and hearts: and I will give unto every one of you according to your works," Rev. ii. 23. God fays to Jeremiah,

remiah, " I the Lord fearch the heart, I try the reins, even to give every man according to his ways, and according to the fruit of his doings," Jer. xvii. 10. Here God has declared himfelf the fearcher of hearts. Is there any other fearcher of hearts? None. But Jefus Chrift declares that he is he that fearcheth the hearts: as there is none other that fearcheth, and that Jefus Chrift has declared that he fearcheth, Jefus Chrift is none other than God Almighty, one with the Father; " the Lord of hofts, that judgeth righteoufly, and trieth the reins and the heart," Jer. xi. 20; " the Lord of hofts, that trieth the righteous, and feeth the reins and the heart," Jer. xx. 12. And the unity of the Godhead of the Lord, the King of Ifrael, and his Redeemer the Lord of hofts, is thus afferted by the one firft and laft; " Thus faith the Lord the King of Ifrael, and his Redeemer, the Lord of hofts, I am the firft, and I am the laft, and befides me there is no God," Ifa. xliv. 6.

CXI.

" I am alpha and omega, the beginning and the ending, faith the Lord, which is, and which was, and which is to come, the Almighty," Rev. i. 8. To the proof already given, that thefe words are fpoken by Jefus Chrift, I will add this, that the declaration follows a defcription of the coming of the Lord, exactly correfponding to that given by our Saviour of the coming of the Son of man; " then fhall all the tribes of the earth mourn, and they fhall fee the Son of man coming in the clouds of heaven, with power and great glory," Matth. xxiv 30. " Behold, he cometh with clouds; and every eye fhall fee him, and they alfo which pierced him: and all kindreds of the earth fhall wail becaufe of him," Rev. i. 7. He then proceeds to declare himfelf to be the Lord, which is, and which

was,

was, and which is to come: to Jesus Christ the Lord, then, the four beasts " rest not day and night, saying, holy, holy, holy, Lord God Almighty, which was, and is, and is to come," Rev. iv. 8.

CXII.

" I am he that liveth, and was dead; and behold, I am alive for evermore. Amen." Rev. i. 18. That these words are spoken by Jesus Christ, cannot admit of a doubt. " And when those beasts give glory, and honour, and thanks to him who sat on the throne, who liveth for ever and ever, the four and twenty elders fall down before him that sat on the throne, and worship him that liveth for ever and ever, and cast their crowns before the throne, saying, thou art worthy, O Lord, to receive glory, and honour, and power: for thou hast created all things, and for thy pleasure they are, and were created," Rev. iv. 9, 10, 11. Such is the honour ascribed in heaven to him who is " alive for evermore. Amen." And shall we, who are a part of his creation, " by whom are all things, and we by him," alone withdraw ourselves from the worship of the " one Lord, Jesus Christ," " by whom all things consist?" And shall we not rather join our voice to the voices in heaven, and say, " hallowed be thy name. Thy will be done in earth, as it is in heaven?" Matth. vi. 9, 10; see also 1 Cor. viii. 6, and Col. i. 17.

CXIII.

The following words of our Saviour to St. John, to be delivered by him to the church of Philadelphia, warrant our preferring that petition of the Lord's prayer to him, " lead us not into temptation, but deliver us from evil," Matth vi. 13. " I will also keep thee from the hour of temptation, which shall come upon all the world, to try them that dwell upon the earth," Rev. iii. 10.

CXIV.

"As many as I love, I rebuke and chasten," says Jesus Christ to St. John, Rev. iii. 19. "Behold, happy is the man whom God correcteth," Job v. 17. "For whom the Lord loveth he chasteneth, and scourgeth every son whom he receiveth. If ye endure chastening, God dealeth with you as with sons. for what son is he whom the Father chasteneth not?" Heb. xii. 6, 7.

CXV.

"Grace be unto you, and peace from him which is, and which was, and which is to come; and from the seven spirits which are before his throne; and from Jesus Christ, who is the faithful witness, and the first-begotten of the dead, and the Prince of the kings of the earth: unto him that loved us, and washed us from our sins in his own blood, and hath made us kings and priests unto God and his Father; to him be glory and dominion for ever and ever. Amen." Rev. i. 4, 5, 6. If it be allowed that there is an errour in the manuscript whence our translation of the first chapter and fifth verse of the apocalypse was taken, there is but very little lost by the concession; for substituting the words $\tilde{\tau}\omega$ $\alpha\gamma\alpha\pi\eta\sigma\alpha\nu\tau\sigma\varsigma$ $\kappa\alpha\iota$ $\lambda\nu\sigma\alpha\nu\tau\sigma\varsigma$ instead of the accepted reading $\tilde{\tau}\omega$ $\alpha\gamma\alpha\pi\eta\sigma\alpha\nu\tau\iota$ $\kappa\alpha\iota$ $\lambda\nu\sigma\alpha\nu\tau\iota$, and then adopting Mr. Lindsey's own translation, I do not see that the doxology contained in the passage, is by any means turned away from its proper object, Jesus Christ; for, taking the whole together, it runs thus, "grace be unto you, and peace from him which is, and which was, and which is to come; and from the seven spirits which are before his throne; and from Jesus Christ, who is the faithful witness, and the first-begotten of the dead, and the Prince of the kings of the earth, *who hath* loved us, and washed us from our sins, in his own blood, and hath made us kings and priests unto God

and

and his Father; to him be glory and dominion for ever and ever. Amen." Rev. i. 5, 6. It is difficult to imagine how any man fhould conceive " him" to be referable to any preceding term in the fentence, befides that to which the multitude of epithets is referred; and that this is Jefus Chrift, does not admit of a doubt. This I fay even upon a fuppofition that Mr. Lindfey has taken the text as it was actually written; but I will now withdraw that conceffion, upon an affurance that the commonly accepted reading is fupported by at leaft equal authority as that of Dr. Mill, and that the tranflators of our Bible have thought it the preferable one. But if I were altogether to relinquifh this text, which will however admit of no other fenfe than that I have afcribed to it, it would avail this gentleman but very little, for the 13th verfe of the 5th chapter affords a doxology which I will not refign fo eafily as he may expect. " Bleffing and honour, and glory, and power be unto him that fitteth upon the throne, and unto the Lamb for ever and ever," Rev. v. 13. Is this doubtful? No, nor a doubt pretended: but Jefus Chrift is in fight, and therefore, fays Mr. Lindfey, an object of worfhip. God only, fays this gentleman in another part of his book, is the proper object of worfhip; but here Jefus Chrift in fight is a proper object of worfhip: I will draw the neceffary conclufion; therefore Jefus Chrift in fight is God. And, " am I a God at hand, faith the Lord, and not a God afar off?" Jer. xxiii. 23. Is this to be acceded to? If Jefus Chrift be a creature, he is not an object of worfhip; and my turning my eye upon him can never confer infinity and eternity on that which was before local and temporary; but Mr. Lindfey perfifting in it that he is a creature, has given the beholders a power of *looking him* into the one Creator. This is too abfurd to dwell on. I fhall only afk, if Jefus Chrift has not any right to our adoration, how he is

X authorized

authorized to demand it on fight? and, if he be in any cafe entitled to our adoration, " the incommunicable honour and prerogative of God alone *," and that therefore he be God, whether it be not the depth of ftupidity, as well as impiety, to deny that our Lord and Saviour Jefus Chrift is one with the Father, God? " Grow in grace, and in the knowledge of the Lord and Saviour Jefus Chrift: to him be glory both now and for ever. Amen." fays St. Peter; and one fuch declaration, that glory is his for ever and ever, is equal to a thoufand; and, were every other one to be given up, this would remain a fufficient eftablifhment of the eternal glory of Jefus Chrift; but, when we find glory once fo afcribed, I do not fee any reafon for doubting fuch doxologies as repeat the praifes of our Lord and Saviour; for, one eftablifhing the right, it is but reafonable to believe, that men, who faw with the fame enlightened underftanding as Peter did, fhould equally afcribe to him the glory which they muft have equally feen to be his due.

CXVI.

" The kings of the earth, &c. hid themfelves in the dens, and in the rocks of the mountains; and faid to the mountains and rocks, fall on us, and hide us from the face of him that fitteth on the throne, and from the wrath of the Lamb: for the great day of his wrath is come; and who fhall be able to ftand?" Rev. vi. 15, 16. This fpeaks for itfelf. There is in context with it a remarkable paffage, by which Jefus Chrift, coming to judgement, acts exactly in correfpondence with thofe words which are addreffed to him by the Father upon his afcenfion into heaven; " The heavens fhall perifh, and wax old as doth a garment, and as a vefture fhalt thou fold them up," Heb. i. 12. " And the ftars of heaven fell unto

---

* Apology, p. 137.

unto the earth, even as a fig-tree casteth her untimely figs when she is shaken of a mighty wind: and the heaven departed as a scrowl when it is rolled together," Rev. vi. 13, 14.

CXVII.

"And I saw another angel fly in the midst of heaven, having the everlasting gospel to preach unto them that dwell on the earth, and to every nation, and kindred, and tongue, and people, saying with a loud voice, Fear God, and give glory to him, for the hour of his judgement is come: and worship him that made heaven and earth, and the sea, and the fountains of waters," Rev. xiv. 6, 7. Paul, who had often termed himself "a prisoner of Jesus Christ," Philemon 9. and who tells the Romans, "I am not ashamed of the gospel of Christ," Rom. i. 16. says to Timothy, "Be not thou therefore ashamed of the testimony of our Lord, nor of me his prisoner," 2 Tim. i. 8; and also says to the Philippians, that though some do preach Christ out of contention, and some of love; yet, being "set for the defence of the gospel; what then? Notwithstanding every way, whether in pretence, or in truth, Christ is preached; and I therein do rejoice; yea, and will rejoice," Phil i. 17, 18. These passages precisely ascertain the meaning of the words *preaching the gospel*, and shew them to be of the same import as *preaching Christ*, or *bearing the testimony of Christ*. Now, in the text before us, we see an angel flying in the midst of heaven *to preach the everlasting gospel*. And, as we well know that it is "the Lord Jesus Christ, who shall judge the quick and the dead at his appearing, and his kingdom," 2 Tim. iv. 1. what does this cœlestial harbinger of our Judge proclaim? "Fear God and give glory to him, for the hour of his judgement is come." "We have one Lord Jesus Christ, by whom are all things, and we by him," 1 Cor. viii. 6.

"All things were created by him, and for him, and he is before all things, and by him all things confift," Col. i. 16, 17. But the angel proceeds, " worfhip him that made heaven and earth, and the fea, and the fountains of waters." A new and heavenly preacher of the gofpel, that is, of Chrift, here directly afcribes to our Judge the name and attributes of God: let us then, upon the teftimony of this herald, " fear and give glory to the Lord Jefus Chrift," the final preacher of whofe gofpel has declared him to be one with the Father, God.

CXVIII.

" The lamb fhall overcome them : for he is the Lord of Lords, and King of kings," Rev. xvii. 14. " The King of kings, and Lord of lords" appears again in the 19th chapter and 16th verfe, mounted upon a white horfe, and followed by the armies in heaven; he is affailed by the beaft, and the kings of the earth, and their armies; but the beaft is taken, and his armies are overcome; and " the remnant were flain with the fword of him that fat upon the horfe; and all the fowls were filled with their flefh," Rev. xix. 21. In the 17th verfe of this chapter, before the war, in which the King of kings and Lord of Lords overcame and flew the beaft, and the armies, and the kings, " an angel cried with a loud voice, faying to all the fowls that fly in the midft of heaven, come and gather yourfelves together unto the fupper of the great God; that ye may eat the flefh of kings, and the flefh of captains, and the flefh of mighty men, and the flefh of horfes, and of them that fit on them, and the flefh of all men, both free and bond, both fmall and great," Rev. xix. 17, 18. The war immediately enfues; and he that fat upon the horfe, having overcome and flain thofe who came againft him, " filled all fowls with their flefh;" fo that we find that fupper given to them by the King of kings, and Lord of lords, to which they are invited by an angel as to the supper of the great God. Him then we must believe to be the great God, who supplied it to them who were called to come to it: but Jesus Christ supplied it to them; Jesus Christ is therefore one with the Father, that great God.

CXIX.

"His name (that sat upon the horse) is called the Word of God," Rev. xix. 13. As there is not the least doubt that it is Jesus Christ who sat upon the horse, we may venture to explain the beginning of the first chapter of St. John's gospel by this declaration, that " his name is called the Word of God;" and whatsoever is there spoken of the Word of God, must be allowed to have been said of him who sat upon the horse, even Jesus Christ, " the victorious Lamb, the King of kings, and Lord of lords;" and there it is expresly declared that " the Word was God," John i. 1; that " the Word was made flesh, and dwelt among us, and we beheld his glory," John i. 14; that " the same (Word) was in the beginning with God, and that by him, who was in the world, and who came unto his own, the world was made," John i. 2, 10, 11. And as " in the beginning God created the heaven and the earth," Gen. i. 1. " that all things were made by him (the Word); and without him was not any thing made that was made;" that " in him was life, and the life was the light of men," John i. 3, 4. To the same purpose are the following texts: " I am the light of the world," says our Lord; and " he that followeth me, shall not walk in darkness, but shall have the light of life," John viii. 12. " We declare unto you, that God is light," says the same Evangelist, 1 John i. 5. " We have looked upon, and our hands have handled of the Word of life; (for the life was manifested, and we have seen it, and bear witness, and

shew

shew unto you that eternal life which was with the Father, and was manifested unto us)" 1 John i. 1, 2. "God was manifest in the flesh," says St. Paul, 1 Tim. iii. 16; and that "the Word of God liveth and abideth for ever," is the declaration of St. Peter, 1 Pet. i. 23. "Through faith we understand that the worlds were framed by the Word of God," Heb. xi. 3. "By whom also he made the worlds," Heb. i. 2. Here every attribute of God is ascribed to the Word of God, to have been from the beginning; to have been the original and author of all created things; or, to use St. John's expression, "the beginning of the creation of God," Rev. iii. 14; to have life in him, and to be the light. But it is farther added, that this Word came in the flesh, in which it was manifest, seen, and handled in the world; this therefore is evidently spoken of Jesus Christ. But the Word of God (here seated on a horse, and declared to be Jesus Christ himself under that appellation) is expresly said to be God: Jesus Christ therefore being that Word manifest in the flesh, and that Word being God, Jesus Christ is therefore one with the Father, God. The gospel is the testimony of Christ, "but the Word of the Lord endureth for ever. And this is the Word which by the gospel is preached unto you," 1 Pet. i. 25. John Baptist was certainly the appointed forerunner of our Lord, and it was of him therefore that John gave testimony. "John bare witness of him," John i. 15. It is very remarkable that these words are not once preceded, in St. John's gospel, by the name of Jesus Christ; but that they immediately follow a declaration, that "the Word was made flesh and dwelt among us;" the Word therefore is Jesus Christ, and "the Word was God;" Jesus Christ is therefore one with the Father, God.

As

As to Mr. Lindsey's laborious dissertation on the Chaldee Targums and the word Mimra, I have nothing to say to it, it does not properly come within my province; one short remark, however, I will make on it. If the word Mimra signify both " word and self," as it is certain that Jesus Christ is " the word of God," the word being the same as the self of God, Jesus Christ is therefore the " self of God; or, to use a more common expression, Jesus Christ is therefore God's own self *. This I infer from Mr. Lindsey's own premises; and so obvious is the conclusion from the manner in which he has supplied them from half a dozen writers, that I wonder how it escaped even his own observation. I will take occasion here to say, that I wave all advantage that I might derive from the idiomatick plurals of the Hebrew language (if only idiomatick they be) preceding verbs of the singular number. They may afford argument to those who, with better knowledge than I am possessed of, shall look for it among them: but I am in pursuit of truth, and not of system; I am in pursuit of truth too momentous to be trifled with, and, while I call upon men to yield their assent to a proposition essential to the happiness of their immortal souls, God forbid that I should knowingly call one sophism into proof, or offer that as argument to my readers, which did not carry conviction to my own breast. At the same time that I relinquish this argument, it is but for myself I do, or can relinquish it.

CXX.

When Mr. Lindsey has declared the office of a priest to be " to offer up the prayers of others," Apol. p. 127, he should not therefore have precluded prayer to Christ, and the practice of making him the object of religious worship, unless he were very certain that no priesthood had been appointed to him; but " they shall be priests of God and of Christ," Rev. xx. 6. I have brought
this

* Glorify thou me with thine own self, John xvii. 5.

this verse to establish the Divinity of our blessed Redeemer, upon a foundation which negligence or blinded prejudice overlooked; but upon which I now demand the acquiescence of the Unitarians in the Godhead of Jesus Christ; we see it allowed an argument if it can be brought, and here it is for them. It is remarkable also that these priests of Christ are those who are partakers of the first resurrection, of whom it is said "that they are blessed and holy:" to those then who are blessed and holy we have reason to conclude, that this mystery of the Godhead of Christ will be more manifestly displayed than to us; who are yet to taste of death. Surely there can be no more uncomfortable conviction than that all the stores of God's wisdom are open to us here, and that in a future state there can be found nothing to add to knowledge; the very expectation of seeing farther into the government of the universe, directed by power and wisdom that are infinite, is a motive to obedience; and a full insight into a mystery which is the means of our own entrance into eternal happiness, is a hope so delightful in itself, that it should make us thankful for such a revelation as intimates it to us, yet withholds the full manifestation for a part of our reward " who wait patiently the coming of the Lord," " for behold, we count them happy which endure," James v.

Jesus Christ was indeed on earth a priest, and accordingly here discharged his sacerdotal office, by offering up the one sufficient sacrifice of himself for all mankind, and " by the blood of sprinkling, that speaketh better things, than that of Abel," which cried from the ground, he has made us a party to the covenant of which he is himself the mediator; and by his blood which does not cry against us, but on the contrary maketh intercession for us, (that body from which it was poured out being our expiation) he has extended salvation

tion to all that believe on him. The writer to the Hebrews has so clearly pointed out to them how their own ritual was a type of Christ's prepared body and blood shed as a sacrifice for the sins of all men; so literally pronounced him our atonement; and so explicitly laid open the nature of his priesthood, and the subsequent mediation of his sufferings in our behalf; that I should ask my reader's forgiveness for so frequently entering into that subject: but when the whole doctrine of atonement by the death of our Saviour is denied, and that he is declared to have died only as a proof that he had lived, I cannot but think it necessary to speak of it, as the occasion offers, in the course of my enquiry; and the rather, when I consider how vastly more probable it is, that even my book shall be read by the Unitarians than the Bible.

CXXI.

"And I saw the dead, small and great, stand before God; and the books were opened: and another book was opened, which is the book of life: and the dead were judged out of those things which were written in the books, according to their works. And the sea gave up the dead which were in it; and death and hell delivered up the dead which were in them: and they were judged every man according to their works. And death and hell were cast into the lake of fire; this is the second death. And whosoever was not found written in the book of life, was cast into the lake of fire," Rev. xx. 12, 13, 14, 15. I need not repeat the numerous passages in which it is set forth, that " the Son of man shall come in his glory, and all the holy angels with him, then shall he sit upon the throne of his glory. And before him shall be gathered all nations; and he shall separate them one from another," Matth. xxv. 31, 32. " Then shall he (the Son of man) reward every man according to his works," Matth. xvi. 27; and that

that "things which offend, and them that do iniquity; he (the Son of man) fhall caft into a furnace of fire; there fhall be wailing and gnafhing of teeth," Mat. xiii. 41, 42. Here every act of our Saviour's office as the judge of the world, who has declared his own determination to call all flefh to account, is given to God, before whom St. John fees the dead, fmall and great, ftand, and all nations gathered to receive judgement, " every man according to his works," and by whom " they that do iniquity" " are caft into a furnace of fire." There can be no truth in fuch a vifion, if it be not that the very fame thing is prefented to the view of St. John, which is foretold by our Saviour; and that he who declared that he would judge, even Jefus Chrift, has, according to his declaration, proceeded to judge, and to teftify himfelf to be one with the Father, God. The book of life is faid, in another place, to be " the Lamb's book of life," Rev. xxi. 27. It is declared that, " the Father judgeth no man, but hath committed all judgement unto the Son," John v. 22. And a reafon is given for this appointment, " (the Father) hath given him (the Son) authority to execute judgement alfo, becaufe he is the Son of man." As the Son of man only he could receive an appointment, and to him who, as a Son of man, has called us brethren, and can have a feeling of our infirmities, it is moft mercifully made. All men are here affembled to judgement before the great God; but " the Father judgeth no man;" before the Son then are they affembled: but they are before God; the Son therefore is one with the Father, God.

CXXII.

" The Lamb which is in the midft of the throne, fhall feed them, and fhall lead them unto living fountains of waters," Rev. vii. 17. Jefus faid to John, " I am alpha and omega, the beginning and the end, the first and the last," Rev. xxii. 13. "And he (that sat upon the throne) said unto me it is done. I am alpha and omega, the beginning and the end: I will give unto him that is athirst, of the fountain of the water of life freely. He that overcometh, shall inherit all things, and I will be his God, and he shall be my Son," Rev. xxi. 6, 7. Here every attribute of him who has called us, if we shall prove victorious, his sons, is equally the Son's as the Father's; he is enthroned; he leads to the living fountains of water, and he is the one first and last; therefore he is with the Father, one God. What an invitation do the Unitarians decline!

CXXIII.

In the holy Jerusalem, "I saw no temple therein: for the Lord God Almighty and the Lamb, are the temple of it. And the city had no need of the sun, neither of the moon to shine in it: for the glory of God did lighten it, and the Lamb is the light thereof," Rev. xxi. 22, 23. "For the Lord God giveth them light," Rev. xxii. 5. "The throne of God and of the Lamb shall be in it; and his servants shall serve him, and they shall see his face; and his name shall be in their foreheads," Rev. xxii. 3, 4. Here God and the Lamb are but one temple, shed one light, which is the one incommunicable glory of God, and possess one throne, present one face to the view of *his* servants, and *his* servants serve *him*, that is God and the Lamb, spoken of in the singular number as but one God. To the trinal unity of God, then I am not afraid to ascribe the excellent doxology of Dr. Tucker, who, when he used it, remembered that there *is* but one God, and that there *are* three persons; "to *him* therefore, Father, Son, and Holy Ghost, let these miracles of divine mercy be ever ascribed; and to *them* be glory, praise, majesty, and dominion, both now and for evermore."
"The personal pronoun *him*," says Mr. Lindsey, "evidenly

dently points to one person, one individual intelligent agent *;" so that as God and the Lamb are, in the passage before us, pointed to by this same personal pronoun *him*, let God and the Lamb, even Jesus Christ, be acknowledged to be one individual intelligent agent, one God blessed for ever. " I will write upon him my new name," says our Saviour, Rev. iii. 12. " A Lamb stood on the mount Sion, and with him an hundred-forty and four thousand, having his Father's name written in their foreheads," Rev. xiv. 1. Conformable to the superscription of the name of the Father, and the new name of the Son, our Lord says, " I will write upon him the name of my God," Rev. iii. 12.

CXXIV.

The angel who spoke to John, and signified to him those things which he was sent by Jesus Christ to reveal to his servant John, Rev. i. 1. testifies as follows, " the Lord God of the holy prophets sent his angel to shew unto his servants the things which must shortly be done," Rev. xxii. 6. And our Saviour immediately after, speaking of this very angel, which has said that he was sent by, and has called himself the angel of the Lord, declares, " I Jesus have sent mine angel to testify unto you, these things in the churches," Rev. xxii. 16. Jesus Christ, who sent his angel, which was sent by the Lord God, is therefore one with the Father, the Lord God.

CXXV.

Such farther evidence as I mean to produce from the holy scriptures, to prove the Godhead of our gracious Redeemer, I shall reserve till I come to consider and confute the arguments by which Mr. Lindsey has endeavoured to depose him from the throne of his glory: and as I closed the apostolical testimony of our Saviour's divinity, by shewing that the appointed witnesses of Jesus

* Apology, p. 199.

sus Christ had brought God himself to speak the fact, and to pronounce that he who had been slain, and had taken that body, by the blood of which we are cleansed, into heaven, there for ever to remain, is one with himself, " God Almighty, whose throne endureth for ever and ever, and the sceptre of whose kingdom is a sceptre of righteousness;" so I shall conclude this chapter by bringing together those doxologies with which all things both in heaven and in earth have glorified the Son of man; and if by these also, the kingdom, and the power, and the glory be ascribed to him, who, of ransomed mankind, admitted to fellowship with him, can then refuse to " magnify the name of the Lord Jesus," and to unite his voice with " ten thousand times ten thousand, and thousands of thousands of angels, who rest not day and night, saying, holy, holy, holy, Lord God Almighty, which was, and which is, and which is to come," " worthy art thou, O Lord, to receive glory, and honour, and power *," " worthy is the Lamb that was slain to receive power, and riches, and wisdom, and strength, and honour, and glory, and blessing †," " and with every creature which is in heaven and in earth, and under the earth, and such as are in the sea, and all that are in them, saying, Blessing, and honour, and glory, and power, be unto him that sitteth on the throne, and unto the Lamb for ever and ever. Amen ‡." " Salvation to our God which sitteth on the throne, and unto the Lamb §," " which is in the midst of the throne ‖ ?" for such is the song of angels, and of every creature " created by him, and for him **; such are the grateful hymns of those who are redeemed by the blood of the " slaughtered Lamb ††," which have come out of great tribulation, and have washed their robes, and made them white in the blood

of

---

* Rev. iv. 8, 11.   † Rev. v. 12.   ‡ Rev. v. 13.
§ Rev. vii. 10.   ‖ Rev. vii. 17.   ** Coloss. i. 16.   †† Is. liii. 7.

of the Lamb," and who " therefore are before the throne of God, and ferve him night and day in his temple," " a great multitude, which no man could number, of all nations, and kindreds, and people, and tongues ſtanding before the throne, and before the Lamb clothed with white robes *". To theſe the glorious company of the apoſtles have added their praiſe, ſaying " to the King of kings, and Lord of lords †," " who only hath immortality, dwelling in the light which no man can approach unto, whom no man hath ſeen, nor can ſee, be honour and power everlaſting. Amen ‡." " To our Lord and Saviour Jeſus Chriſt be glory both now and for ever. Amen § :" " to whom be praiſe and dominion both now and for ever. Amen ∥." " Wherefore ſeeing we alſo are compaſſed about with ſo great a cloud of witneſſes, let us lay aſide every weight, and the ſin which doth ſo eaſily beſet us, and let us run with patience the race that is ſet before us, looking unto Jeſus, the author and finiſher of our faith, who, for the joy that was ſet before him, endured the croſs, deſpiſing the ſhame **," which was undergone for our redemption; and let us " with every tongue confeſs that Jeſus Chriſt is Lord, with every knee, of things in heaven, and things in earth, and things under the earth, bow our knee alſo at the name of Jeſus ††;" and knowing that the ſame Lord over all is rich unto all that call upon him, let us alſo call upon the name of the Lord, and be ſaved; and to him that ſitteth on the throne, and the Lamb, one God, the Father and the Son, with the whole hoſt of heaven and earth, and all created beings, join in aſcribing " bleſſing and honour, and glory, and power. Amen."

CHAP.

* Rev. vii. 9, 14, 15. † Rev. xvii. 14. ‡ 1 Tim. vi. 15, 16.
§ 2 Pet. iii. 18. ∥ 1 Pet. iv. 11. ** Heb. xii. 1. †† Phil. ii. 10.

CHAP. IV.

Controverted Evidence of our Saviour's Divinity established.—Objections answered.—The Divinity of the Holy Ghost proved from the Scriptures.

"RELigious worship," says Mr. Lindsey, "is the incommunicable honour and prerogative of God alone," Apology, p. 137. Among the multitudinous proofs which I have already given of our Lord's divinity, I have produced many instances of prayer, of praise, and thanksgiving, preferred to him both in earth and in heaven; by angels and those who have already become partakers of the benefits of his passion in heaven; and in earth, by men filled with the Comforter, the holy spirit of truth, to whom " the testimony of Jesus" * was given. These I look upon to be acts of religious worship; but this honour and prerogative of God alone is ascribed to Jesus Christ; it is incommunicable, and must therefore perfectly and essentially distinguish the possessour; but Jesus Christ is the possessour; Jesus Christ is therefore one with the Father, that God alone whose incommunicable honour and prerogative it is to be the object of our religious worship and adoration.

Mr. Lindsey is so exceedingly anxious to emancipate himself from the service of Jesus Christ, whose servant and Prisoner Paul declares it is his joy and glory to be; he bends so reluctantly under the easy yoke, the light burden of the gospel; he so boisterously dashes about the bonds of peace, and so fretfully endeavours to cast the cords from him; and with such a foaming hydrophobia flies from " the fountains of living waters," that he has really become a very melancholy spectacle, and therefore

* Rev. xix. 10.

fore I feel it a duty incumbent upon me to force, as strongly as I can, this conviction upon him, that if he will drink of these waters, they will refresh him, and he shall not thirst again; that if he return to Christ, the great shepherd and bishop of our souls, however sorrowful and heavily laden he may be, he shall find rest to his soul; that if he knock, Christ shall open; and, that " if he ask any thing according to his will, the Son of God will hear him, and he shall have the petition that he desired of him *," Let me therefore now, presuming that Christ at hand is not different from Christ afar off; and that no merits can put any created being into possession of the incommunicable prerogatives of God, or render inferior natures worthy of the honour which belongs to God alone, recapitulate, and once again present him with an instance of each; of prayer, by that of Stephen, " Lord Jesus receive my spirit;" " Lord, lay not this sin to their charge." Of praise, by that in the Revelation, " Blessing, and honour, and glory, and power, be unto him that sitteth upon the throne, and unto the Lamb for ever and ever;" " salvation to our God which sitteth upon the throne, and unto the Lamb;" and of thanksgiving, by that of St. Paul, " I thank Christ Jesus our Lord, for that he counted me faithful, putting me into the ministry."

There is yet another species of religious worship, which I have intentionally omitted to take notice of in its course; it is Benediction; and my reason for deferring to observe upon it, is, that it demanded a separate consideration, on account of Mr. Lindsey's doctrine concerning it. He denies benediction to be any evidence at all; and, till I had established its competency, it is therefore easy to see I should have produced it out of its place before. Mr. Lindsey's assertion, Apology, p. 131,

* 1 John v. 14.

p. 131, concerning such passages as 1 Cor. i. 3. * is, " that they are only pious wishes, not prayers." Admitting for a moment only this distinction between prayers and pious wishes, and the conclusion thence inferred, I believe these same pious wishes will be found to be very impious wishes, and a wish that God should have an assistant in conferring blessings on mankind, be acknowledged rather derogatory from the all-sufficiency of his power: but I do not see how any inference can be drawn from a wish different from that which follows from a prayer, they both equally acknowledge the power which they desire to have put into exertion; and if the power be acknowledged by a declaration of it to a third person, entrusted with an assurance that I wish it to be exerted, I cannot imagine why the possessor of it should not be addressed and let into the secret also, he may not else know my mind, and the power may not therefore be quite so beneficially exerted as I could piously wish. Is it that a Being, whose power is to be acknowledged adequate to the gift of blessings, is unintelligent and unable to hear our prayers? or are we not to address him, because he is unable to grant them? If the latter, we reject our own conclusion, and waste our wishes; and I believe the inconsistency of the former supposition is too apparent to require a comment. The same consequence is inferred, I say, by our wishes as by our prayers, and if the power of God is acknowledged by prayer to be in Jesus Christ, by our wishes also that he would exert that power, it is equally acknowledged; so that even this (I think disingenuous) evasion will not invalidate the force of that testimony which is afforded to this dreaded position, that Jesus Christ is one with the Father, God, by the benedictions of the apostles, the appointed witnesses of our Lord.

* " Grace *be* unto you, and peace from God our Father, and from the Lord Jesus Christ."

Of these benedictions I need only produce one from St. Paul, because it comprehends in it the substance of all the rest, which he has bestowed upon his hearers, "Grace, mercy, and peace from God the Father, and the Lord Jesus Christ our Saviour," Titus i. 4. From God alone can the blessings of grace, mercy, and peace proceed; but I will shew that they have all proceeded from Jesus Christ; for St. Paul himself, who knew the ability of him whom he thus invoked, and that "he is able to succour," says, "I thank Jesus Christ our Lord, who hath enabled me, for that he counted me faithful, putting me into the ministry; who was before a blasphemer, and a persecutor, and injurious. But I obtained *mercy*, because I did it ignorantly in unbelief: and *the grace of our Lord* was exceeding abundant," 1 Tim. i. 12, 13, 14. Here we find grace and mercy bestowed by the searcher of hearts, who, thro' the veil of blasphemy and persecution, distinguished that faith which enabled Paul to be put into the ministry by the Lord Jesus Christ. We do not find this accurate apostle ever say grace, mercy, and peace from Apollos or Cephas; he knew that they, on whom he bestowed his blessing, were not of Apollos nor of Cephas, who were only fellow-labourers with himself; and that, had he been to the end of time calling down grace and mercy from them, they had it not to impart; from Christ, that God who gave the encrease, when they watered what he himself planted, he called for blessings; from God alone, to whom belong mercies, it was fit that he should call them down, because that he alone could answer and confer them. "My peace I give you," says Jesus Christ, "not as the world giveth give I," John xiv. 27. If grace, mercy, and peace then be in the power of our gracious and merciful Redeemer to bestow, every benediction of the apostle of the gospel of peace is to be considered as a short prayer pre-

ferred

ferred to him; and benedictions being thus considered as a part of religious worship, it is easy to see the conclusion, that Jesus Christ, to whom it is offered, is one with the Father, that God, whose incommunicable prerogative and honour religious worship is. " Let us therefore, beloved," " being called unto the grace of Christ," Gal i. 6. " not separate ourselves, having not the spirit, but building up ourselves on our most holy faith, praying in the Holy Ghost, keep ourselves in the love of God, looking for the mercy of our Lord Jesus Christ unto eternal life," Jude 19, 20, 21; and " believe that through the grace of our Lord Jesus Christ we shall be saved," Acts xv. 11.

But it has been said that the interposal of the conjunctive *and*, enumerates distinct natures between the Father *and* Son; and that grace, mercy, and peace may proceed from, or glory, honour, and dominion be ascribed to one part of the subject, without affecting the other. Not to insist on the absurdity of introducing a name, to say nothing about it, in any proposition; on other grounds also, the distinction between God *and* Lord, how well soever it may have been supported by an epigram *, seems to me not only weak but insincere. " From God the Father *and* our Lord Jesus Christ," are words that occur perpetually in St. Paul's epistles; and I think that candour will allow that " the Father, and our Lord Jesus Christ," are, in such passages, put in apposition to " God," and mark a distinction of persons indeed, but undoubtedly an unity, an identity of Godhead; for, were that copulative *and* to be taken as a mark of any other distinction, and insisted on as introductory of a second power, however subordinate it may be to the Father, and acting under him; the consequences of such a manner of understanding it might prove very fatal to the cause it is brought to support; for the same copulative is used by St. James, in

* Apology, p. 6.

in a manner that would deſtroy the Godhead of the Father himſelf; for by it the word " Father" is ſet apart from God. He ſays, " true religion, and undefiled before God *and* the " Father," where the copulative is uſed exactly in the ſame manner as by St. Paul: If it be admitted then that the perſonal terms ſtand in appoſition to the general name of " God," all is at once accounted for; whereas, on the other hand, if it be inſiſted upon, that, in the one caſe, the conjunctive enumerates diſtinct natures, a conſequence will neceſſarily follow, which even an Unitarian would ſtart at drawing from it. St. James does not ſtand alone in this manner of diſtinguiſhing between God *and* the Father; St. Paul has afforded many inſtances of a like nature, " giving thanks to God and the Father," Col. iii. 17. " Now, God himſelf, and our Father, and our Lord Jeſus Chriſt, direct our way unto you," 1 Theſſ. iii. 11. " In the ſight of God and the Father," 1 Theſſ. i. 3. How uncandidly then does even this honeſt and diſintereſted man deal by himſelf, in making uſe of, or yielding his aſſent to ſuch weak ſophiſms; but I am ſorry to ſay that every thing ſeems an argument in his eyes, that only appears to make againſt " the acknowledgment of the myſtery of God, and of the Father, and of Chriſt," Col. ii. 2. " Now, unto God and our Father, be glory for ever and ever. Amen." Phil. iv. 20*.

In

---

* If it be inſiſted upon, that the following words, " Peace from God our Father, and the Lord Jeſus Chriſt," have any other meaning than that the Father and the Lord Jeſus Chriſt are the one God, by which name the three perſons of the Trinity is comprehended, I ſhall inſiſt upon the diſtinction between " God and the Father" here, and maintain that they have diſtinct meanings alſo, and that the Father is therefore not intended by the word God in this doxology.—But in that caſe the word God is without any meaning at all. To this I anſwer, that it has a meaning, and ſignifies the Son, our Lord Jeſus Chriſt, to whom, as well as to the Father, glory is aſcribed. I give Mr. Lindſey his choice how he will interpret; for, let him take it either way, the divinity of our Lord follows.

In the Jewish ritual, the necessity of repeating the sacrifice is made use of as a proof of the insufficiency of any single victim, to establish those who came to the altar: for, had any one offering been answerable to so great an end, the daily sacrifice had been taken away, that work for which it had been appointed being finished. Just such is the case with Mr. Lindsey's arguments; the sacrifice of to-day manifested the weakness of the sacrifice of yesterday; and the offering now made upon the altar of sophistry, manifests the insufficiency of that which has preceded it, to establish the votary, that doctrine, of which he stands the priest; it acknowledges the weakness of the priesthood, and that it is not faultless; like that of the Jews, therefore, I entertain a chearful hope that the whole shall at length vanish away. This gentleman, accordingly, very justly considering all that he has already urged as no argument at all, proceeds to insinuate, rather than say, (for he has not put it into so many words) that the junction of the name of Christ, in doxologies and benedictions, with the name of God, which is invoked or glorified in them, does not afford any proof that Jesus Christ is God, because that to their names sometimes other names also are joined. Had the fact been as here stated, I should have allowed it some weight, and therefore looking on it as material, I did literally "search the scriptures," and throughout could find but that one instance in which Mr. Lindsey has exemplified the rule. It is the benediction of St. John in the first chapter and fourth verse of the Revelation, "Grace be unto you, and peace from him which was, and which is, and which is to come, and from the seven spirits, which are before his throne; and from Jesus Christ," Rev. i. 4, 5. And here it must be granted, that unless the seven spirits be God also, the junction of the name of Jesus Christ is not a proof that he is God; but I may possibly surprize Mr. Lindsey by an assurance that these seven spirits also are God; and this is a position easily explained to any man who remembers that "Noah found grace in the eyes of the Lord*;" "The seven spirits are the eyes of the Lamb †;" and grace, in the eyes of the Lamb, is surely a blessing devoutly to be implored, when we consider who that Lamb is, even our Lord Jesus Christ himself, " the Lord of Lords;" and when we reflect on the advantages that accrued to Noah from his having found favour in his eyes before. According to Mr. Lindsey's mode of arguing, we might as well declare that St. Paul meant to distinguish between God and the hands of God, when he says, " It is a fearful thing to fall into the hands of the living God," Heb. x. 31. For, if these terms be not only different appellations of the same Being, I will then allow that to find grace from God, and from the eyes of God, have likewise distinct meanings.

This is the only benediction against which this charge is brought, and I hope I have shewed its inability to affect the Godhead of our blessed Lord; had it been proved I should have allowed it an argument, as it is true that God alone is the fountain whence grace and mercy can flow, and from which alone the apostles, with the spirit of truth, could seek to draw them: but surely if the names of other Beings be found joined with that of God in the performance of actions, of which other Beings are capable, it can never be admitted an argument against the divinity of Christ, whose name is often found joined with God, and invoked to perform actions of which God alone is capable. To Timothy St. Paul says, " I charge thee before God and the Lord Jesus Christ, and the elect angels," 1 Tim. v. 21; and on this passage Mr. Lindsey

---

* Gen. vi. 8.   † Rev. v. 6.

sey makes the same observation as that above, saying, "the angels being here joined with God and Christ, shews that when God is joined with other Beings in the most solemn manner, no equality can be inferred from such a conjunction;" Apology, p. 107. Now I deny that God is in this instance joined with other Beings in the most solemn manner, the conferring of a charge upon Timothy was an act of which every Being, upon whom God had bestowed the powers of discernment, was a proper and competent witness before whom he should confer it, and therefore, had the apostle joined man and every intelligent nature to the name of God, and of Jesus Christ, and the elect angels, it could not in the least derogate from the dignity of God, or ever be interpreted as conferring upon them a claim to Godhead. That it should argue against Christ's divinity, it is necessary to shew that it proves too much, and therefore nothing, and that too-much, which it is supposed to prove, is, that the angels are God also; but does any such consequence follow? Certainly not; and therefore this most solemn conjunction cannot impeach the divinity of our Lord. I do not desire the aid of this verse in proof of our Saviour's Godhead, there being no greater power called into exercise than that of witnessing a charge to which the witness of God will add solemnity indeed, but which is an act that he has given power to inferior natures to perform. "Ye are my witnesses, and God also," 1 Thess. ii. 10, says St. Paul: now which does this most solemn conjunction of God and the Thessalonians prove, the Thessalonians to be God, or God a Thessalonian? Neither one nor the other; for the conduct of Paul, which he called upon God and them to testify to be just and holy, was performed equally before God and them, and they being endowed with adequate faculties, were therefore equally competent witnesses of it. But with respect to

the

the passage before us, the apostle, about to send forth a preacher of the gospel of Jesus Christ, and recommending perseverance and constancy in " the testimony of our Lord," has, with peculiar accuracy, selected the witnesses to his charge to Timothy, remembering that Jesus Christ, coming to judgement, is to be attended by the holy angels, who are therefore on that day, when all flesh shall be assembled before God, to be witnesses to the manifestation of all the hidden things, and the counsels of all hearts: before them therefore Paul has judiciously chosen to give his charge, as in their presence Timothy well knew he should in the end render an account of his apostleship, and, according to the discharge of his holy function, " have praise of God," or " be made a spectacle to angels," 1 Cor. iv. 9; for Jesus Christ has himself said, " whosoever shall confess me before men, him shall the Son of man also confess before the angels of God," Luke xii. 8. &c.

I have now brought to an end, not indeed the whole of the evidence of our Saviour's divinity afforded by the scriptures, but the whole of that which I intend to produce; for, " if they should be written every one, I suppose that even the world could not contain the books that should be written." Somewhere however I must pause, and therefore consider myself as well warranted to do so now, as I should be after a much more voluminous work: for, to my apprehension, I have already exhibited proof amply sufficient to establish my point, and therefore sincerely hope for the concurrence of my intelligent, and not " unlearned reader," in this conclusion from the whole, namely, that our Lord and Saviour Jesus Christ is with the Father the one " first and last, which was dead and is

alive

alive for evermore, the Almighty, besides whom there is no God," If. xliv. 6. Rev. i. 8, and ii. 8.

I by no means consider every one of the scriptural proofs which I have made use of, as equally able to sustain the argument by itself; for some among them may be of disputable interpretation, but at the same time, being united with such as are incontrovertible, (for many such I am bold to declare there are) they borrow light from them, and strength to support their part of the burden: but let me carry this idea to the utmost, and suppose every assertion that Christ is God, which I have brought from scripture, confuted and shewed to be misapplied, one only excepted, that one to which no answer can be given must remain as compleat a proof of our Saviour's divinity as ten thousand repetitions of it could afford; for all scriptures being written by inspiration, there is no assertion for the truth of which God himself is not responsible, and that which God has once said requires no farther confirmation: but if it be found that he has once declared the Godhead of Jesus Christ, that fact is immutably established; and being established, may well be allowed a matter of sufficient importance to be frequently referred to, nay, (though not necessarily for the confirmation of God's truth, yet for the more extensive information of mankind) to be frequently repeated. If then many texts in scripture, upon inconteftible proof of Christ's Godhead from any one, admit of an easy interpretation by referring them to that great truth, why should we hesitate to interpret them by it, instead of wresting them to senses that they will not endure; Procrustes-like, torturing them down to the diminutive bulk of our own imaginations; and thereby rendering the word of God, which alone is true and wise, inexplicable and inconsistent with itself?

It is only the facts which are revealed, and not the manner of relating the facts contained in scripture, that are said to be to the Greeks foolishness; were the relation inconsistent with itself, it would be justly chargeable with folly before God himself, who cannot lye. That folly which St. Paul apprehends the Greeks will lay to the charge of his gospel, is, that it did not coincide with their doctrines. Inconsistency with itself is inconsistency with God, who sees things only as they really are, and consequently not as they are not; whereas inconsistency with my opinion may be wisdom, though to me foolishness; for I may have seen things as they are not, or not have seen them as they really are. What God relates cannot be but true; he cannot relate contradictions; our belief therefore is not required to contradictions. A God crucified in the flesh, in which he had humbly taken the form of a servant, and submitted to feel the infirmities of man, was, to the philosophical religion of the Greeks, foolishness indeed; for, with it, it was altogether inconsistent; but it was nevertheless the wisdom of God, and the power of God unto salvation to every one that believeth. To the Jews, who had long known the one true God, and who had experienced prosperity or adversity as his mighty arm was stretched out to lead or to chastise them, the bleeding body of our Lord suffering death under their own hands, was indeed a stumbling-block; for it was altogether inconsistent with their idea of the Almighty Jehovah. A plurality of persons in the God who had declared his name to be "one," was to the Jews an unsurmountable difficulty; it transcended their faculties, and, as they conceived themselves in possession of a full acquaintance with the incomprehensible nature of their Maker, it was altogether inconsistent with their vain presumptions. To the Jew and to the Unitarian it is alike a stumbling-block, "For unquestionably the Trinity is one of those doctrines that prejudice them most against christianity," Apology, p. 88.

If it be asked, as indeed it is, though not in direct terms, why a fact of such great importance to us to believe is not laid down in so many words, by the witnesses of our Lord, in any of their epistles? it is not difficult to give an answer to such as will consider, that the epistles were written to men already in possession of it; not with a view of introducing them to a new object of faith, but of establishing them in a faith already imparted; for, not to insist upon the circumstance of Paul's having visited all those people to whom he afterwards addressed his epistles, the Romans and the Colossians excepted; nor to weary my less active reader by taking him in pursuit of this vigilant apostle through all the dangers that he encountered for the sake of propagating " the gospel of God our Saviour" in every region; I can prove, from internal evidence, that he only wrote to those who had already obtained grace to be faithful, and who therefore needed not that he should now instruct them in the object of their faith. From Corinth, where he had first known and taught Aquila and Priscilla, he wrote to the Romans; and when he wrote his epistle to them, Aquila and Priscilla were at Rome, for he salutes them there. To these fellow labourers of Paul, Apollos was indebted for his knowledge of the gospel: it is therefore highly probable that so faithful and diligent preachers of the word had not been inactive in bearing the testimony of our Lord to the Romans also; for Paul directs his letter to them in the following terms: " To all that be at Rome, beloved of God, called to be saints, and whose faith is spoken of throughout the whole world," Rom, i. 7, 8. If such was their faith already, to what end should the object of it be pointed out anew; but perseverance and constancy were indeed properly to be recommended, and a stedfast adherence to that which they had known. He had already planted; his object now was to water only; to cultivate and assist the growth of the infant gospel; to cause it to extend its boughs; to gather the faithful under its peaceful shade; and to point out to their observation the blessed fruit with which the branches of this tree of life were laden, saying, in the day that thou eatest hereof thou shalt surely LIVE. To the Corinthians he wrote from Philippi, and addresses himself " to them that are sanctified in Christ Jesus, called to be saints with all that in every place call upon the name of Jesus Christ our Lord, both theirs and ours," 1 Cor. i. 2. Is not this a direct acknowledgment that they were already well informed, and needed not now to be told that he, on whose name they called, the object of their religious worship, even Jesus Christ, their Lord and ours, was one with the Father, God? This he had taught them before when he was present, and had baptized Crispus and Gaius among them; and to what end should he now renew the superfluous information? The Galatians he chides, not indeed for having relinquished the gospel which he had before preached to them, but for having listened to some who had endeavoured to introduce the ceremonies of the law into the practice of christianity. To these therefore he is more explicit, as they were perverted, and that it was necessary to bring them back; and though he does not, in direct terms, declare the Godhead of our Saviour, he uses words very nearly synonimous, words fully sufficient to recall former knowledge, and revive the memory of what he had before communicated; for he says, that " he was not taught the gospel of Christ by man, but by the revelation of Jesus Christ; that he had himself once been as zealous of the law, as they could now be, but that, notwithstanding

he

he had, through Zeal for the traditions of the Jews, persecuted the church of God: being now called to be a servant of Jesus Christ, he saw and preached that justification came by faith in Christ, and not by such works as are enjoined by the fleshly ordinances of the law," Gal. i. In his epistle to the Ephesians, to whom he wrote from Rome, after he had been transmitted thither by Festus, and some years after his last visit to them, he says, " I cease not to give thanks for you, after I heard of your faith in the Lord Jesus," Eph i. For the faith of the Philippians also he thanks God, and directs his epistle " to all the saints in Christ Jesus, which are at Philippi," Philip. i. To them and to the Colossians he wrote while a prisoner at Rome, and to these latter he addresses himself " to the saints and faithful brethren in Christ, which are at Colosse," " we give thanks to God since we heard of your faith in Christ Jesus," Colos. i. *At Thessalonica Paul was severely treated by the unbelieving Jews, who, after his departure, not only pursued him to Berea, but continued to persecute the few of their own countrymen who had believed, and " consorted with Paul and Silas:" to this little " church of the Thessalonians, which is in God the Father, and in the Lord Jesus Christ;" it is that St. Paul writes, " remembering without ceasing their work of faith, as they had become followers of the Lord, having received the word with much affliction, wherefore they were ensamples to all that believe," 1 Thess. i. 1. Now the word of God which Paul had preached at Thessalonica, and for which he was driven out, was charged against him by his persecutors, to have been his " saying, contrary to the decree of Cæsar, that there is another *King*, one Jesus;" so that we find, that, though to a faithful people, he did not think it necessary to tell what was the object of their faith, which it is probable Paul was of opinion they

Acts xvii.   knew

knew themselves; he nevertheless on his first visit let them into an acquaintance with the one meaning of the words *God* and *Christ*, and that Jesus Christ is with the Father, the one God, the Lord of hosts, the *King* of glory. Timothy and Titus he calls " his own sons after the faith;" and we well know that they had accompanied, and assisted him in diffusing the light of the gospel; his epistles to them contain a charge to " bear the testimony of our Lord," and a rule for their demeanor as men appointed to so great a trust. His letter to Philemon, " his dearly beloved fellow labourer," seems little more than of a private nature. The object of this " Jew of Tarsus," in writing to his own countrymen the Hebrews, is to remove their adherence to the law of Moses, which was the grand obstruction to their belief, and to shew that it was not, as they conceived, altogether profitable, and therefore not immutably permanent, but that it might be done away; and this even according to their own prophets, to which he therefore refers them. It is not my purpose here to paraphrase the epistles of this great preacher of Jesus Christ; it answers my end to shew that there is a sufficient reason for his not having summed the doctrine, which he conveys in them, into the one short proposition, that " Jesus Christ is one with the Father, God." It seems to be the intention of " James, a servant of God, and of the Lord Jesus Christ," to comment on the epistles of St. Paul, and to stand up against the misrepresentations of the unlearned and unstable, who wrested such things as were hard to be understood in them to their own destruction. He did not undertake to point out an object of faith, but to shew " with what respect we should have the faith of our Lord Jesus Christ, the Lord of glory;" he presupposes the faith of his hearers, and is grafting the morality of a Christian upon it; he opposes himself to
some-

something very like modern methodism, built upon an erroneous acceptation of St. Paul's doctrine of justification by faith alone; shews that the works which that apostle precludes are the ceremonies of the law, as inconsistent with the liberty of the gospel, but that, by works of " pure and undefiled religion, spotless and benevolent *before God*, the faith in our blessed Redeemer is made perfect," he prescribes, not what faith we should entertain, but how we should entertain that of which we were before possessed. Peter writes to the " elect, who, not having seen Christ, yet love him; who believe, and therefore rejoice with unspeakable joy full of glory;" and this " servant of Jesus Christ" addresses his second epistle " to them that have obtained like precious faith with us, through the righteousness of our God and Saviour Jesus Christ," 2 Pet i. 1. For so it stands (not in the French perhaps, but) in the Greek, as the margin of our Bible also acknowledges. St. John writes his first epistle, " not because ye know not the truth, but because ye know it," 1 John ii. 21; and then proceeds to establish his hearers against those who seduce them, by doctrines which hardly differ from the direct proposition; but of which I have already taken notice. He rejoices greatly that the " elect lady," to whom he directs his second epistle, and Gaius, to whom he addresses his third, " walk in the truth." " St. Jude, the servant of Jesus Christ," writes " to them that are sanctified by God the Father, and preserved in Jesus Christ, and called," and declares the sufficiency of once delivering the faith. To what end now should any one of the apostles, in direct terms impart the divinity of our blessed Lord, when every person, to whom they wrote, was already apprized of the fact? But it may be said that they wrote for the information of posterity, as well as of those to whom they more

im-

immediately addressed themselves, and that therefore they should have done it. And have they not sufficiently done it? have they not sufficiently revealed it to such as will, in obedience to the precept of our Lord himself, "search the scriptures"? When I hear that there is but one God; when I hear our Saviour, in the vail of the flesh, say, " Father, if it be possible let this cup pass away from me;" and when knowing that Jesus Christ died for our redemption, I hereby " perceive the love of God, because he laid down his life for us," 1 John iii. 16: what need have I of a farther explanation to enable me to form the proposition myself, and say that as the Father is God, and as the Son is God, and yet as there is but one God, the Son, even our Lord Jesus Christ, is therefore one with the Father, that one God. But it may still be objected, that we see the apostles frequently, on their first appearance among the different people to whom they preached, and that therefore we might expect to hear the fact related expresly in their Acts; and do we not? has not Paul charged the Ephesian elders at Miletus " to feed the church of God, which he hath purchased with his own blood?" Acts xx. 28. Was not every prescript made by the apostles, made to all that would hear the word? and were not the doctrines delivered by them to any one church, written for the profit of all? and was not that which was delivered to all of that generation, written in one code, and transmitted through time for our use and information? That code is the Bible; and from the whole of the Bible, this one proposition is to be deduced; the whole Bible therefore, and nothing less than the whole, is to be pronounced the gospel or testimony of our Saviour Jesus Christ, and thence it is, that this proposition is as deducible as any conclusion resulting from any premises, even in the mathematical

tical Elements of Euclid, namely, that Jesus Christ is one with the Father, God.

I shall, for the future, consider my point as proved, and therefore admitted, and henceforward address myself more directly to Mr. Lindsey's book, and weigh the objections which he has made to our Saviour's Divinity; and as I have but little doubt that I shall be able to shew these wanting in the balance, I shall dismiss them with what expedition I possibly can. He tells us that there were very early heresies in the church; and in the next passage says, that "all *Christian people for upwards of three hundred years after Christ, till the council of Nice, were* generally *Unitarians* *." I do not mean to enter the lists with this gentleman on the ground of ecclesiastical history in general; but in this point I will dare to meet him, and I will not use "the authorities of men, which are nothing. It is holy scripture alone which can decide this important point, and to that we must make our final appeal †." To that I do appeal; and thence I learn, and think that even I have thence rendered it evident, that not one of the apostles of our Lord was an Unitarian. The first of these three centuries then I must use the liberty of taking away from Mr. Lindsey's bold and unsupported assertion; for to the close of it was the life of the beloved disciple of Jesus Christ extended; and therefore *all* Christian men were not Unitarians: but perhaps the less extensive word "*generally*" came into the latter end of the sentence as a saving term, and with intention to subtract from "*all*" in the commencement of it, and so to leave St. John the remainder; a single instance of a retrograde character, who, notwithstanding the weight of general example, very obstinately

* Apology, p. 24.   † Apology, p. 23.

stinately persisted in the belief of the spirit of truth, from whom he had learned a contrary doctrine. Holy scripture is silent with respect to the two succeeding centuries; I shall therefore here decline the combat, and suppose the fact to be as this gentleman has stated it, and, on that supposition, refer to what he has himself said, that, " at the first planting of the gospel a crop of evil weeds, and wild opinions grew up, together with the plant of heavenly *truth*," Apology, p. 20 *.

" Disbelief of the Trinity, no blameable heresy," is the marginal title of a short section of Mr. Lindsey's Apology. I shall not enlarge on the merit or demerit of belief in the doctrines of Christianity, but must say, that I look upon a disbelief in the Trinity to be the same with a disbelief in Jesus Christ, as revealed to us in the holy scriptures.

I should be sorry that any reader of my book should impute a spirit of intolerance to me, because I altogether reject the testimony of fire and faggot, undergone by some Unitarians in maintenance of their tenets. I have at least equal compassion for their sufferings, with that which Mr. Lindsey can feel; but as I cannot infer the truth of their profession from their miseries, so neither can I admit the cruelty which inflicted them to be any argument of the falsehood of the religion embraced, or rather professed by their barbarous tormentors; for, if this be insisted on to be of weight against the profession of faith in the Trinity, " the transitory triumphs of the Arians," notwithstanding the brevity of their prospe-

rous

---

* I should here ask Mr. Lindsey's pardon for the abridgment of his beautiful metaphor, in which he has sowed *light* upon a busy mind, and, instead of reaping a fine crop of young luminaries, has, on account of the rankness of the soil, only been able to gather in evil weeds and wild opinions of baleful *shade*.

rous days, can furnish me with means to make the opposite scale greatly preponderate. Were recrimination my object, or were I to admit but for a moment, that sufferings are of any value in evidence, good God! how many witnesses might I call to prove the truth of the doctrines which I maintain! But why should I call? from whom shall I receive my answer? They are for ever silent who should have rendered it; the poor dumb mouths, which once eloquently poured forth the doctrines of our Redeemer, now tongueless, can only pour forth that blood which they have shed to testify their belief in him. Yet even here I seek not a testimony of the truth of my own tenets, nor of the falsehood of theirs, who, to shun the confutation, put those to silence who could have uttered it. But as I have treated of this mode of argument before, I shall now finally dismiss it, with an assurance to Mr. Lindsey, that I do, as warmly as he can, compassionate all men who have suffered for their sincerity, and as utterly abhor the execrable zeal of their infatuated persecutors as he can possibly do.

The immutable nature of truth can never be affected, she remains equally spotless, whether she be assailed by an ingenious opponent, or an absurd advocate. The ingenuity of sophism is in like manner unable to alter the nature of falsehood, neither can she borrow strength from the weakness of her adversary. To this short position I refer that great body of human authority cited by Mr. Lindsey, and to which, however able the men who compose it may be, I cannot pay any respect while they stand opposed to the word of God. To this head I also refer such absurdities as that uttered by Anselm, Archbishop of Canterbury; the truth remained unchanged, even tho' he abetted it with violence. I do not desire to have it considered that every man who believes with me is therefore wife, and can give a reason for the faith that is in him. If I be found a defective advocate myself, let not my deficiency be transferred to my cause.

Mr. Lindsey says, " Authorities of men are nothing: it is holy scripture alone which can decide this important point, and to that we must make our final appeal," Apology, p. 23. After this assertion one might expect a candid enquiry into what the apostles have said upon this important point. But here we are severely disappointed, and scarce find a text quoted throughout his book but at second hand; nay, scarce a page of original writing through the whole work. Holy scripture is not once appealed to; and this same Nothing, the authorities of men, is the foundation of his system; and such as the foundation is, such indeed is the superstructure. But all this is very soon accounted for, and a perfectly new mode of argument is most ingeniously devised and introduced; and in the very next sentence to that in which he makes the scripture the final appeal, he proposes that " the matter is to be put to the vote, as it were." Now, though he never appeals to his final appeal, he does not in the same manner desert his own darling invention; but has instant recourse to as very an electioneering trick as ever was played at Brentford or Shoreham; for he flatly assures " the less learned" reader, that, upon enquiry, he shall find that to be undeniably true, which I have already shewed to be undeniably false; namely, that " all christian people for upwards of three hundred years after Christ, till the council of Nice, were generally Unitarians." This is a method of procuring votes with a witness; the whole interest of " the less learned" is obtained at one bold stroke; and in another passage of his book he has solicited the suffrages of the absolutely " unlearned;" and

having

having thus obtained the ear of the populace, he trumpets forth a multitude of names of men, and sacrifices every consideration of the authority of scripture to the establishment of their authority with the unlearned reader. To some of these I will allow that he may have done but justice, and I will not disturb the ashes of those on whom he has poured unmerited incense. I fear not his host of Unitarians, so long as I am abetted by the word of God, against which he has arrayed them. But in his diligent canvass I am surprized that he should think of the names of the Voltaires, the Morgans, and the St. Johns: does he mean to poll these men too? Are these the apostles of the gospel to which Mr. Lindsey appeals? But errour cannot, forsooth, escape their quick-sighted eyes; I sincerely believe it; they are active in pursuing and embracing errour, and I shall therefore allow them well qualified to vote with him on this occasion. But when did their quick-sighted eyes discover or pursue truth? In a few pages after we are astonished at seeing David Hume advance to give his suffrage in the contest; his vote, however, I must admit to be unexceptionable; he is excellently qualified to abet Mr. Lindsey's tenets, having undertaken to subvert the religion and liberties of this country. Whenever the bonds of religion are loosed, and the restrictions of conscience taken away, a substitute must be found to controul mankind, and an earthly tyrant be established on the throne of a deposed God, to bind in fetters those hands which have rejected the easy yoke of their Creator, and emancipated themselves from obedience to the mild sway of their merciful Redeemer. Thus far the cunning, for I cannot call it the manly understanding, of Mr. Hume, has been able to penetrate; and accordingly, when with talents exactly adequate to mischief, propensities to put them into exercise, and a disposition to enjoy the perpetrated

petrated crime, he has, by shallow sophistry, seduced mankind into the paths of vice; he rushes on the villain he has made, and, like Jonathan Wild, consigns to chains the wretch who has deserved them from his own persuasion. When, as an essayest, with just enough of art to withhold a fraud from the eyes of an indolent or willing reader, he has obliterated every virtue by which we can deserve or enjoy freedom, and has rendered the heart of an Englishman no strenuous foe to despotism, he becomes the voluminous pamphleteer of the Stuarts, and, with just enough of plausibility to conceal a falsehood from one who has no longer an interest in detecting it, to the consenting slave points out the acceptable tyrant, and to the tyrant the hands which he has fitted to his chains *.

Mr.

* I may seem here to have stepped out of my way unnecessarily; I cannot, however, admit that I have. The peace and tranquillity of mankind are my object, and to the maintenance of them it is necessary that I should strike at their enemies as they cross me, and put my fellow creatures on their guard against the invader of their happiness; such I consider Mr. Hume to be, and accordingly point him out as a Being that has waged eternal war with the welfare of mankind, both here and hereafter; who has untied, or, rather like a rat, nibbled at, the bonds of religious duty, that a necessity might thence arise of imposing the manacles of civil slavery; who frees us from our God that he may enthral us to man; inflicts the heaviest ills upon us in this life, and with a merciless hand tears away that hope of a future recompense, which was the only consolation that remained to the wretch he had enslaved.—Let it not be said that, in what he has done to these ends, he is himself also deceived. No man can ignorantly falsify in the relation of important historical facts; he therefore who has so falsified must have done it knowingly, and he who is capable of imposing known falsehood upon the public ear, is capable of broaching known sophisms: but this man has by falsehood struck at our liberties, and, by premeditated sophistry, at our religion. The necessity of their aid to the promotion of his design, is no mean proof of our right to enjoy the invaluable blessings of freedom and hope, and argues them to stand upon the firm basis of truth; and surely that he has had recourse to them for such a purpose as that of subverting all human felicity, is a sufficient reason for us to despise the wretch whose treachery and malice prepense has aimed a blow against our religious and civil rights.—When I have just repeated that I look upon our liberty to be so intimately connected with our virtue, and our virtue with the religion of the gospel, that, on the

ever-

Mr. Whiston may give his voice for Mr. Lindsey; he preferred the *apoſtolical* conſtitutions to the canonical books of the New Teſtament, declared them more ſacred and quite divine, becauſe they favoured his Arian ſentiments *. This book was written in the fourth century; and, as it teaches a doctrine not found in the ſcriptures, has, from this *apoſtolic* old man, obtained a preference. But I ſhall ceaſe to purſue this idea farther; for, however deſerving of ridicule Mr. Lindſey's argument may be, the ſubject calls on me to be ſerious.

Mr. Lindſey dwells upon the prejudices of mankind taken in with their nurſes milk, upon doctrines darkened and perplexed by early prepoſſeſſions. It is true, and I thank God and my pious parents for it, that, with my nurſe's milk, I did imbibe the doctrine which I now maintain; and at the ſame time I embibed a belief, that graſs was green, that fire was hot, that ſnow was cold, and that two and two make four. With ſuch various errours was my infancy turned aſide from truth, and ſo radically have they been eſtabliſhed in my mind by education, that I have never ſince that fatal time, when my inſtructors cruelly took advantage of my ſuſceptible and tender years, been able to comprehend that clear evidence which is of force to ſet aſide ſuch abſurdities. This childiſh and commonplace objection to the truth, becauſe it was early known, does not deſerve a ſerious refutation. If the ſcriptures afford a ſufficient teſtimony now, is it an argument to the contrary of that which they teſtify, that our teachers have read and aſſented to them, and that they have thought the word of God fit to be

com-

overthrow of the latter, one undiſtinguiſhed ruin muſt overwhelm them all together, my indignation will probably meet not the pardon only, but the approbation of *ſome* of my countrymen.

* Apology, p. 68.

communicated to their children? But I will now put a question to Mr. Lindsey, to which, if he does not find the answer on the surface of his heart, let him search the inmost recesses of it, and thence inform me, whether even his disinterested conduct, whether the doctrine of Unitarianism, of which he is the strenuous advocate, are pursued by him without one prejudice? I do not speak of those which are instilled by education, but others which, perhaps, he has not found so conquerable. This, however, is a delicate point, and must not be pursued farther. I mean not to wound nor diminish the public regard of this worthy gentleman, but choosing to put my rule by an instance, rather than in a general way, have fixed upon his name, as affording me an argument *à fortiori* in its behalf.

Such objections as turn meerly upon words I shall leave unanswered, they merit contempt and not consideration; but I must show that, upon such a supposition as the existence of the Trinity, that chain of absurdities and contradictions, which Mr. Lindsey thinks would follow, are by no means the natural consequence of the doctrine: there may be much that Mr. Lindsey cannot look into, I grant it; but did God take council of Mr. Lindsey; or has he revealed himself to him as he did to the apostles and prophets? Bishop Pearson's words keep the first and second persons in the Trinity distinct; the Father and the Son are not said in the scriptures to be jointly one Father, or one Son, but they are declared to be one God. And as to the assertion, that we who join in the four invocations, at the beginning of the litany, can be but ill defended against the charge of holding four Gods, to wit, the Father, the Son, the Holy Ghost, and the Trinity, (declared by him to be a fourth intelligent agent); it is about as wisely put as if we should say,

say, that the government of Rome was administered, not by three, but by four men, to wit, Octavius, Lepidus, Anthony, and the Triumvirate, " which is the u' oſt confusion imaginable." Apology, p. 124.

' To the consequences of offering up divine honour to Jesus Christ our Lord, which are brought together in the 136th page of the Apology, I oppose all that I have already brought in proof of the one Godhead of the Father and the Son; for this one position being admitted, our Saviour has directed prayer to be made to himself.—There is authority for so doing in the writings of the apostles.—The object of our worship is not inferior to the Father, with whom he is one God;—and therefore there never can be a distraction in the mind of the sober worshipper, who, holding in sane memory the unity of the Godhead of the Father, and of our Lord Jesus Christ, will never entertain " a doubt, when he is to pray to God, and when to Christ, when it is right, and when amiss to do it;" he will always find one God the object of his adoration, who, remembering his mercies vouchsafed to man in the flesh, will hear the prayer preferred to him, with gratitude and reliance upon him, who has already so graciously redeemed him by laying down his own life for him, 1 John iii. 16.

Mr. Lindsey, having allowed that it is Jesus Christ who is to judge the world, by disallowing his Godhead, and consequently the direction of prayer to him, has actually conferred upon God the Father, the office of Mediator with Jesus Christ, who is to judge us: for if the Godhead be not in Christ, our merits, of which no creature can have cognizance, are to be handed over for his information; and God the Father, to whom alone they can be known, is to stand forth before the seat of judgement, as our accuser or excuser: so that here we find a change of office between the Father and the Son; an absurdity at least as great as any that appears to Mr. Lindsey's reason, on the establishment of my tenets; an absurdity, in which no man can acquiesce, because it contradicts the principles whence our argument proceeds, and directly opposes itself to revelation: whereas the difficulties arising from an acquiescence in the doctrine of our Saviour's divinity, are only in matters not submitted to reason, and upon which we never should pronounce that the facts are not so, because we do not see how they are so with faculties not equal to the intuition.

The argumentum ad absurdum to which Mr. Lindsey's authors have frequent recourse, is to be judged of according to the nature of the absurdity which it would point out, as a consequence of admitting the fact it is opposed to; and if that be only such, or said to be such, because our reason cannot solve it from its incomprehensibility, it affords no confutation of the position it tries to confute: whereas, if the absurdity result from inconsistency with revelation, which must fall upon its establishment, it is a good argument; nothing being to be admitted which can militate against the truth of God. This general rule, (a rule so obvious, that nothing but having seen a book written without any regard to it, could have induced me to set it down) the reader of Mr. Lindsey's Apology will do well to hold constantly in mind, for by referring what he reads there to it, there is very little contained in the book to which it does not afford a compleat answer.

Having believed the scriptures to be the revelation of God, I have ever avoided the glosses of commentators, influenced by interest or prejudice, and have made the

unperverted

unperverted original my study, in order thence to derive a religion for myself, and I must acknowledge that I have often conceived, both from St. John's first epistle, and from several passages in the epistles of St. Paul, that they particularly opposed themselves to an opinion, prevalent in their day, that Jesus Christ had not come in the flesh; that he had not like infirmities and temptations as we have, but that the senses of mankind were imposed upon by the appearance of a body only. But as I have said that the truth most difficult to be conceived by mankind is, not that God had descended to dwell on earth, or that a man Jesus had lived on earth; but that an union of the two natures of God and of man had subsisted in Jesus Christ, a man living among them, I inferred the following conclusion, " that the apostles had preached him as God only, leaving it to their own knowledge of him, to prove that he was man; that having seen the power with which the testimony of the apostles was attended, the hearers yielded credit to that which they witnessed, and forthwith acknowledged Jesus Christ to be God: but that not being able to understand the compatibility of divine perfection and human imperfection, and therefore concluding that such an union could not have subsisted, they considered their senses imposed upon by an apparent body only, and rejected their belief in the manhood of Christ, not believing him to be man, whom they had acknowledged to be God; and that the apostles, on seeing such a doctrine arise, found themselves now under a necessity of preaching him as man, whom they had already taught to be God, and obliged to make use of the testimony of the Holy Ghost, to re-establish a fact which they had at first left to the testimony of the senses; a testimony which they had considered as sufficient then, but now saw superseded by that of their preaching."
Mr. Lindsey has proved that I was not mistaken in this;

and his account of these erroneous tenets is very correspondent to the idea which I had formed of them from scripture: for, of those who entertained them, he says, " They could not allow that a pure emanation of deity, such as they presumed Christ to be, could have any connection with so impure a substance as a human material body; and so they invented this solution of the difficulty, that he was a man in appearance only, and not in reality." Apology, p. 154. I cannot, for my part, exceedingly wonder at the errour into which these hearers fell; for I frankly acknowledge, that had I been a witness of the birth, life, death, burial, resurrection, and reascension of Jesus Christ into heaven; and had I afterwards heard him, by the assisted preaching of the apostles, declared to be God; the reality of that body, in which I had seen him, and in which I had seen him act such a part, would have come into suspicion with me; I should have doubted of the reality of a body so differently endowed from the bodies of all other men: " metuissem credere in carne natum, ne credere coactus fuissem ex carne inquinatum," St. Austin, quoted by Mr. Lindsey, Apology, p. 158, and I should have believed that he was all God without manhood. But I sincerely return thanks to the divine spirit that has testified of the flesh of our blessed atonement, and redeemed me from an errour whereby my spirit would have been proved not to have been of God. I care not to what Genus this Linnæus of divinity, who has so skilfully classed the opinions of mankind, will refer me; let him only remember that I do not now embrace such errours; for that philosophy, by which I should have said that he who is God, is therefore not man, is superseded; and I yield my faith obedient to his word, whose word alone is true; and, by consequence, I believe that Jesus Christ is come " a man as concerning the flesh," and that he is also " over all, God blessed for ever."

The truth as set forth in the scriptures, I have all along acknowledged my reason incapable to comprehend; but Mr. Lindsey thinks it ought to be comprehensible, and will not allow that God had a right to retain a power greater than he has given us abilities to search into; or wisdom, the exercise of which he has not endowed us with a capacity to understand; and therefore he thinks we had better reject all that surpasses our faculties; for, by so doing, he is of opinion that we should have a perfect union in the church. Let us for a moment grant that we should obtain this union; what is it? An union in errour; and is such an union to be desired? is this the object of his wishes? does he look upon a concurrence in falsehood as a compensation for rejected truth? But the ruin of truth, he says, and quotes Dr. Clayton for it, is not likely to result; for the gates of hell shall never prevail against the Christian religion. That they never will is my sincere belief, and therefore it is my sincere belief, that Mr. Lindsey's proposed union in errour will never take place; for, is the rejection of a point, on which nothing less than the essence of Christianity depends, is the denial of his divinity, whom we worship, no subversion of his religion? I think that the object of my worship, and of my religion is one; and if my worship be deprived of its object, I know not where to find that of my religion; and should, on seeing " the King of kings" degraded from the throne of his glory, the " God who purchased us with his own blood," torn from the supplication of his adorers, then say that the gates of hell had prevailed against his church; an event which I trust that, of his infinite mercy, and according to his immutable

mutable promise, he will avert. But I shall now resume the concession I made, for a while, and oppose Mr. Lindsey's assertion, that union would be the consequence of a legal establishment, or admission of his tenets; for we of the church, as now established, might, in that case, think fit to be dissenters from his doctrines, as he dissents now from ours. I know that, for my part, I should oppose them to the utmost of my power. But the true meaning of his words is easily comprized in this short but profound proposition, That if all mankind will agree with Mr. Lindsey, Mr. Lindsey will not disagree with all mankind: yet even this I must take the liberty to doubt.

It is a very weak assertion, that faith in the divinity of Jesus Christ leads to the admission of many objects of worship, and that the church of Rome has thence taken occasion to adore the Virgin Mary, the apostles, and martyrs, and such other persons as her own favour has been pleased to rank among her saints: for as the ground of faith in Jesus Christ, as God, is by no means pretended to be the ground for the adoration of any besides him, it is not true that the saints are worshipped, because he is revealed to be God. Jesus Christ is revealed to be God; the saints are not revealed to be God: does it therefore follow that the saints are to be worshipped? Certainly not. But very particular care has been taken to guard against the adoration of the Virgin Mary, and the apostles, and to prevent their being considered as proper objects of worship, though she was declared blessed among women, and they were highly favoured above men, having been entrusted with the testimony of Jesus Christ, who also wrought many miracles by their hands in support of their witness. It seems to have been with a view of preventing mankind from looking upon such circumstances as a ground of worship,

worship, that our Saviour has, in more passages than one, spoken with seeming disrespect (if I may dare to use the expression of him who was without sin) to his mother: " woman, what have I to do with thee?" John ii. 4. " Who is my mother?" Mark iii. 33. Peter, when Cornelius met him and fell down at his feet, and worshipped him, " took him up, saying, stand up, I myself also am a man," Acts x. 25, 26. And Paul and Barnabas, when they heard that the priest of Jupiter, with the people at Lystra, would have done sacrifice unto them, " rent their cloaths, and ran in among the people, crying out, and saying, Sirs, why do ye these things? We also are men of like passions with you; and yet with these sayings scarce restrained they the people, that they had not done sacrifice unto them," Acts xiv. 14, 15, 18. And even the angel, than whom man is made a little lower, declined the worship of St. John, saying, " I am thy fellow servant, and of thy brethren that have the testimony of Jesus, worship God," Rev. xix. 10. From the exercise of miraculous power, from supernatural endowments, we find mankind easily persuaded to conclude divinity, or at least an adorable superiority in those who are so endowed. To guard against this facility of superstition, and to shew that from an absolute revelation only we are to believe the divinity of any, the several texts which I have cited, seem to have been written. It is true a revelation that Jesus Christ is God, one with the Father, conveys an idea different from that of Mr. Lindsey, that the Father only is God, and so may afford an analogy, by which, faith, in a multitude of persons in the Godhead, might be facilitated, if revealed, but by no means a proof that there are more persons than are revealed: let us still remember the limits of reason, and not perpetually fly beyond her confines: she will conduct us very safely, if we do

not

not obtrude premises upon her which are not within her district: with respect to scripture truths, the peremptory word of the God of truth, is the ultimate boundary of her province. Our terms of salvation are prescribed, and God does not require our ingenuity in finding more points of faith than he has offered for our assent in order to secure it; and if he has not revealed, he does not need our belief, however like we may conclude our own suggestions to be to that which he has made known. Analogy may indeed facilitate conception, and make us more readily enter into a position laid down; yet it is but a bad ground to argue upon, for no certain conclusion can ever follow from it. I shall myself use it now to illustrate; and as I have denied that it can, from the divinity of Jesus Christ, shew the divinity of any other not revealed to be divine, I only ask its assistance in procuring a more easy assent to the divinity of that which is revealed to be divine; and this will, I presume, not be withheld by those who have carried its use so much higher than I dare to do. If then the Holy Ghost be revealed to be one with the Father, and the Son, God, it may be some ease to the mind in giving its assent to the existence of a third person in the Godhead, to reflect that it has already acquiesced in the admission of a second. It is not my intention to examine into the evidence of the divinity of the Holy Spirit so extensively as I have already done into that which is afforded to the Godhead of our blessed Redeemer; it is not so strenuously opposed; besides my attentive reader has, in all probability, inferred it for himself, from several contexts which I have laid down already, though I have not directly pointed it out as a conclusion. I shall therefore now content myself with a very few passages proving the Holy Ghost to be God also, reminding my reader of what I have already offered

fered concerning the sufficiency of any one assertion, for the truth of which God himself is responsible.

" He shall be great, and shall be called the Son of the Highest." " The Holy Ghost shall come upon thee, and the power of the Highest shall overshadow thee: therefore also that Holy Thing which shall be born of thee, shall be called the Son of God," Luke i. 31, 35. That which is conceived in her, is of the Holy Ghost," Matth. i. 20. That which is conceived of the Holy Ghost, is therefore called the Son of God; the Holy Ghost therefore, of whom the Son of God is conceived, is one with the Father and the Son, " the Highest."

" I will pray the Father, and he shall give you another Comforter, that he may abide with you for ever, even the Spirit of Truth." " I will not leave you comfortless: I will come to you." " If a man love me, he will keep my words: and my Father will love him, and we will come unto him, and make our abode with him," John xiv. 16, 17, 18, 23. Here the Father, Son, and Holy Ghost, one God, are, or is, the Comforter, the witness to the truth, which shall come and abide, or make abode with him who loveth the Son, and keepeth his words. The identity of the Godhead of the Holy Spirit with that of the Father, and of the Son, is here expressly declared.

" Why hath Satan filled thine heart to lie to the Holy Ghost?" " thou hast not lied unto men but unto God," Acts v. 3, 4. Here also the Holy Ghost is directly pronounced to be one, with the Father and the Son, God.

" The things of God, knoweth no man but the Spirit of God;" " which things also we speak, not in the words which man's wisdom teacheth, but which the Holy Ghost teacheth," 1 Cor. ii. 11, 13. Here the Holy Ghost is one and the same with the Spirit of God; and in the 16th verse he is called " the mind of Christ;" he is therefore one in Godhead with the Father and the Son, from both of whom, one God, he equally proceeds.

" What, know ye not that ye are the temple of the Holy Ghost which is in you, which ye have of God, and ye are not your own? For ye are bought with a price," 1 Cor. vi. 19. What now is the price paid for this purchase wherewith we are bought? are we not " the church of God which he hath purchased with his own blood?" Acts xx. 28. Being then redeemed by the blood of Jesus Christ shed for our ransom, we have therefore become the temple of the Holy Ghost. But " know ye not that ye are the temple of God, and that the Spirit of God dwelleth in you? If any man defile the temple of God, him shall God destroy; for the temple of God is holy, which temple ye are," 1 Cor. iii. 16, 17. The Father is God, and the Son is " God, who purchased us with his own blood;" and the Holy Ghost, whose temple we are, is here declared to be God. But there is but one God; the Father, Son, and Holy Ghost are therefore that one God, that Trinity in Unity which is to be worshipped. This may seem to 'the natural man', Mr. Lindsey, to be *hay and stubble*; but let him lay aside the vanity of thinking himself in the least degree a judge of spiritual things, and believe that which God has witnessed; " Let him become a fool, that he may be wise, for the wisdom of this world is foolishness with God," 1 Cor. iii. 18, 19; " Let him account of the apostles as stewards of the mysteries of God," 1 Cor. iv. 1. " and not be taken as wise in his own craftiness." " We are the house of Christ, if we hold fast the confidence and the rejoicing of the hope firm unto the end," Heb. iii. 6. " Know ye not your ownselves, that Jesus Christ in you, except ye be reprobates?" 2 Cor. xiii. 5. " Ye are the temple of the Holy Ghost which is in you." " Ye are the temple of the living God; as God hath said, I will dwell in them, and walk in them; and I will be their God, and they shall be my people," 2 Cor. vi. 16. Is this to be resisted?

That it was God who spoke by the prophets, is not denied. But by the mouth of the prophet David God has said, " To-day if ye will hear his voice, harden not your hearts as in the provocation, and as in the day of temptation in the wilderness: when your fathers tempted me, proved me, and saw my work. Forty years long was I grieved with this generation, and said, it is a people that do err in their heart, and they have not known my ways. Unto whom I sware in my wrath, that they should not enter into my rest," Pf. xcv. 7, 8, 9, 10, 11. Of him who has thus sworn, and who was thus provoked for forty years in the wilderness, even that God who led the children of Israel out of the land of Egypt, and out of the house of bondage, and said, " I am the Lord thy God," it is thus declared by St. Paul, " the Holy Ghost saith, to-day if you will hear his voice, harden not your hearts, &c." Heb. iii. 7, 8, 9, 10, 11.

Our Saviour himself says, " The spirit of truth, which proceedeth from the Father, he shall testify of me," John xv. 26; and accordingly St. Paul having declared to the Hebrews, that they who had heard the Lord confirmed his great salvation unto us, " God also bearing them witness," Heb. ii. 3. proceeds to preach the sufficiency of the one sacrifice of Christ's body once offered for sins, and the kingdom of heaven opened

opened to all believers by his having overcome the sharpness of death, and "an entrance into the holiest by the blood of Jesus, by a new and living way which he hath consecrated for us," "whereof the Holy Ghost is a witness to us," Heb. x. 15. "It is the Spirit that beareth witness, because the spirit is truth." "If we receive the witness of men, the witness of God is greater: for this is the witness of God, which he hath testified of his Son. He that believeth on the Son of God, hath the witness in himself: he that believeth not God, hath made him a liar, because he believeth not the record that God gave of his Son," 1 John v. 9, 10. These words amply explain the meaning of St. Paul's direction to the Thessalonians, "Quench not the Spirit," 1 Thess. v. 19; and, upon the whole, we so frequently find the testimony of Jesus Christ borne by God and by the Holy Ghost, that we must conclude the Holy Ghost, who "is a witness unto us," to be one with the Father and with the Son, God, who hath given the record of his Son, "that witness who is in him that believeth on the Son of God." This may perhaps afford more provender for Mr. Lindsey. I should hope however that he may, by this time at least, have begun to doubt the tenets which he has professed, and reflect on the very destructive consequences of his errour, if he can be persuaded to consider his doctrine to be such. To this purpose, and as the last argument which I shall produce to the divinity of the Holy Ghost, and his unity with the Father and Son, I shall add the declaration of our Saviour himself, who declared to the Scribes, who said, "He hath Beelzebub, and by the prince of the devils casteth he out devils;" "all sins shall be forgiven to the sons of men, and blasphemies, wherewith soever they shall blaspheme: but he that shall blaspheme against the Holy Ghost hath never forgiveness, but is in danger

of

of eternal damnation: becaufe they faid, he hath an unclean fpirit," Mark iii. 22 to 30. Here the context requires the following interpretation, 'Ye have faid that I have a devil; it fhall neverthelefs be forgiven you: but if ye fhall hereafter ufe like blafphemy, ye fhall never have forgivenefs: I came not to bear record of myfelf, and therefore difpenfe with your unbelief; whereas, when the Holy Ghoft fhall in due time bear witnefs, that ultimate teftimony upon which the faith of mankind is to be required; when the whole of that evidence fhall be afforded to the world, upon which God has thought right to demand the faith of men, and to which he will not add; then, if ye blafpheme, or lay fuch a charge againft the Son of man, declared by the Holy Ghoft to be God, ye refift the united Trinity, and fin againft God, who fhall bear me witnefs; and whofe witnefs is greater than that of man, which as yet ye are pardonable for conceiving me only to be.' The manner in which St. Luke has related the fame event, greatly corroborates this manner of underftanding the declaration of our Lord, " He that denieth me before men, fhall be denied before the angels of God. And whofoever fhall fpeak a word againft the Son of man, it fhall be forgiven him: but unto him that blafphemeth againft the Holy Ghoft, it fhall not be forgiven;" for our Saviour is in context with the declaration appointing the apoftles to be witneffes unto him; and for the purpofe of rendering them competent and irrefiftible without fin, he goes on to fay, " Take ye no thought how or what thing ye fhall anfwer, or what ye fhall fay: for the Holy Ghoft fhall teach you in the fame hour what ye ought to fay," Luke xii. 9, 10, 11, 12. On this place it is to be remarked, that our Lord has declared of him who fhall fpeak againft the Son of man, that he fhall be forgiven; and alfo, that he who denieth him,

him, shall be denied also. Here are two contradictory assertions made, and consequently two distinct circumstances are to be understood for the sake of reconciling them to truth, and to sense, which easily results, upon admitting that two distinct times are intended; and that " he who now denies me is pardonable; but that he who shall hereafter deny me, shall himself also be denied. Ye have not now the manifest testimony of God; but hereafter the Holy Ghost shall bear me witness: and in the hour when the Holy Ghost shall teach my appointed witnesses what they ought to say: ye shall not be forgiven if ye withhold belief." I desire my reader will refer this argument to the doctrine of my second chapter.

I have now proved to my own, and I hope also to my reader's, entire satisfaction, that the Son is God, and that the Holy Ghost is God: that the Father is God, and that there is but one God, are conceded points; and, having been admitted, I have been exempted from the necessity of proving them. But as there is but one God, and that each of the three persons is God, does not a Trinity in unity necessarily follow? But Mr. Lindsey does not find this conclusion drawn in so many words, and so will not believe that it results. Had Mr. Lindsey told me how many miles it measured from Richmond to Catterick, I apprehend he would charge me with great stupidity if I could not conclude for myself how many miles from Catterick to Richmond; and yet even this obvious inference does not offer itself more perspicuously to the understanding than that with which he quarrels. The promises are all fairly stated; and which am I to charge it to, the account of obstinacy, want of discernment, or a composition of both, that he will not look upon the necessary conclusion, which is, that the object

of

of our religious worship is a holy, blessed, and glorious Trinity, three persons and one God?

That each of the three persons is God, seems to me a fully sufficient reason why I should prefer to each my prayer, my praise, and my thanksgiving; that the three persons are one God, is in like manner a reason why I should address my adoration to this trinal unity. That this is a stumbling-block to the Unitarians and to the Jews, I grant; that to the Greeks it is foolishness, I grant also; that it altogether surpasses my own faculties, I as freely acknowledge; but that it is revealed by the God of truth I know, and therefore I yield my faith to what he has declared concerning his own inscrutable nature,

AND WHERE I CAN'T UNRIDDLE LEARN TO TRUST.
PARNELL.

I can clearly see that the insolence of reason, or rather of pride under her abused name, meets in this point the object of its contempt; but " behold ye despisers, and wonder and perish; for I work a work in your days, a work which ye shall in nowise believe, though a man declare it unto you," Acts xii. 41. I do not apply these words uncharitably, I use them to shew that God had beforehand ordained a difficulty to the conceptions of mankind, that they who withstand his testimony, because they have not been admitted of his council, are impeached of contempt, and threatened with eternal destruction. " Knowing therefore the terrour of the Lord," I would persuade men to humility, to obedience, to faith unto salvation, that they may escape the " vengeance taken upon them that obey not the gospel of Jesus Christ."

It is not my office to stand forth the panegyrist of the liturgy of the established church, and therefore I refrain from entering into a scriptural vindication of
it:

it: if it indeed remain neceſſary now, I have taken a great deal of pains to very little purpoſe; for I ſhould conceive an intelligent reader of the arguments I have already cited in proof of the divinity of Jeſus Chriſt and of the Holy Ghoſt, muſt, without any more particular diſcuſſion of the point, be very well able to vindicate it himſelf, and to ſet forth the propriety of offering up his adoration to them with the Father, one God. Were I diſpoſed ſo to do, I could draw together alſo the opinions of ſome of the wiſeſt men that have ever adorned our iſlands; who have conceived our book of common prayer one of the fineſt compoſitions that has flowed from the pen of man: but even this human compoſition I ſhall not maintain by human authority, though I could bring ſtronger hands to ſupport the fabric of our church, than thoſe of either Dr. Clarke or Mr. Lindſey, which have been deſperately employed in dilapidating; or, to uſe Mr. Lindſey's leſs-confuſed metaphor, in *ſmothering the fabric*.

This gentleman, after he had deprecated all human authority as a ground of faith, we have already ſeen making uſe of it, and nothing elſe, in ſupport of his doctrines. But he has attacked human authority in another ſenſe of the words alſo; and, to the great conſternation of every Briton, who ſhall meet it in his way, has emphatically and concluſively pronounced it A Monster. But the terrified reader of his book may calm his breaſt when he comes to know that this ſame monſter is nothing worſe than "a legal eſtabliſhment of the church of England." An eſtabliſhment, the neceſſity of which, I am ſorry to ſay, grows every day more and more obvious; and to whoſe good purpoſes, Mr. Lindſey's own conduct bears an incontrovertible teſtimony. A farther vindication of this alſo exceeds the limits of my deſign; but methinks a gentleman, who has experienced ſuch lenity from our eſtabliſhment,

blishment, should at least acknowledge, from the tolerated altar of his new synagogue, that the church of England is not a very fierce monster.

As the limits are, however, of my own appointment, I will take the liberty of transgressing them a little here. The articles of religion, when first prescribed, were chiefly intended as a barrier to divide our new reformation from Popery, which it had just escaped, many of the particular tenets of which are formally abjured in them. Though access to the scriptures were now permitted to all men, it was thought necessary to assist the weak, in forming their conclusions upon the whole, and to sum up in brief those doctrines which lie diffused in the sacred writings. Moderation appears also to have been a principal object in forming them; for as abhorrence must naturally succeed the detection of the self-interested frauds of the church of Rome, it seems a reasonable apprehension, that every tenet which it had held, would fall into contempt, if not conspicuously held forth, as retained by the leaders of reformation; hence the Trinity is formally avowed, in which we continued our agreement. I am far from maintaining that the body of the people should be obliged to subscribe to any articles of faith; but it appears to me absolutely necessary that certain articles of faith should be subscribed by the pastors in our church, otherwise we must cease to be a church; and, instead of a general amity amongst men, the gospel will be converted into a source of universal discord, and bring indeed, not peace, but a sword; we shall, instead of a church of England, have as many churches as parish ministers; every parish, zealous to maintain the doctrines of its polemic pastor, will war on its neighbour, and think they do God service by reducing those, who dissent from them, to opinions which they have been instructed

structed to esteem necessary to be entertained. Subscription to these doctrines, as a security for the maintenance of the imposed faith, will be required, and that which is now established in peace, will be, if relinquished, again exacted by the very consequences of having relinquished it; for, however exceptionable those articles which are now subscribed may be thought, I greatly doubt whether they who complain would agree together in forming a set that would be less liable to objection; and that subscription would again be required and submitted to, as the purchase of tranquillity, I do not entertain the smallest doubt. Articles, summing up in few words the essential doctrines diffused in the scriptures, ought to be prescribed to those who are authorized to teach; and these alone should they be permitted to promulgate, whatever they might privately think. It is true the conscientious man who does not acquiesce in their truth, and therefore cannot subscribe to them, is excluded from the office of a teacher, and withheld: but from what? from an opportunity of propagating opinions contrary to those which the wisest men have conceived deducible from scripture, for by such I conceive these articles to be formed. It is to be hoped that many a weak man has a tender conscience; by this then he is restrained from uttering his trifling suggestions; while he who has less scrupulously acquiesced in what he doubted, has, by his subscription, given security to mankind that he will not propagate pernicious or silly tenets. I do not wish to confine the private sentiments of the heart, but I do to restrain the liberty of teaching and imparting such notions as a weak man may instill into a credulous or unthinking congregation. Anabaptism itself pretended to the sanction of scripture, and may again, to the utter subversion of all religion and virtue. The church of Catterick may set up against that of Northallerton, and

whe

who shall decide which is right, if there be no prescript? The more extensive diocesan churches may disagree, and when the church of Carlisle shall make inroads into the neighbouring churches of Durham and Chester, who shall restrain the arm that declares itself raised for the propagation of truth? Intestine wars and universal confusion may at length leave the decision in the hands of victory, and vanquished truth shall then subscribe to articles dictated by its erroneous conquerour. Such would be the process: and let not those who now complain of the necessity of subscribing the articles of the church of England, flatter themselves that matters would be rendered more agreeable even to themselves, if they should be indulged in their desires. Perhaps, when every species of disturbance and puritanical absurdity had raged through the nation, and robbed them of their tranquillity, they would then begin to acknowledge the happiness they enjoyed when protected by that barrier which they had themselves broken down, and become the first to replace it; the want would teach the value of that which they now overlook, because they possess it. But the subscription of articles of faith is no such mighty grievance as some would intimate; it may be a severity to a few who are not admitted into the pulpit, because they cannot accede to them: but surely it is a great happiness to the body of the people that they are under the guardianship of an establishment that protects them from the necessity of listening to the whimsical interpretation of weak teachers. It is therefore necessary, so long as there is no compulsion on the laity to learn and give their faith to the doctrines of the clergy, that the conclusions which are to be drawn from holy writ should be prescribed to those who are appointed to teach: if they cannot subscribe, let them let it alone, a church with which they cannot concur, is even better without them.

them. Is it for the admiffion of a few individuals that a door is to be opened, by which every fpecies of abufe may enter?

I honour and concur with Mr. Lindfey's patriot wifh, that England fhould ever fet the example of improvement; but it is very weakly urged, that religion fhould keep pace with fcience in improvement, and that a fubfcription to articles muft always impede its progrefs; for nothing can be more abfurd than the idea of a progreffive religion, which, being founded upon the declared, not the imagined will of God, muft, if it attempt to proceed, relinquifh that revelation which is its bafis, and fo ceafe to be a religion founded upon God's word. God has revealed himfelf, and all that he has fpoken, and confequently all that is demanded of us to accede to, is declared in one book, from which nothing is to be retrenched, and to which nothing can be added. All that it contains was as perfpicuous to thofe who firft perufed it, after the rejection of the Papal yoke, as it can be to us now, or as it can be to our pofterity in the fiftieth generation. If we look for any thing new, it is not in the fcriptures that it is to be found; and if we add, it is not religion that has improved, for truth will never defert her own foundations, nor follow our fantaftic imaginations. The progrefs of every fcience has been to the difcovery of fomething new, derived from new combinations of principles within our comprehenfion, and confequently capable of being compared for the fake of additional knowledge. Is fuch a progrefs to be defired in religon? What novelty do we feek for, or what advantage do we propofe from the introduction of novelty into religion? Such an idea feems to intimate

As if religion were intended
For nothing elfe but to be mended. HUDIBRAS.

CHAP.

CHAP. V*.

ΤΩ͂Ν ΠΕΡΙ' ἙΑΥΤΟ͂Υ.

MY name appearing prefixed to this edition will put it out of doubt that I am in truth, as I formerly stated myself, a Layman, and I conceive that my book has rendered it unneceſſary for me to ſay that I am altogether unread in theological diſputations; of theſe two circumſtances, however, I am now about to make my advantage, for I ſtill deſire to have the end kept in view, and to convert even myſelf into ſome ſort of argument in behalf of it.

On the publication of Mr. Lindſey's Apology, as I have already ſaid, I was drawn by curioſity to look into it; but finding it to contain a doctrine which I had not in the leaſt ſuſpected, (as I really had never known any thing of the gentleman before) I placed the Bible by my ſide, happy in finding the beſt, the only evidence in this caſe offered to the examination of every man. With perfect freedom from prejudice, nay, I am almoſt aſhamed to confeſs it, with the firſt ſerious conſideration of ſo important a point that I had ever entered into †, I ſat down to read Mr. Lindſey's book, and, for the truth of every poſition contained in it, appealed to the word of God himſelf, that I might thence learn how truly it was advanced; when, to my utter aſtoniſhment, I ſoon found that this was the only book upon the ſubject, which the diligent Apologiſt had not critically read, and that in every particular it directly oppoſed itſelf to him, and to his frequent quotations. It grew into a matter

---

* This chapter is for the moſt part a parody of Mr. Lindſey's concluding chapter, and title is the ſame with his.

† I would not have it underſtood that I had never read the Bible before, but that I never read it to this point, or in a like inquiſitive manner as now.

matter of wonder with me, what could influence a man to surrender his worldly competence in defence of a contradiction to the only witness that bears any testimony concerning the fact which he contradicts. As I had received an education among men not unlettered, I was not altogether unacquainted with the laws of argument, and soon perceived his errour to proceed from his having drawn from a wrong source, from his having laid aside the Bible, and said, " my reason does not acquiesce in a Trinity of Persons in the one God, and my reason is competent; this is a matter submitted to my faculties, and I am skilled to affirm or deny concerning a comprehensible God." As I found difficulties in lifting up my own faculties to God, I conceived Mr. Lindsey's no better able to soar to such unsurmountable heights; and having found that my Maker *had* spoken, looked upon his word as the fountain from which all argument concerning him should flow, and accordingly I have stated my own idea of the manner of pursuing this enquiry in my first chapter. Under this persuasion I noted my Bible, and to what purpose my reader is empowered to judge from my third and fourth chapters: but, as I went along, the degrees or different species of testimony afforded to the divinity of our Lord and Saviour Jesus Christ, offered themselves to my observation; and this also I have in my second chapter submitted to public censure. Such was the process of an enquiry entered into by a man who set about it for his own information only; but the substance of which, as it has afforded perfect conviction to himself, he has at length decided to be due to mankind; at length decided, I say, because that many scruples delayed my determination. First it occurred to me that, being a Layman, it was, properly speaking, no business of mine; that an established clergy was appointed for the defence of religion; that at the head of this Clergy there was a respectable and venerable body of

learned

learned Bishops, who were daily acquiring more weight by the accession of a numerous Nobility to their bench; by which accession, if the body should lose (as in all human probability they will) on the side of learning, they were sure of obtaining consequence on the side of fashion; and therefore that it was not to be supposed that the conduct of one country clergyman could long continue of any national importance. But when, on the other hand, I considered how ready the world was to impute partiality to any body of men who should write on a subject in which their private interest was so deeply concerned, and that their own silence shewed they were themselves aware of this, I thought that a Layman writing upon the subject, a man totally unconnected with their profession, would probably be more attended to. Another objection which occurred to me, was my entire ignorance of controversial theology, and particularly my having never looked into any controversy upon the Trinity, except what I have seen in Mr. Lindsey's book; but being by Mr. Lindsey's book convinced that the Bible was the only guide to be depended upon, I then thought that the reading that with attention would be a sufficient preparative for writing; that my very ignorance in controversy would turn to account, and that it might be considered as a corroborating proof of the truth of what I should write; that the Bible alone had been found sufficient to convince *one young man*; and accordingly, thro' the whole course of my enquiry, the Bible alone have I consulted, and this (notwithstanding that I have acknowledged myself educated in these doctrines) without a single prejudice, either my own, or borrowed from any other. Perhaps I have been too nicely scrupulous in this respect; for, through the fear of imbibing one prejudice on so important a question, I have worked only on my own ideas derived from scripture, shunned the superior suggestions of wiser men, and diligently withheld myself from an acquaintance with any thing
that

that had ever been said upon the subject before. I knew not thro' what foul or crooked channels the course of the stream had been turned, but was very certain that the well-head was pure, and thence only I therefore determined to draw. From this circumstance I also entertained some hope, that, being totally unbiassed, I might possibly strike out some new lights; or, where I should accidentally agree with any former writers, put an old argument in so different a manner, that it should convey a new impression, and convince such of my readers as affect novelty; for of novelty, if that be a recommendation, they have undoubtedly a chance, as all contained in my work is my own, whether any of it may have been stated before or not.

May I have leave to say, without blame, that having been born a gentleman, a farther difficulty opposed my resolution to publish; the inconsistency of such doctrines as I was about to maintain, with the modish practices and easy principles of the polite world suggested itself to me; why then, it often occurred to me, why must I be so singularly nice and scrupulous as not to comply with what men of fashion accommodate themselves to? why disturb others, and not give way to a more chearful way of thinking; why promulgate that veneration for a Deity which a free communication with the world may disperse or remove? and why render myself obnoxious to men who must detest the doctrines which restrain their will, and not rather wait patiently for a change in the morals of the age? These considerations altogether were of weight to divert me for a while from the thought of publication; not that I now justify myself therein: yea rather I condemn myself, and have at length decided to offer to mankind those arguments which have already afforded conviction to myself *.

I

---

* See Apology, p. 210, of which this paragraph is only a parody.

I am very confcious that my ftyle would admit of great improvement; but if it be confidered that I did not fee Mr. Lindfey's book till * late in the month of January, I fhall readily be forgiven by the ingenuous and candid reader, who will fee that I have employed that time in the purfuit of matter, which, had I lefs regard to an argument of fo high importance to him and myfelf, I might have beftowed in polifhing a lefs convincing work. But why then fhould I not have withheld it longer from the world, and rendered it better able to fuftain their criticifm? For this fhort reafon: a deadly poifon has been adminiftered to the publick, I have hafted to prepare the antidote, and have not paufed to fugar over the brim of the veffel in which I offer it to their lips. He muft love the poifon who rejects the antidote that is not feafoned to his palate. I am as fenfible of the charms of language as my faftidious reader may be, and could perhaps, even without his affiftance, have rendered my own ftyle more agreeable to his ear, and greatly fhortened what I have been forced, thro' hafte, to exprefs in unfelected terms. If, however, he be fuch a man as cannot pardon me, I do not afk his pardon.

I fhall here take occafion to explain what I have written with refpect to Mr. Lindfey himfelf. I have heretofore confidered him in the character of a Sectary and Writer only, and confequently have been under a neceffity of fpeaking concerning him in terms, which I have always uttered with regret. I am not, however, going to retract a fingle fyllable which can only affect him in his public character; but, on the contrary, more fummarily to avow the fubftance of what I have already laid down. As a Sectary then, I think he would be a dangerous man, had he not himfelf diminifhed

---

* I did not fee it till the 21ft of January, and the former edition of this volume was finifhed from the prefs May 5, 1774.

nished his importance by becoming the advocate of his own tenets; for as a Writer, I consider him to be perfectly harmless; yet still from that character, in which I shall henceforward address him, I dread the Schismatick, and have therefore opposed myself to a book, which, had it not come from the self-denying hand of this gentleman, might, for me, have gradually subsided in its congenial oblivion. His conduct, however, might support it for a time; my effort therefore is more expeditiously to dismiss it from existence.

It may look a little quarrelsome, that I cannot let even so much of his book, as corresponds with the title page, pass without a censure. But this gentleman has thought it necessary to make an apology for the most unexceptionable conduct that he could possibly have pursued; for a sincere obedience to the dictates of his conscience; for having made a sacrifice to what he esteemed the truth, however mistaken; for having looked upon pardon as inconsistent with the retained offence; and for having convinced mankind that " he had escaped the pollutions of the world by his former knowledge of the Lord and Saviour Jesus Christ," 2 Pet. ii. 20. Had he indeed pursued a contrary course, and continued to profess when he had ceased to believe, then would an apology have been truly necessary, and we should not perhaps have admitted it to be satisfactory, though he had even yielded to the importunity of stronger motives than those which he has resisted. Had his power of doing good been far more extensive, and had the subscription of a doctrine, which he did not believe, afforded his benevolent propensities an opportunity of propagating the opposite tenet which he did believe, and think necessary to be received by all men, not even so good an end should exempt the means from the charge of falshood, nor the perpetrator

from

from the imputation of holding "the damnable doctrine of doing evil that good may come of it." Had a dignified character extended his influence still wider; had the pastoral office been committed to his hand; and had the emblem of the descending spirit sat upon him, he could but ill defend himself from the justice of universal condemnation, though thus, meditating, he should address his mitre, the symbol of a cloven tongue, "thou art the symbol of a double tongue, and thou shalt sanctify duplicity; thou shalt be my warrant for *hypocrisy and prevarication*; for thee will *I keep up all these forms* of subscribing what I do not believe, *till relieved by proper authority*, and vested with dignities without the necessity of falsifying, in order to obtain them; for thee *I will ministerially comply with what I am not able to remove, and patiently remain in my post, however invidiously misrepresented*; for thee, and under thy sanction, I will utter two languages; I will tell a lye for the sake of telling truth; enter into terms for the purpose of infringing them; and comply with such proposed conditions as shall afford me an occasion of shewing that they ought not to be complied with. At the door of the vineyard I will say that *the wild branches* are but the fine luxuriance of nature, and that their growth ought to be encouraged, so shall I obtain the power of *pruning them away*; I shall create to myself an opportunity of *rooting out some of* what I take to be *the rankest weeds*, by telling the owner of the vineyard that I think them the most beautiful plants, and engaging that I will diligently cultivate them: thus shall I trick him into his own advantage, and prove, by having dispensed with truth in order to get admission, that his service, and not my profit, was the only motive to the fraud, the pious fraud by which I induced him to admit me †. Had Mr. Lindsey, I say, thus pondering, lulled

himself

† See considerations on the propriety of requiring a subscription to articles of faith.

himself into a hope that none *would suspect him of hypocrisy and prevarication*, he should have found it vain; every whisper would be interpreted into censure, and every breeze of opinion, prove a storm sufficient to disturb the tranquillity of his soul. Is there any man who can have thus dealt by himself? To him I call to descend from his throne, to seek for happiness in self-approbation, and for public applause, by conspicuous and exemplary virtue; let him place the mitre upon other brows, and put upon his own " the helmet of salvation." There are men in England who can profess with sincerity, and maintain what they have professed; who do not need the picklock of equivocation, nor the burglary of more open falsehood, to obtain an entrance into the ministry, from which I thus boldly call, in the name of each man's conscience, upon every person, whether he be Archbishop, Bishop, Priest, or Deacon, who has subscribed with insincerity, or who cannot now overcome his scruples, to retire, and follow the worthy example which is afforded them by Mr. Lindsey.

As a good man, I honour Mr. Lindsey; as a man strenuous in the maintenance of his faith, though I believe it erroneous, I respect him; and if his understanding were but nearly commensurate with his honesty, I believe that the church which he has deserted, would have found in him, who is now her weak opponent, an advocate truly able to maintain her cause; for I do not remember in my life to have met with a man, in whom the excellencies of head and heart had united, who did not submit his own understanding to the word of his Maker, and believe, because that his immutable truth is a fully sufficient ground of faith.

As I am now about to conclude, I must call back the mind of my reader, and having brought my argument

ment to an end, refer to him the issue upon which he is to determine.

Either Jesus Christ is one with the Father, God, or he is not; either the Holy Ghost is one with the Father and the Son, God, or he is not.—On supposing that the negative side of this dilemma can be assumed, (and for argument's sake it must be supposed, however irksome) a consequence ensues, horrible to thought. The God of peace becomes a firebrand of contention; tenfold confusion proceeds from God, " who is not the author of confusion ;" the Spirit of truth is a lyar; the simple and guileless zeal of the apostles, is crafty and designing duplicity; the wisdom of God, folly, beneath the foolishness of men; and the revelation of the God of truth, from end to end, scarce the word of designing falsehood, it must have proceeded from a dupe to his own artifices. I shudder while I write: but it is acknowledged that the scriptures are the word of God, and the application of this description to them I will leave with men who can persist in the denial of this great mystery: Whereas, on the other hand, three persons and one God being acknowledged, a fact is established concerning the things of God, incomprehensible to us, who have not spiritual things to compare with spiritual, and which therefore, though it may transcend, can never contradict our reason. Our belief, which is all that is required, may be yielded to the evidence of the fact without any violence offered to our understanding; and therefore, however incomprehensible the object of the testimony may be, there can be no difficulty in making the affirmative, which does not equally attend upon pronouncing the negative of the proposition, and one of the two we are under an absolute necessity of adopting.

In

In whatsoever God acts, he must condescend. The whole extent of created nature bears to him but a like proportion as an atom; he is equally the God of a fraction as of the universe; and a fraction is as commensurate to his infinity as the universe. But his love is infinite, and we have been the object of it, an object as observable by him as all worlds; for, little as we are, we bear the same proportion to him. Let us then lay aside that pride, which, in the pretence of humility, withdraws mankind from the eye of his Maker; from that microscopick eye, by which even the hairs of our head are numbered; that equal and all-pervading eye, which as accurately sees and marks the fall of a sparrow, as the crush of worlds. When we thus consider him, doubts will vanish; we shall see that we may possibly be within his contemplation, the objects of his favour; we shall acquiesce in a revelation of the benefits he has conferred upon us, and acknowledge that we *have been* the objects of his favour; our ignorance shall be dissipated, our pride deposed; and reason (rightly so called) assuming her proper dignity, conduct us with certainty so far as her own prescribed boundaries extend; instruct us where to pause; teach us the limits of our own faculties, and the illimitable extent of our Maker's; put an end to idle speculation; point out God as our revealed Benefactor, not the subject of our inquisitive curiosity; dictate confidence and hope in him; and make us, because he has revealed it, " to acknowledge the mystery of God, and of the Father, and of Christ."

F I N I S.

INDEX
TO THE

Texts *of* Scripture *quoted in the third Chapter, according to the Order in which they stand compared.*

I.
		Ch.	V.	Page
Isaiah	—	vii.	14.	50

II.
Isaiah	—	ix.	6.	50

III.
Isaiah	—	xliv.	6	} 50
Revelation	—	ii.	8	

IV.
Isaiah	—	lii.	9	
			10	
			15	
Isaiah	—	lii.	10	
Isaiah	—	liii.	1	} 51
Luke	—	iii.	6	
John	—	xii.	38	
			41	
1 Corinthians	—	x.	9	

V.
Isaiah	—	xl.	10	
			11	
Revelation	—	xxii.	12	} 52
John	—	x.	11	
Hebrews	—	xiii.	20	
			21	

VI.
Isaiah	—	lii.	7	} 52
Romans	—	x.	15	

VII.
Psalm	—	viii.	2	} 53
			1	
Matthew	—	xxi.	16	

VIII.
Psalm	—	xliv.	22	} 53
Romans	—	viii.	35	

IX.
Matthew	—	vi.	10	
			13	} 54
Matthew	—	xxiv.	30	
			31	

		Ch.	V.	Page
Matthew	—	xxv.	31	
			32	
			33	
			34	
Mark	—	viii.	38	
Matthew	—	xiii.	41	
Matthew	—	xvi.	27	} 54
Luke	—	ix.	26	
Ephesians	—	v.	5	
2 Timothy	—	iv.	1	
2 Peter	—	i.	11	
Luke	—	xvii.	20 to 30	

X.
Matthew	—	xi.	27	} 56
Luke	—	x.	22	

XI.
Matthew	—	xxviii.	20	
Mark	—	xvi.	20	} 57
Hebrews	—	ii.	3	
			4	

XII.
Mark	—	ix.	24	57

XIII.
Luke	—	v.	20 to 25	
Isaiah	—	xliii.	25	} 57
Nehemiah	—	ix.	17	

XIV.
Luke	—	vi.	22	
			23	
Acts	—	vii.	52	} 58
			59	
1 Peter	—	iv.	13	
			14	

XV.
Luke	—	viii.	38	
			39	
Mark	—	v.	19	} 59
			20	
John	—	xi.	35	

	Ch. V. Page		Ch. V. Page
XVI.		**XXIII.**	
LUKE — xxiii. 42 ⎫		John — xiv. 8 ⎫	
43 ⎬ 60		9 ⎬ 68	
Luke — xxiv. 26 ⎭		10 ⎪	
		11 ⎭	
XVII.		**XXIV.**	
JOHN — ii. 19 ⎫		John — xiv. 12 ⎫	
21 ⎬ 61		13 ⎪	
Acts — ii. 32 ⎭		14 ⎪	
XVIII.		John — xvi. 23 ⎬ 69	
JOHN — iv. 10 ⎫		Exodus — iii. 15 ⎪	
14 ⎪		1 Timothy — iii. 16 ⎪	
Jeremiah — xvii. 13 ⎪		1 John — i. 1 ⎪	
Revelation — xxii. 1 ⎪		John — i. 1 ⎭	
17 ⎪		**XXV.**	
John — iv. 14 ⎬ 61		JOHN — xvi. 7 ⎫	
Isaiah — lv. 1 ⎪		John — xiv. 26 ⎪	
Isaiah — xliv. 3 ⎪		John — xv. 26 ⎪	
John — vii. 37 ⎪		2 Peter — i. 21 ⎬ 72	
38 ⎪		1 Peter — i. 11 ⎪	
Acts — xx. 28 ⎪		John — xvi. 14 ⎪	
John — iv. 42 ⎪		15 ⎭	
Isaiah — xii. 3 ⎭		**XXVI.**	
XIX.		JOHN — xvii. 1 ⎫	
JOHN — v. 17 ⎫		Hebrews — ix. 24 ⎬ 73	
18 ⎪		John — xvii. 5 ⎪	
John — v. 26 ⎪		24 ⎭	
27 ⎪		**XXVII.**	
Hebrews — ii. 18 ⎪		JOHN — xviii. 37 ⎫	
Hebrews — iv. 15 ⎬ 63		1 Timothy — vi. 13 ⎬ 74	
John — v. 21 ⎪		John — i. 49 ⎭	
25 ⎪		**XXVIII.**	
28 ⎪		JOHN — xx. 28 ⎫	
John — vi. 69 ⎪		29 ⎬ 75	
John — ix. 38 ⎭		John — xx. 16 ⎭	
XX.		**XXIX.**	
JOHN — v. 24 ⎫		ACTS — i. 24 ⎫	
John — iii. 18 ⎪		John — xv. 27 ⎪	
John — iii. 13 ⎪		Mark — xvi. 15 ⎪	
John — iii. 31 ⎬ 65		Romans — i. 5 ⎪	
John — vi. 62 ⎪		John — ii. 25 ⎪	
John — xvi. 28 ⎪		Acts — i. 21 ⎪	
29 ⎭		22 ⎪	
XXI.		Acts — ix. 5 ⎬ 76	
JOHN — viii. 58 ⎫		6 ⎪	
Revelation — i. 4 ⎬ 66		13 ⎪	
Exodus — iii. 14 ⎪		14 ⎪	
John — iv. 26 ⎭		15 ⎪	
XXII.		1 Corinthians — i. 17 ⎪	
JOHN — x. 30 ⎫		Luke — xi. 49 ⎪	
John — x. 33 ⎬ 67		Matthew — xxiii. 34 ⎪	
John — x. 38 ⎭		Acts — ix. 20 ⎪	
		21 ⎭	

Acts

INDEX.

	Ch.	V.	Page
Acts	ix.	2	
		15	
Acts	xxii.	14	} 76
John	xxi.	17	
John	xiii.	37	
		38	

XXX.
Acts	iii.	12	
Acts	iv.	10	
		21	} 81
Acts	ix.	34	
		35	

XXXI.
Acts	vii.	54	
		55	
		56	
		57	
		58	
		59	
		60	
John	xvi.	13	
Psalm	xxxi.	5	
Revelation	xxii.	9	} 82
Jeremiah	xxiii.	23	
Acts	vii.	56	
		57	
Matthew	xxvi.	64	
		65	
		67	
Matthew	xiv.	61	
		to	
		65	

XXXII.
| Acts | ix. | 40 | } 88 |
| | | 42 | |

XXXIII.
Acts	xi.	18	
		20	
		21	} 89
		22	
		23	
Acts	xv.	11	

XXXIV.
Acts	xiii.	45	
		46	
		47	
Isaiah	xlix.	6	
Matthew	xv.	24	} 89
Acts	xiii.	48	
		49	
Acts	xiv.	1	
		3	

	Ch.	V.	Page
Matthew	xxviii.	20	
Mark	xvi.	20	
Hebrews	ii.	4	} 89
Acts	xix.	10	
		11	

XXXV.
Acts	xvi.	14	
		15	
		16	
		17	
Luke	xxiv.	45	} 92
Mark	i.	34	
Romans	i.	1	
Philippians	i.	1	
Titus	i.	1	

XXXVI.
Acts	xvi.	30	
		31	
		32	} 93
		33	
		34	

XXXVII.
Acts	xvii.	18	
Acts	xvii.	23	
		24	
		28	} 94
Colossians	i.	16	
		17	
Isaiah	xlii.	8	

XXXVIII.
Acts	xviii.	8	
		9	
		10	} 95
		11	
Acts	xxiii.	11	

XXXIX.
Acts	xviii.	24	
		to	} 96
		28	

XL.
Acts	xix.	10	
Acts	xix.	17	
		18	} 97
		19	
		20	

XLI.
Acts	xxi.	11	
		to	} 97
		14	
Matthew	vi.	10	

XLII.
| Acts | xxii. | 16 | 98 |
| | | | Acts |

	Ch.	V.	Page
XLIII.			
Acts	xxii.	17, 18, 19, 20	98
XLIV.			
Acts	xxiv.	5, 14	99
John	v.	39	
XLV.			
Romans	i.	1, 9	99
XLVI.			
Romans	ii.	3	100
John	v.	22	
Matthew	xvi.	27	
Romans	ii.	6	
XLVII.			
Romans	ii.	4	100
Acts	xi.	18	
1 Timothy	i.	16	
2 Peter	iii.	15, 9	
XLVIII.			
Romans	iii.		101
Romans	iv.		
Hebrews	xi. xii.		

The whole of each chapter referred to.

	Ch.	V.	Page
XLIX.			
Romans	viii.	9, 11	101
L.			
Romans	ix.	5	102
LI.			
Romans	x.	12, 13	102
LII.			
Romans	xiv.	6 to 9	103
1 Corinthians	x.	31, 28	
LIII.			
Romans	xiv.	10, 11, 12	103
Isaiah	xlv.	23, 21, 22	
2 Corinthians	v.	10	
Hebrews	x.	31	

	Ch.	V.	Page
LIV.			
Romans	xiv.	14	104
LV.			
Romans	xv.	16, 19	105
LVI.			
Romans	xvi.	16	105
1 Corinthians	i.	1, 2, 3, 4	
LVII.			
1 Corinthians	i.	7, 8	106
1 Corinthians	iv.	5	
2 Corinthians	x.	14 to 18	
LVIII.			
1 Corinthians	i.	11, 12, 13	107
1 Corinthians	i.	10	
1 Corinthians	iii.	5, 6	
1 Corinthians	i.	8	
LIX.			
1 Corinthians	i.	14, 15	108
LX.			
1 Corinthians	i.	26, 27, 28, 29	109
1 Corinthians	i.	21, 31	
2 Corinthians	x.	17	
Jeremiah	ix.	24	
LXI.			
1 Corinthians	ii.	8	110
Acts	iii.	15, 17	
James	ii.	1	
Psalm	xxiv.	10	
Genesis	ii.	7	
LXII.			
1 Corinthians	ii.	7 to the end.	110
LXIII.			
1 Corinthians	vii.	25	110
Daniel	ix.	9	

LXIV

		Ch.	V.	Page			Ch.	V.	Page
LXIV.					**LXXII.**				
1 Corinthians		viii.	4		Ephesians		iv.	8	
1 Corinthians	—	viii.	6					9	
Acts	—	xiv.	7	111				10	122
			15		Ephesians	—	iv.	14	
1 Corinthians	—	xii.	2					15	
1 Corinthians	—	xiv.	3		**LXXIII.**				
			33		Ephesians	—	vi.	5	
LXV.								6	
1 Corinthians		x.	20					7	123
			21	115				8	
2 Corinthians	—	vi.	15		Colossians	—	iii.	22	
			16		**LXXIV.**				
LXVI.					Philippians	—	ii.	6	
2 Corinthians		iv.	5	116				7	124
2 Timothy	—	i.	8					8	
LXVII.					Colossians		i.	15	
2 Corinthians		xii.	5		**LXXV.**				
			7		Philippians	—	iii.	20	
			8	116	1 Timothy		i.	1	
			9		1 Timothy		ii.	3	124
			10		1 Timothy		iv.	10	
LXVIII.					Titus		i.	3	
Galatians	—	i.	1		Acts		ix.	5	
Galatians	—	i.	11	118	**LXXVI.**				
			12		Colossians		i.	15	
LXIX.								16	125
Galatians	—	i.	10					17	
Galatians	—	vi.	12	119				18	
			17		**LXXVII.**				
LXX.					Colossians	—	ii.	9	128
Galatians		iv.	6		**LXXVIII.**				
Galatians	—	iii.	8		Colossians		iii.	11	
Romans	—	viii.	11	119				12	128
			14					13	
			15		**LXXIX.**				
1 Corinthians	—	xii.	3		Colossians		iii.	24	
LXXI.								25	
Ephesians	—	i.	7		Romans		ii.	5	
Ephesians	—	iii.	8					11	128
			14		Ephesians		vi.	6	
			15					9	
			16		James		ii.	1	
Romans	—	ii.	4		**LXXX.**				
Romans	—	ix.	23		1 Thessalonians		ii.	2	
Ephesians	—	iii.	18	121	1 Thessalonians	—	ii.	8	
			19					9	128
			17		1 Thessalonians	—	iii.	2	
Ephesians	—	iv.	13		John		xvi.	13	
Ephesians	—	iii.	7		1 Thessalonians	—	ii.	3	
Ephesians	—	iv.	7		**LXXXI.**				
Romans	—	xi.	33		1 Thessalonians	iv.	2	129
			34					3	

G g 2 LXXXI.

	Ch.	V.	Page		Ch.	V.	Page
LXXXII.				**XCI.**			
2 Thessalonians	i.	6	} 130	Hebrews	—	ii. 16	} 137
		7		Colossians	—	i. 16	
		8		Hebrews	—	x.	
		9		Hebrews	—	vii.	
		10		Hebrews	—	viii.	
Matthew	—	vi. 9		Hebrews	—	ii.	
1 Peter	—	iv. 17		**XCII.**			
LXXXIII.				James	—	v. 8	} 142
2 Thessalonians	—	ii. 16	} 130			9	
		17				10	
2 Thessalonians	—	iii. 3				11	
LXXXIV.				James	—	v. 14	
2 Thessalonians	iii.	5	} 132			15	
2 Corinthians	—	ii. 14		Acts	—	ix. 34	
		17		Luke	—	viii. 48	
LXXXV.				Luke	—	v. 13	
1 Timothy	—	ii. 5	} 132	**XCIII.**			
		6		James	—	i. 1	} 143
		7		James	—	ii. 1	
		8				5	
LXXXVI.						9	
1 Timothy	—	iii. 16	} 133			13	
1 Timothy	—	i. 10		**XCIV.**			
		11		1 Peter	—	v. 1	} 144
LXXXVII.						2	
1 Timothy	—	iv. 10	} 133			3	
1 Timothy	—	i. 15				4	
2 Timothy	—	ii. 8		John	—	xxi. 14	
		10				15	
LXXXVIII.						16	
1 Timothy	—	vi. 13	} 134			17	
		14		John	—	x. 13	
		15				14	
		16		1 Peter	—	ii. 25	
2 Corinthians	—	v. 16		Hebrews	—	xiii. 20	
Revelation	—	xix. 16		Acts	—	xx. 28	
LXXXIX.				James	—	i. 12	
2 Timothy	—	iv. 1	} 135	James	—	ii. 5	
		8		1 Corinthians	—	ix. 25	
Titus	—	ii. 13		2 Timothy	—	iv. 8	
XC.				1 Peter	—	iv. 11	
Titus	—	ii. 13	} 136	**XCV.**			
		10		2 Peter	—	i. 1	} 146
Revelation	—	i. 5		1 Timothy	—	i. 1	
Titus	—	iii. 4		**XCVI.**			
		5		2 Peter	—	i. 11	146
		6		**XCVII.**			
Titus	—	i. 3		2 Peter	—	iii. 10	} 146
		4				11	
						12	
				2 Peter	—	iii. 15	
				1 Timothy	—	i. 16	
				2 Peter	—	iii. 18	
				XCVIII.			

INDEX.

XCVIII.
1 John	—	ii. 22	148

XCIX.
1 John	—	iv. 3	148

C.
1 *JOHN*	—	v. 7	148

CI.
1 John	—	v. 13, 14, 15	} 148
1 John	—	iii. 21, 22	

CII.
1 John	—	v. 20	
1 John	—	v. 11, 12, 13	} 149

CIII.
2 John	—	9	
1 John	—	ii. 23	} 151
1 John	—	iv. 15, 12	

CIV.
Jude	—	1	
Philippians	—	i. 1	} 151
Titus	—	i. 1	
1 Corinthians	—	i. 1	

CV.
Jude	—	151

CVI.
1 John	—	iii. 16	153

CVII.
Acts	—	xx. 28	
Isaiah	—	xl. 11	} 153
Acts	—	xx. 29, 30	

CVIII.
Hebrews	—	i. 8, 10 to 12	} 154
Hebrews	—	i. 9	
Romans	—	ix. 5	
Hebrews	—	xiii. 8	

CIX.
Revelation	—	ii. 8	
Isaiah	—	xliv. 6	
John	—	xiii. 31, 32	} 157
Revelation	—	i. 8	
Revelation	—	xxii. 13	

Ch. V. Page
CX.
Revelation	—	ii. 23	
Jeremiah	—	xvii. 10	
Jeremiah	—	xi. 20	} 157
Jeremiah	—	xx. 12	
Isaiah	—	xliv. 6	

CXI.
Revelation	—	i. 8	
Matthew	—	xxiv. 30	} 158
Revelation	—	i. 7	
Revelation	—	iv. 8	

CXII.
Revelation	—	i. 18	
Revelation	—	iv. 9, 10, 11	
Matthew	—	vi. 9, 10	} 159
1 Corinthians	—	viii. 6	
Colossians	—	i. 17	

CXIII.
Revelation	—	iii. 10	} 159
Matthew	—	vi. 13	

CXIV.
Revelation	—	iii. 19	
Job	—	v. 17	} 160
Hebrews	—	xii. 6, 7	

CXV.
Revelation	—	v. 13	
Revelation	—	i. 4, 5, 6	} 160
Jeremiah	—	xviii. 23	

CXVI.
Revelation	—	vi. 15, 16	
Hebrews	—	i. 12	} 162
Revelation	—	vi. 13, 14	

CXVII.
Revelation	—	xiv. 6, 7, 9	
Philemon	—	i. 16	
Romans	—	i. 16	
2 Timothy	—	i. 8	
Philippians	—	i. 17, 18	} 163
2 Timothy	—	iv. 1	
1 Corinthians	—	viii. 6	
Colossians	—	i. 16, 17	

CXVIII.

INDEX.

CXVIII.
	Ch. V. Page
REVELATION — xvii. 14	
Revelation — xix. 21	
16	} 164
17	
18	

CXIX.
REVELATION — xix. 13	
John — i. 1	
14	
2	
10	
11	
Genesis — i. 1	
John — i. 3	
4	
John — viii. 12	
1 John — i. 5	} 165
1	
2	
1 Timothy — iii. 16	
1 Peter — i. 23	
Hebrews — xi. 3	
Hebrews — i. 2	
Revelation — iii. 14	
1 Peter — i. 25	
John — i. 15	

CXX.
REVELATION — xx. 6	} 167
James — v.	

CXXI.
REVELATION — xx. 12	
13	
14	
15	
Matthew — xxv. 31	
32	} 169
Matthew — xvi. 27	
Matthew — xiii. 41	
42	
Revelation — xxi. 27	
John — v. 22	

CXXII.
	Ch. V. Page
REVELATION — xxii. 13	
Revelation — vii. 17	} 170
Revelation — xxi. 6	
7	

CXXIII.
REVELATION — xxi. 22	
23	
Revelation — xxii. 5	
3	} 171
4	
Revelation — iii. 12	
Revelation — xiv. 1	

CXXIV.
REVELATION — xxii. 6	
Revelation — i. 1	} 172
Revelation — xxii. 16	

CXXV.
REVELATION — iv. 8	
11	
Revelation — v. 12	
13	
Revelation — vii. 10	
12	
Colossians — i. 16	
Isaiah — liii. 7	
Revelation — vii. 9	} 172
14	
15	
Revelation — xvii. 14	
1 Timothy — vi. 15	
16	
2 Peter — iii. 18	
1 Peter — iv. 11	
Hebrews — xii. 1	
Philippians — ii. 10	

INDEX

TO THE

Texts of Scripture *quoted in the third Chapter according to the Order in which they stand in the Bible.*

	Page
Genesis i. 1	165
—— ii. 7	110
Exodus iii. 14	66
—— iii. 15	71
Nehemiah ix. 17	58
Job v. 17	160
Psalms viii. 1	53
—— viii. 2	53
—— xxiv. 10	110
—— xxxi. 5	85
—— xliv. 22	53
Isaiah vii. 14	50
—— ix. 6	50
—— xii. 3	62
—— xl. 10, 11	52
—— xlii. 8	95
—— xliii. 25	58
—— xliv. 3	62
—— xliv. 6	50, 157, 158
—— xlv. 21, 22, 23	104
—— xlix. 6	90
—— li. 9, 10, 15	51
—— lii. 7, 10	51
—— liii. 1	51
—— 7	173
—— lv. 1	62
Jeremiah ix. 24	61
—— xi. 20	158
—— xvii. 10	158
—— xvii. 13	61
—— xx. 12	158
—— xxiii. 23	86, 161
Daniel ix. 9	111
Matthew vi. 9	130, 159
—— vi. 10	54, 98, 159
—— vi. 13	54, 159
—— xi. 27	56
—— xiii. 41	55, 170
—— xiii. 42	170

	Page
Matthew xiv. 61 to 65	82
—— xv. 24	91
—— xvi. 27	55, 100, 169
—— xxi. 16	53
—— xxiii. 34	78
—— xxiv. 30	158
—— 31	54
—— xxv. 31, 32, 33, 34	54, 169
—— xxvi. 64, 65, 67	87
—— xxviii. 20	57, 92
Mark i. 34	93
—— v. 19	59
—— viii. 38	55
—— ix. 24	57
—— xvi. 15	77
—— xvi. 20	57, 92
Luke iii. 6	51
—— v. 13	143
—— v. 20 to 25	58
—— vi. 22, 23	58
—— viii. 38, 39	59
—— viii. 48	143
—— ix. 26	55
—— x. 22	56
—— xi. 49	78
—— xvii. 20 to 30	55
—— xxiii. 42, 43	60
—— xxiv. 26	60
—— xxiv. 45	92
John i. 1	71

INDEX.

Reference	Page
John i. 1 to 14	165
—— i. 15	166
—— i. 49	74
—— ii. 19, 21	61
—— 25	77
—— iii. 13, 18, 31	65
—— iv. 10, 14	61
—— iv. 42	62
—— iv. 26	67
—— v. 17, 18, 26, 27	63
—— v. 21, 25, 28	64
—— v. 22	100, 170
—— v. 24	65
—— v. 39	99
—— vi. 62	65
—— vi. 69	64
—— vii. 37, 38	62
—— viii. 12	165
—— viii. 58	66
—— ix. 38	65
—— x. 11	52
—— x. 13, 14	145
—— x. 30	67
—— x. 33	67
—— x. 38	68
—— xi. 35	60
—— 38	52
—— xii. 41	52
—— 12, 13, 14	69
—— xiii. 31	156
—— 32	156
—— xiv. 8 to 11	68
—— xiv. 12 to 14	68
—— xiv. 26	72
—— xv. 26	72
—— xv. 27	77
John xvi. 7	72
—— 13	84, 129
—— 14, 15	73
—— 23	70
—— 28	66
—— 29	66
—— xvii. 5, 24	73
—— xviii. 37	74
—— xx. 16, 28, 29	75
—— xxi. 14, 15, 16, 17	145
Acts i. 21, 22	77
—— 24, 25	76
—— ii. 32	61
—— iii. 12	81
—— 15, 17	110
—— iv. 10, 21	81
—— vii. 51	59
—— 52	58, 59
—— 53	53
—— 54	59, 82
—— 55	59, 82
—— 56	59, 82
—— 57	59, 82
—— 58	59, 82
—— 59	59, 82
—— 60	82
—— ix. 2	79
—— 5	77, 125
—— 6	77
—— 13	78
—— 14	78
—— 15	78
—— 20	78
—— 21	77, 78
—— 22	77
—— 26	78
—— 34	82, 143
—— 35	82
—— 40	88
—— 42	88
—— xi. 18	89, 100
—— 20	89
—— 21	89
—— 22	89

Acts

INDEX.

	Page
Acts xi. 23	89
—— xiii. 45	90
46	90
47	90
48	91
49	91
—— xiv. 1	91
3	91
7	112
15	112
—— xv. 11	89
—— xvi. 14	93
15	93
16	93
17	93
30	93
31	93
32	93
33	93
34	93
—— xvii. 18	94
23	94
24	95
25	95
—— xviii. 8	95
9	95
10	95
11	95
24	97
25	97
26	97
27	97
28	97
—— xix. 10	92, 97
11	92
17	97
18	97
19	97
20	97
—— xx. 28	62, 145, 154
29	154
30	154
—— xxi. 11	97
12	97
13	97
14	97
—— xxii. 14	80
16	98
17	98
18	98
19	98
20	98
—— xxiv. 5	99
14	99
Romans i. 1	93, 99
5	77

	Page
Romans i. 9	100
16	163
—— ii. 3	100
4	100, 128
5	128
6	100
11	128
—— iii. 26	101
—— iv.	101
—— viii. 9	101
11	101, 128
14	120
15	120
35	53
—— ix. 5	102, 157
23	121
—— x. 12	102
13	102
15	53
—— xi. 33	122
34	122
—— xiv. 6	103
7	103
8	103
9	103
10	103
11	103
12	103
14	104
—— xv. 16	105
19	105
—— xvi. 16	105
1 Corinthians i. 1	105, 151
2	105
3	106
4	106
7	106
8	106, 107
10	107
11	107
12	107
13	107
14	108
15	108
17	78
21	109
26	109
27	109
28	109
29	109
31	109
—— ii. 7 to the end	110
8	110
—— iii. 5	107
6	107
—— iv. 5	106

H h   1 Corinthians

INDEX.

	Page
1 CORINTHIANS vii. 25	111
———— viii. 4	111
6	112, 159, 163
———— ix. 25	146
———— x. 9	52
20	115
21	115
28	103
31	103
———— xii. 2	115
3	115, 120
———— xiv. 33	115
2 CORINTHIANS ii. 14	132
17	132
———— iv. 5	116
———— v. 10	104
16	134
———— vi. 15	115
16	115
———— x. 14	107
15	107
16	107
17	107, 109
18	107
———— xii. 5	117
7	117
8	117
9	117
10	117
GALATIANS i. 1	118
10	119
11	119
12	119
———— iii. 8	120
———— iv. 6	119
———— vi. 12	119
17	119
EPHESIANS i. 7	121
———— iii. 7	122
8	121
14	121
15	121
16	121
17	122
18	121
19	121
———— iv. 7	122
8	122
9	122
10	122
13	122
14	123
15	123
———— v. 5	55
———— vi. 5	123

	Page
EPHESIANS vi. 6	123, 128
7	123
8	123
9	128
PHILIPPIANS i. 1	93, 151
17	163
18	163
———— ii. 6	124
7	124
8	124
10	174
———— iii. 20	124
COLOSSIANS i. 15	124, 125
16	95, 125, 138, 163, 173
17	95, 125, 159, 163
18	127
———— ii. 9	128
———— iii. 11	128
12	128
13	128
22	123
24	128
25	128
1 THESSALONIANS ii. 2	128
3	129
8	129
9	129
———— iii. 2	129
———— iv. 2	129
3	129
2 THESSALONIANS i. 6	130
7	130
8	130
9	130
10	130
———— ii. 16	130
17	130
———— iii. 3	131
5	132
1 TIMOTHY i. 1	125, 146
10	133
11	133
15	133
16	100, 147
———— ii. 3	125
5	132
6	132
7	132
8	132
———— iii. 16	71, 133, 166
———— iv. 10	125, 133
———— vi. 13	74, 134
14	134
15	134, 174
16	134, 174

INDEX.

Reference	Page
2 Timothy i. 8	116, 163
—— ii. 8	134
10	134
—— iv. 1	55, 135, 163
8	136, 146
Titus i. 1 —	93, 151
3 —	125, 137
4 —	137
—— ii. 10 —	136
13 —	136
—— iii. 4 —	136
5 —	136
6 —	136
Philemon 9 —	163
Hebrews i. 2	166
8	155
9	155
10	155
11	155
12	155, 162
—— ii.	139
The whole referred to.	
3	57
4	57, 92
16	137
17	140
18	63, 140
—— iv. 15	63
—— vii.	140
The whole referred to.	
—— viii.	140
The whole referred to.	
—— ix. 24	73
—— x.	139
The whole referred to.	
1	140
5	140
6	140
20	139
31	104
—— xi.	101
The whole referred to.	
3	166
—— xii.	101
The whole referred to.	
1	174
6	160
7	160
8	157
—— xiii. 8	157
20	52, 145
21	52
James i. 1 —	143
12 —	145
—— ii. 1 —	110, 128, 144
5 —	144, 146
9 —	144
James ii. 13 —	144
—— v.	168
The whole referred to.	
8 —	142
9 —	142
10 —	142
11 —	142
14 —	143
15 —	143
1 Peter i. 11	73
23	166
25	166
—— ii. 25	145
—— iv. 11	146, 174
13	59
14	59
17	131
—— v. 1	144
2	144
3	144
4	144
2 Peter i. 1	146
11	55, 146
21	72
—— iii. 9	101
10	146
11	147
12	147
15	100, 147
18	147, 174
1 John i. 1 —	71, 165
2 —	165
5 —	165
—— ii. 22 —	147
23 —	151
—— iii. 16 —	153
21 —	149
22 —	149
—— iv. 3 —	148
12 —	151
15 —	151
—— v. 7 —	148
11 —	149
12 —	149
13 —	149
14 —	149
15 —	149
20 —	149
2 John 9 —	151
Jude, the whole,	151
Revelation i. 1	172
4	66, 160
5	136, 160
6	157, 160
7	158
8	157, 158

Reve-

INDEX

		Page				Page
REVELATION	i. 18	159		REVELATION	xix. 13	165
————	ii. 8	51, 157			16	134, 164
	23	157			17	164
————	iii. 10	159			18	164
	12	172			21	164
	14	166		————	xx. 6	167
	19	160			12	169
————	iv. 8	159, 173			13	169
	9	159			14	169
	10	159			15	169
	11	159, 173		————	xxi. 6	171
————	v. 12	173			7	171
	13	161, 173			22	171
————	vi. 13	163			23	171
	14	163			27	169
	15	162		————	xxii. 1	62
	16	162			3	171
————	vii. 9	174			4	171
	10	173			5	171
	14	174			6	172
	15	174			9	85
	17	170, 173			12	52
————	xiv. 1	172			13	157, 170
	6	163			16	172
	7	163			17	62
————	xvii. 14	164, 174				

ERRATA.

Page.	line.	for.	read.
19	17	the inscrutable	his inscrutable
33	23	the Lord shall	the Lord God shall
101	32	synonimous.	*dele* the full point
160	31	ׁלֹא	ׁלֹא
164	12	the Lord	*dele* the

There are, besides, a few typographical errours of less importance, which are therefore left unnoticed. The reader is requested to pardon these, and the omission or misplacing (if any there be) of the inverted commas, by which quotations are marked.

PAGE 40—Pliny's Epistle to Trajan, giving him an account of the professours of Christianity, is alluded to; in which he says of them, "Carmenque Christo quasi "Deo dicere secum invicem."

PAGE 195—The horrid persecution carried on in Africa, against the Believers in the Godhead of our Saviour, by the Arian tyrant HUNERIC, in the fifth century, is alluded to—See Mosheim's Ecclesiastical History, Vol. I. p. 401, Octavo, 1768.

PAGE 198—In support of what I have said concerning Mr. Hume, see his works *passim*. Or rather save yourself the disagreeable labour, and attentively read Dr. Beattie's manly and convincing *Essay on the Nature and Immutability of Truth, in opposition to Sophistry and Scepticism*; in which you will find Mr. Hume already detected. — See also Harris's well-authenticated *Historical and Critical Account of Charles* I. p. 264, Octavo, 1758, where the Infidelity of the Historian is pointed out.

www.ingramcontent.com/pod-product-compliance
Lightning Source LLC
Chambersburg PA
CBHW021403230426
43666CB00006B/622